304.8

GSHEL

19/5/14

CW00523914

LES PALADINS DU MONDE OCCIDENTAL:

L'Histoire Profane Inédite, by Laurence Talbot, 1965:

In this remarkable book, which testifies to an original and independent mind, the authoress tries to prove that a great and highly developed civilisation which preceded historic times, left many relics in European cultures that followed. This civilisation was that of the Atlantics, who founded a mighty empire in Europe and Northern Africa. The "Paladins", who brought elements of their Megalithic culture to Greece, Asia Minor, Egypt, Syria, Mesopotamia and even to India, were the heroes and demigods of Greek mythology and were in reality deified leaders of colonising groups of Atlantics and Northerners. (*Mankind Quarterly*, 1971. Shortened)

Originally Published by:
Editions Marocaines et Internationales
Tangiers

C0000 00163 2997

Knights-Errant of the Western World

Laurence Talbot

Translation by Myron Kok

Published in 2012 by Myron Kok
36 Barrow Rd, Cambridge CB2 5AS
First published in 2009
Design by comfybadger
Printed and bound in the UK by Kall Kwik Cambridge

ISBN 978-0-9568533-2-5

Contents

Translator's Foreward

Madame Talbot covers a very wide field of enquiry, and reference books which I have consulted to help me find my way include :

> *A Smaller Classical Dictionary of Biography, Mythology and Geography* (abridged), William Smith D.C.L. and LL.D (John Murray, Albermale St. London, 1876 and 1926).
> Harrap's: *French – English Dictionary*, 2002
> Harrap's: *Dictionary of French Slang*, 1988
> Cassel's: *New Latin Dictionary.*
> *Everyman's Dictionary of non – Classical Mythology* (Egerton Sykes), 1968.
> Penguin: *Dictionary of Classical Mythology.*
> *Oxford Dictionary of Classical Myth and Religion* (Price & Kearns), 1984.
> *Encyclopedia Britannica* and *Chambers Encyclopedia.*

I didn't find everything I was looking for, but I hope that the translation and notes (in spite of errors and possible misinterpretations on my part) will interest readers as much as they have interested me.

NB:
Madame Talbot, when dealing with the Classical World, sometimes uses Latin names, sometimes Greek. On the whole she writes Hercules rather than Heracles, Juno rather than Hera: however she seems to prefer Zeus to Jupiter and Pallas Athene to Minerva. To avoid puzzlement, both forms will be given to this translation, when the occasion arises.

In the main text numbers in brackets refer to Mme. Talbot's own notes after the last chapter. Asterisks are the translator's interpolations which are explained at the end of the relevant chapter.

INTRODUCTION

An ecumenical civilisation, powerful and of genuine quality, existed before those times we call 'historical'. It was a civilisation Mankind could be proud of. We do not know what it was really like because men forget, but also because every new conqueror throughout the ages has always cloaked the vanquished foe in total darkness.

In this book I have tried to throw some light on the darkness.

In attempting to do this, I have followed my own instincts. I have tried to give a bird's eye view of the subject, and by showing those aspects of past ages which still survive in one form or another, I have tried to breathe new life into dead bones. This way of writing history may cause some surprise as it does not conform to academic norms, and there will of course be criticism of its inadequacies: lack of ordered categorization, useless repetition, too many abridgements. The reason for this is that causes lead to multiplicity of effects. When clearing a jungle to make a path, one cannot hope to proceed in a perfect straight line along which the traveller can make his way in peace and quiet. This task will one day be tackled by the experts and they will clean up the edges to achieve the best possible result. But the bold explorer who opened up the way will only have the satisfaction of having braved the dangers.

These dangers are considerable. To maintain that the earliest great migrations did not take place from East to West, but from West to East; to maintain that a vast Atlantic kingdom pre-dated all the others and was indeed the father of those civilisations is by no means new. There is too much evidence to support this argument for it not to have been noticed by several historians, and not just in recent times. But those who have done so have always (and for obvious reasons) been the object of derision and even hostility. And this has made them withdraw, despite their convictions.

And yet the rumblings of real history continue unabated, a history which can explain all the obscurities of Antiquity and of Pre-History. But to prove this history, to make it known, necessitates an examination of such a mountain of error and falsification that it will take more than one person to clear it all out of the way. As everyone knows, it is easier to discover the truth than to get it accepted.

And even to discover the truth is difficult enough since all our sources of information have been most carefully destroyed or suppressed. Fortunately, however, distance (in history as in optics) puts many things into perspective. By making use of this advantage to develop a new method of research, I have in this first book been able to clear the way a little. I do not claim to have given a full account of the Great Atlantic Epic – it is too early for that. But I have managed to light a few torches here and there to dispel the shadows.

In a second book this process will be continued.

If you wish to understand the true nature of things, you must look carefully at the names they are given.

It is by symbolism alone, that we shall be able to read the thoughts of men long gone.

At the start of our history life was simplicity itself.

Isha Schwaller de Lubicz Her-Bak

1

THE HAIR AND THE FEATHER

*"Tell me the meaning of words
and I shall tell you the history of the world."*
(Thiers)

When (at the end of an upheaval like World War II) the mob cuts off the hair of women whose behaviour is judged to have been unworthy; and when (on the morning of his consecration) the novice has his hair cut off to signify that he has finally entered the Church, do we know to what ancestral rules these acts are related? Do we know that we must seek the answer to these questions from the Pelasgians, who brought civilisation to Greece and to the Middle East?

We think ourselves very sophisticated, and yet we are still conditioned by all kinds of influences, such as ancestral memory, to quote just one example. We can be sure that the first men to go to the moon will take some charm or other with them – which could quite easily be the hair of an elephant.

In his *Lettre au Greco* Kazantzaki tells us that as a child he awaited the blessing of his grandfather as if it were a gift that would work wonders. He writes that he expected to be given "the hair of the ogre, spoken of in fairy tales: one carries it around on one's person as a precaution, in case of need, and when one burns it the ogre will come to the rescue."

But how could ogres be of any interest to the historian? Who believes in ogres? After all, we can read in any dictionary that such things have long since been written off by Science.

Let the scoffer smile, for on the contrary there is every reason to believe that ogres were the last survivors of the race of giants: for, are there not still a few examples of other enormous creatures? Why should Mother Nature have been so perverse as to spare Man (and Man alone) the need to obey the law of gigantism (in both the animal and the plant world) which was such a feature of creation in its pristine youth?

If the word '*ogre*' conjures up for us (conditioned as we are by centuries of Christianity) a creature of myth and evil, that is because to the Pagans (who knew many things of which we are now ignorant) it represented the human race at its best, a race of giants to be revered by these men as their sacred ancestors.

But why the hair, especially?

Because according to *Genesis*, as conceived by this first of all races, everything started with the great sea frost, with *Pelagos* the jellyfish, warmed by the heat of the sun, which gave life to the inert mass from which all forms of animal creation would emerge. Since the initial life-urge manifested itself in the shape of thread-like tentacles (called *pils* or *pelz*), these tentacles came to represent, symbolically, of course, the most important vehicles of creation. And the guiding principle of this realistic cult became so well embedded in the popular mind that in Old French a blade of grass was also called a *poil* (hair), from which the French derive their word for a 'lawn' (*pelouse*). At the same time the tree (in the Icelandic *Edda*) is called the *fields' head of hair* (*chevelure des champs*), while the expression *Gaule chevelue* described a land rich in forests and all kinds of vegetation.

When it is remembered that the hair, or *axil* filament, of the spermatozoon is the element which enables it to move about in order to procreate, one is forced to admit that the origin of the myth in question gives proof of a level of beauty, science and intelligence which does honour to the men of Pre-History.

The main reason for the prestige of the hair (*poil, fil, cheveu* – and in Old French *peulx*) was further reinforced in the eyes of so-called 'ignorant creatures' by the well-observed fact that hair reflects a man's vital force and is also a conductor of electricity. Hence the expression, still used in French, of *having shining hair* (*avoir le poil luisant*), meaning 'to be in perfect health'; or the French expression *getting your second animal coat* (*reprendre du poil de la bête*), meaning 'when a man's health and strength have been restored'. This is, of course, in common parlance, even if it is not elegant speech.

Moreover, every one of us knows that our hair is brittle or dry or without lustre, or soft or split, or straight or curly in relation to our state of health and to the air we breath. For there is something else! Hair is so subtle: it is so well tuned to natural forces that it can undergo a complete metamorphosis. In the winter snow the red-coated hare turns white. In the animal world it is an almost universal law that the coat is renewed annually (yet another reason to admire our distant ancestors, so attentive to the cycle of seasons and to the power of their destructive and restorative magic).

As for the fable – or rather, historical fact – with its vivid imagery (but shortened and compressed so as to reach down to us through the ages, and with a symbolic value which is incomprehensible to modern man), we are immediately reminded of the *golden thread* with which man was attached to life and which was cut by Proserpina to grant him death, as we are told in the *Aeneid.*

We are also reminded of Nisos. Nisos was King of Megara. Scylla, his daughter, loved Minos who was at war with her father (to love the son or the daughter of one's parents' enemy seems to have been an age-old and fatal inclination, favoured by Nature which, as we know, always 'does the right thing' since *Harmony* is the daughter of Ares, God of War). Now Nisos had *red hair* on which the fate of his city, as well as his own life, depended. This is not just an empty statement: it simply means that since he himself was a descendant of the Giants (i.e. of the Nordic race with red hair and blue eyes), he also had their great strength. The young Scylla, overcome by her love for Minos, cut the hair of her father – an act which brought about the ruin of Megara, either because she had found a way of killing Nisos or because she had diminished her father's strength.

Other defeats in bygone ages were explained in the same way – for example, that of Samson in the Bible.

On more than one occasion the Hebrews crossed the paths of giants or the grandsons of giants. Did Moses' scouts in the land of Canaan not come across three members of the tribe of the *Enachides*? And do we not read in Deuteronomy that Og, King of Basan, was the last of the giants to fight Moses?

The hair cult was also extended to animals which were considered by the Ancients to be their cousins.

This could perhaps explain the cult of the cat in Egypt (whose coat is very magnetic); the cult of the black bull; the 'milk-white' ox; the red stag; white and black fur. All these dress colours are connected in some way to a philosophical idea or fact of human history which would take too long to study at this point.

In time, the hair cult evolved, was extended, became more complicated and led to a new cult of the bristle or anything bristly, such as the coat of the porcupine. Thus, the sacred character of the natural, live spike spread to the teeth of combs and to the pointed shape of the beard, until it finally became assimilated to any pointed area of the body and to the male sex in particular, leading in turn to reverence for anything having a point. The fact that spinning was queen's work in

5

Antiquity, as it was in Old France (while in the Middle Ages, the silk manufacturer, the furrier and wool merchant were still privileged occupations for the Nobility) was not so much a question of the money needed to be able to pursue these trades as of the value attached in Antiquity to a skein of wool or to silk in themselves. This is because, contrary to the present day, everything in times long past bound men to the whole of creation, both in flesh and in spirit – even a thread.

The hair which contained essential oils and secreted nourishing juices, the hair whose very name contains the true root (*pelagos*) of the name of that people from whom our Occident has inherited its whole civilisation (and much more directly than it realises) - this hair has played an important part in our mores. It goes without saying that what was an extremely significant cult for the Sages soon managed to transform itself into an object of superstition and to place its mark on the customs of the people. This is not only true for the whole head of hair but also for the single [thread of] hair.

It is because hair reminds us of the strength and courage of our giant ancestors that our French *cuirassiers* wear a horse tail in their helmets, and the guardsmen of the English a busby.

A man 'with hair on his chest' (*homme à poil*, or *homme à quatre poils* - literally, *man with four hairs*) is how we French like to describe the 'rough, tough customer': and we may well wonder by what subconscious memory of ancient myths in the minds of men the French called their First World War heroes the 'hairy ones' (*poilus*).

Long ago the Gauls considered it to be a mark of great refinement to pull out a hair from their heads on meeting a friend, and to give it to him.

Splitting hairs (*couper un cheveu en quatre* meaning 'cut a hair into four pieces') is a way of exploring every avenue of an argument beyond the limits of endurance: unless, of course, it can be traced back to an ancient custom of making a quarter share of your lottery ticket, as it were, when you were fortunate enough to have a giant's hair in your possession.

In Ancient Gaul people swore oaths on a hair.

The long hair of the Gauls was a demonstration of freedom as well as a trademark. History tells us that Caesar ordered them to cut off their hair when he had conquered them.

But the cult persisted. Chroniclers of the 8th Century relate that the great lords entrusted the first hair cut of their children to the person in whom they placed the most trust, and that those who were thus honoured became the child's spiritual parent (1).

Everything changed under the Capetians. Around 1116 long hair was frowned upon by the Church. It was a reminder of pagan days gone by. In 1196 a church law prohibited entry into religious buildings for all those who wore their hair long, and on Christmas Day, at Mass, Godefroy, Bishop of Amiens, refused at St. Omer, in the presence of Robert, Count of Flanders, the offerings of anyone who persisted in keeping long hair.

For Churchmen, the tonsure was proof of their renunciation of the freedom of the life temporal and of submission to the life spiritual.

Outside the Church, cutting off someone's hair was to shame that person. Members of a conspiracy were often condemned to cut off each other's hair.

The Red Indians' practice of scalping may well have a similar myth at its origin; so too the sacred character of Mohammed's hair and the long tress dear to the Ancient Chinese. Wearing the hair long was, for the Koreans, a sign of resolute nationalism.

* * *

The passage from the hair cult to the feather cult is easily explained. The structure of the pointed hair closely resembles that of a bird's feather, or so our science book tells us. In the Middle Ages people spoke of a porcupine *feather*. Furthermore, the words used to describe the two things (*pel* and *pen*) resembled each other closely. *Pen* in the Celtic language meant *point*; *insect sting* or *serpent's forked tongue*, *feather*. The word still survives in English. In Medieval France a pen (*plume*) was called *penne*. From this word many other terms are derived, inter alia *pennon* (English 'pennant' – pointed flag cut diagonally). From Latin we get *penna* (pennant) and also *penis* (for obvious reasons).

The famous *plumed serpent* was, from the very earliest days of the distant, distant past, no more than a serpent with a scaly skin and a penis, which was sometimes a slit in the shape of Mercury's rod and curiously covered with pointed hairs.

In the same way, the *jarls* of Normandy take their name from the concept of a pointed hair or feather. It is claimed that the name is of unknown origin. [That is] because we are forgetting the Icelandic hero *Jarl* with the rosy cheeks and blond hair, skilled in handling the javelin. *Jarl* is cognate with *jarre*, a word meaning the *long, hard hair ending in a point*, and which encases a second hair, finer and generally called *down*. *Jarre* is also spelt *jars*. The latter form, which is in turn cognate with the French word *gars*, used to mean *young boy*, and especially (in earlier days) that person who with his weapon (lance or javelin) was identified with the powerful feather charged with protecting the weak, and in particular the young virgin whose emblem was the wild goose (exceptionally fierce), sacred to the people of the North, but also to Gaul under the rule of the Franks. The Norman *jarl* was the Celtic *iarl*, a word which up to the 13th Century was used to describe the Breton princes and the lords of Cambria (Wales). It is also cognate with the English *earl*.

The warrior's plume also goes back a long way. Feathers from the eagle, the peacock, the swan and the ostrich have appeared at the top of Europe's oldest shields [coats of arms, escutcheons] – each animal enhancing the intrinsic prestige of the feather with an entirely personal prestige, charged with a symbolism so important that it would be just as revealing as a source of history as are texts, if we were only intelligent and artless enough – in the proper meaning of the word – to believe in its importance.

Apropos of Romulus, Virgil writes in the *Aeneid*: "Do you see how a double crest is suspended over his head and how his father has already marked him out to a be a god by a sign which only relates to him?"

Crest is indeed a word which is historically of great significance for anyone wishing to explain it, which we shall do on another occasion.

The peacock feather was particularly important since it is connected with the king of birds, displays the semblance of an eye (sacred symbol of the first race) and is also the emblem of divine rule. The subject of the peacock feather could fill a book of 500 pages, but the matter would still not be exhausted. Suffice it to say that, in the early days of Christianity, the peacock feather also served as emblem for the Annunciation. It was on the feathers of this bird that Medieval knights swore their most solemn oath. King Arthur's Round Table and festivities organised by the Duke of Burgundy for the creation of the *Order of the Golden Fleece* served as background for this ancient rite of chivalry - *the peacock oath*. Hence the tradition of *making a vow*, which we still practise when we are served a rare or new dish out of season.

By sending King Pepin a cloak of peacock feathers, Pope Paul III knew he was offering him a royal gift which took due note of his birth.

The coats of arms of English houses were more usually adorned with the *swan's* feathers. No doubt there is a connection between this fact and the king's swans on the Thames. But the *Order of the Swan* is Prussian and is connected with Lohengrin, Knight of the Holy Grail, sent by King Arthur to rescue Elsa of Brabant. *Cygnus* (swan) sounds the same as the word *signus*, and that is important. Its root, *sig* or *zig*, is Nordic. It is this root that we also find in the Ionian letter *sigma* and in the word *zigurat*, but also in the term *seigneur* (lord) - the *seigneur* being the man marked with a *sign* (of his birth, naturally) and the man who *signed* (*signer* = *seigner*) his documents.

As for the ostrich feather it is mostly found (and with good reason) on the coats of arms of Austrian houses and those of Luxemburg (inter alia, [on] that of John of Bohemia, but also on that of the Plantagenets). But these princes were not the only ones to *wear, each one of them on his head, a magnificent steel chauffrin, decorated with very fine Ostrich feathers* (3).

Like the peacock feather, that of the ostrich, used as an emblem, goes back to the very earliest days, since it appears with the name *shoo* amongst the oldest hieroglyphics, and can also be seen on several monuments in the ancient city of Nimrod. If we are to believe A.H. Layard, the famous archeologist, the ancient warriors of Mesopotamia decorated the shafts of their lances with it – just as is done by the Bedouins of the Hedjaz (4).

As an emblem representing birth, it also served to symbolize courage and victory, not because the ostrich is known for being a brave bird, but because of its giant size.

These fabulous times have bequeathed [to us] the prestige of a *feather in the wind*, symbol of that manly audacity displayed with *panache* by the Musketeers of D'Artagnan. The *panache* of the *Bersaglieri*, though not quite so sumptuous, is just as real for all that, because the *Bersaglieri* are a product of the *Berserker*, from whom their name is derived.

The initially sacred, and finally precious (later priceless?) value attached to the feathers of the peacock or ostrich elevated them to one of the most magnificent gifts and greatest marks of honour that princes could bestow on each other. Eventually, they were even required in lieu of ransom money: "the English provided as a ransom for the capture of his son four feathers," we read in the Dictionary of Lacurne de Saint-Palaye.

The custom of obtaining payment in this currency quickly became widespread in countries where these birds were hunted. *All sovereigns and all servants of the Government of Africa, today as in the days of the Egyptians, demand that their subjects or those people administered by them should pay them regular tribute in ostrich feathers. This is why the Arab believes he is talking to a taxman when he is asked for ostrich feathers.*

We need look no further than this old custom when searching for the origin of the modern expression *to be fleeced* (French *to be plucked*). In Old French *pennir* meant *to deprive* or *to strip bare*. This is why the Faithful referred at Easter to the *semaine penneuse*, the week in which they were *deprived of all pleasures*.

Incidentally, this is a very vivid image and reminds us of the torture in which it was customary to *plumer les cheveux et la barbe* (tear out the hair and beard), just as later the nails were torn out.

Pel and *pen* are related, as we have seen: but so too are *pel* and *pal*, in the sense that the *pal* or *pieu* (stake) represents an enormously magnified and pointed animal hair. [This] is why, in heraldry, it symbolises power. And it is also why, in days gone by, in our different countries of the West, a pole was erected in the centre of the circle formed by the assembled clan chiefs.

Hence our French word *paladin* (knight errant) and later still *palais* (palace).

But what does all this tell us about the Pelasgians?

For the Greeks, the Pelasgians were 'the peoples of the high seas' (*pelagos*). When we say *high seas* we don't mean 'the sea beyond the coast', we mean 'the sea of the upper regions', in French the *régions summériennes* (*en sus de*, 'over and above', *mer* 'sea'). With the word *pelagos* there is always an idea of deep sea, or distant sea, and also the idea of migration. For the Hellenes, the expression *People of the Sea* (which, after the Pelasgians, was applied to the Achaeans) always implied in legend something both terrible and grandiose, not suitable for describing local sailors. When Plato, quoting Solon, "the wisest of the seven sages", tells us in his *Timeas* that, at the start of their separate histories, Greece and Egypt had been conquered by Sea Peoples coming from the West, then he is alluding to those people, those of the great western sea; in other words, [of] the North Atlantic. Incidentally, Science speaks of *pelasgians* as fish coming down from the North Sea and spilling over periodically into the … Mediterranean!

Furthermore, the word *pelagos* is also cognate with the idea of French *poil* (hair): i.e. *pel*, now, *Pelagie*, the jellyfish which gave her name to Greece in her most ancient days and whose image is used to decorate archaic Cretan pottery [and] was a sacred symbol for Western Sea Peoples. This inert mass, smooth and naked, represents the smooth, naked sea, *peeled*, so to speak, before life surged from its entrails. The whole story is set out most clearly in the Finnish *Kalevala* (5). In the Danish language, the word *arve* means both *Pelasgian* and *peeled*. This cannot be pure chance. For the Nordic peoples it is beyond all doubt that the idea of water, or rather of the ocean, has been associated from time immemorial with that of a *naked surface*, as opposed to a *hairy earth*. In the Icelandic *Edda* (6), when Thor asks the dwarf Alviss what is the name of the water on which men sail, the latter replies that the giants call it '*dwelling of the eels*' and the Asir call it an '*unbroken surface*'.

The thread-like appendages of the jellyfish, the first signs of life and of movement, are the sons of Pelagos, sons of the sea, those who summoned the others to begin the struggle that is the basis of all civilisation. La Villemarqué tells us that Pelagos in the Breton language is *Morgane*, that is *water virgin*, the water of *the world's beginning*. The masculine form of the name is *Morvan*, meaning 'man of the sea'.

These clues from linguistics point to a Norwegian origin of the Pelasgians in Antiquity.

The Pelasgian world, of which Crete was a part, included ancient Thrace, Thessaly, Phrygia, Lydia, Caria, Phoenicia, Epirus and Illyria, and reached as far as the Samnites and the Oscans. A detailed examination would easily prove that the conquerors of these different countries originated from areas in the North Atlantic. On the one hand, the invaders sailed down the rivers until they reached the point of exit at the *Black Sea*, and on the other, they arrived by sea via the Pillars of Hercules.

The Greeks called the Ocean *Okeinos*, fief of the *Occident*. The French word '*mer*' *(sea)* comes from the Celtic *mohr*. It is cognate with *Maia* or *Maja*, pronounced *Mara* (German *Meer*), name of the eight-legged crab, also a symbol of the jellyfish.

How marvellous it is to see how the water element, in which life was born, and the religious symbol of maternity have so faithfully preserved their linguistic roots through so many millennia.

2

TORCHES AND
LILY OF THE VALLEY

We are talking about May 1st.

Our dictionaries tell us that it was on the occasion of a worker's congress in Paris in 1888 (some say it was 1889) that it was decided to make this day a public holiday. From 1890 it became known as International Labour Day.

But it was not the French who took the initiative in this matter. It was the Anglo-Saxons. To be more precise, the idea was put to the vote by Gabriel Edmonston, and seconded by Thomas J. Doran, at the Chicago Congress of 1884.

The choice of this day was justified by the fact that May 1st (the Festival of *Saint Jacques* in France) falls in the United States on the day when leases come up for renewal (elsewhere this is on *St. George's Day*, or at *Michaelmas*). It was known as *Moving Day*, a very busy day, in the true sense of the word - and also figuratively speaking.

It would be wrong to assume that workers' business, closures of leases and the festivities generally associated with May 1st (which incidentally marks the beginning of the month dedicated by Rome since 1758 *alla gloria della grande madre di Dio*) are not in any way connected. They were, on the contrary, very closely connected in the mental horizons of the men who laid the foundations of our civilisations.

The First of May, or the Calends of May, was a sacred date in the calendars of the Celts and the Nordics. This was known in Gaelic as *Kalamae* or *Kalan*, and also as *Kalanmai*. At Rome the Calends of May were dedicated to *Flora*. But they were in fact introduced into the Empire by the Etruscans and not by the Romans, and they came via Gaul. The word 'calan' is of Celtic origin, and the Celt was in his own language known as *Kalou* or *Calou* (*Keltos* in the Greek). *Calan* was used to describe anything extra special, either in time or in space. The first day of every month was *Day* with a capital 'D', and it is possible that they marked it with a pebble (French *caillou*, a word which, according to Littré, was pronounced *kalou*). This is quite possibly why in French we still call an important day 'a day to be marked with a stone' (*jour à marquer d'une pierre*).

Most scholars claim that the French word *calendes* is derived from the Latin verb *calo* (to call together, assemble). But quite apart from the very old English verb *to call*, it is more than probable that the Latin *calo* has a Celtic root *cal*. This would fit in very well with the theory put forward in the previous paragraph since the *calends* were most certainly a day on which the people 'came together'. And just as we do at our fairs and on market days, the people of those times exchanged their wares, and paid for them with 'coins' which were in fact little pebbles (*kalous*).

In essence, market days were of course in the very nature of things a celebration of work, since these men were exchanging the fruits of their labours. But such days must certainly also have had social significance (perhaps clan leaders came together to discuss plans for the future of the community, and to let clansmen vote on the issues) and there would also have been an important religious element since, in those days, as at the peak of the Christian Era, all human activity, whether political or commercial, was dependent on an all-pervading Spiritual Power. The best proof of this can be seen in the fact that, as late as in the 9th Century of our era, a religious society known in France as the *Frères des Calendes* (Brothers of the Calends) was still very active in France and in the German states.

Because the Gregorian Calendar was 'out of sync' with the Celtic Calendar (which began with the Winter Solstice and divided the year into lunar months), there was for a long period of time confusion between the month of May (Fr. *mois de* Mai) and the month of March (*mois de Mars*). This in turn led to describing the flowering field of May (*champ de Mai*) and the field of March (*champ de* Mars) as the great communal field or *mall* (*mail*). The close link between these concepts is easily explained when it is remembered that the fundamental myth about the god of *war* was allied to the myth of *renewal* (death and rebirth), since it was a basic principle of Paganism that all life *in its entirety* was derived from a union of opposites and the clash of forces. [NB: In French, the month of *March* is (like the God of War, **Mars**) also *Mars*: *Janvier*, *Février*, *Mars* etc.]

In modern times it was above all the old idea of the awakening of nature at the end of winter which predominated on May 1st. It was celebrated more or less all over Europe, but more especially in the old Celtic, Nordic provinces where the myth originated.

In France, as, for example, in Germany, a dummy man, representing winter, was burnt. In other parts a tree was planted, especially a birch. The birch, a tree of the North, was most significant. Its black and white bark is symbolic of day and night, of light and shadow. The same custom was observed in Anglo-Saxon countries where, on this occasion, houses were decorated with green branches. On the other hand, the tree around which the people danced, was denuded of its branches and was simply a pole (*pall*), representing all that remained of the phallic symbol. But it aroused so much enthusiasm that in AD 1642 the English parliament, in a surfeit of Puritanism, forbade the pleasures of the Maypole.

In France, up to the war of 1914 which put a seal on the break with ancient tradition, there was not a single province where a girl ready for marriage did not wake up on that morning to find a *mai* at her door, a large 'garland' of flowers. This was not necessarily the offering of a particular swain, more often than not it was the collective tribute of all the young males in the village. The ribbon or ribbons were especially important. The young men proffering them, having forgotten the old customs, could not have known that the long ribbons flapping in the breeze represented the *threads* with which proliferating Nature spread out her tentacles at the return of Spring. They were symbolic of the life force, emblems of virility, and were also seen at the time attached to the hats of the young conscripts.

* * *

The month of May, *mae* or *mai* (Lat. *maies*) takes its name from *Maia*, the creative power incarnate in the creature known today by the same name: *maia* or spider-crab. In the signs of the Zodiac it is called *Cancer* (French *chancre/crabe*). Its very descriptive symbol ♋ represents infinity, or the **end-joined-up-with-the-beginning**, an esoteric sign from which we take the motif sometimes called the '*69*'. This is a very Celtic motif and is often found in primitive Irish art. The French have, of course, given it a lewd connotation. The sign not only represents the idea of transcendent motherhood but also symbolises the islands which, according to the Ancient Peoples, constituted the *Empire of the Night and of Death*, from which Life was born.

Ireland was once known in France by the name of this fabulous creature, which is still called by modern scientists *maie* or *maia*. It is, however, also called *erine* (the Celtic name for Ireland is *Eirin*) or *arane*. This reminds us of the Isle of *Aran* which seems at one time or other to have been the generic name for all the islands lying in these regions.

The coats of arms of the Isle of Man show three legs of the *aranie* (*araignée de* mer: spider crab). We also see them in archaic Greek art on the shields of the giants. A full representation of the creature appears on Cretan pottery, and also on ceramics sold at Carnac. For the Greeks it symbolised wisdom because it represented great age.

There can be no mistake. In Mythology, *Maia* is described as a daughter of Atlas – and Atlas was a Titan, an Atlantan. We must, however, remember that *atlantan* referred to the whole Atlantic world, where Atlas was one of the kings. According to legend there were ten of them.

That the *maia* (sea-spider, spider crab) should through the ages have symbolised the act of delivering a child is all the more apparent because the art of midwifery is today called *maieutique* in French.

But how could this creature symbolise motherhood? A very important question whose answer confirms the origin of the myth. For although the genesis of the world is described in more or less similar terms throughout Pagan countries, each tribe or nation has nevertheless coloured its description in its own particular way.

Now it so happens that genesis based on the concept of the *maia* is nowhere set out so clearly or so simply as in Nordic cosmogony, and especially in the Finnish *Kalevala*.

In ancient times *Finnish* did not have the limited application the word has today. As noun and adjective the term was applied to all the peoples of northern Europe, generally white and blond. That is the original meaning of the English adjective *fine*, which is a direct derivation.

The hero of heroes in Ireland was called *Fynn*.

There is no need for surprise. National epics, prehistoric Nordic art, archeological discoveries in the North and a comparative study of languages give abundant proof that in the earliest days the inhabitants of Scandinavian countries lived in very close proximity with the Celts.

So, in short, what do we read in the Finnish *Kalevala*? (1) We read that life started when the eagle, catching sight of a mound of turf floating on the water, laid her eggs on it. The eagle *eyalo* (from the archaic Danish) means the *eternally shining,* i.e. the sun. The grassy mound is the knee covered in seaweed which the *Virgin of the Waves* (Lady of the Lake in King Arthur?) one day raised above the surface of the water: a very poetic and beautiful song from the *Kalevala.* The details which emerge from this version of genesis give us to understand that the first *Virgin of the Waves* was the jellyfish which reflects the rainbow whose symbolic importance will be shown later. But the son to whom she gives birth after many torments lasting many centuries is called *Vainamoinen,* and the first syllable of this name *vai* is the equivalent of *mai,* just as *mae* is the equivalent of *vae.* So it seems that at some time or other the spider crab and the jellyfish began to overlap, because *Vainamoinen* also wanders over the Ocean, ceaselessly buffeted by the waves. No doubt both creatures were totems of different clans, although related: but one was more specially Nordic (the jellyfish) while the other was more specially Celtic (the *maia*).

Speaking scientifically, these two creatures were equally entitled to serve as symbol for Creation. That goes without saying, as regards the jellyfish and her thread-like appendages, as we have seen in the previous chapter. It is, however, curious to note that one of the characteristics of the spider crab and the whole family of crustaceans is that they carry seaweed on their backs: first of all for reasons of prudence, as a camouflage against enemies, but more important still, so as not to starve. We can, therefore, see that she fully deserves her reputation for wisdom, and that she also "exposed to the eagle a knee, covered in seaweed."

The Greeks in their Mythology adopted this tradition from the Pelasgians. They told of the *rainbow* which, by touching the *sacred island,* created an explosion of life on earth. Then the Sages of Antiquity, including Solon, confused this little island with the whole Atlantan concept. One can see how this would happen on the back of the Atlantic crab. And then in the age of Classical Greece, which marked the triumph of anthropomorphism, men spoke of Juno, breast-feeding Hercules and spilling her nourishing milk into the hollow of the island, or *hile* (navel of the world) which was thereby fertilised.

But Maia belongs to the North, as do all maritime symbols.

Strange to relate, the same myth is related by the *Winnebagos,* a North American Indian Tribe, whose sorcerers know about *the sacred island, cradle of the race* (2) while a similar concept has taken root in India. Here the Hindu *Maya* or *Maha,* almost identical in origin and with the same symbolic value, has in turn produced the word *maiadan,* which in the East means 'market place, meeting place', and is the equivalent of both the French *mail* (mall/avenue) and the Ancient Breton *marha*, which means exactly the same thing. From this root *mai* or *maj*, containing the idea of great age and, therefore, of superiority and wisdom, we derive our words *magus, major, majesty*, and many others. Similarly, in India, *maha* means *great, superior*. Thus: *maharaja* (or the *raja* of the regional capital) and the *maharani* (whose name suggests our *Mara, Maria* or *Marie*, eternal symbol of divine births).

Is it surprising that in an Irish manuscript of the 12th century, entitled *Togail Troi* (The Fall of Troy) which traces the ancestry of the heroes engaged in this epic, *Maia* should be the name given to Juno, wife of the supreme god? Just as *Mait*, in very ancient times, was the name borne by the Egyptian *Isis*? Or that in the *Vedas* the wife of Vishnu was called *Maya*, while the mother of the Buddha would later be given the same name? And should we also find it surprising that the *May* moon should be the moon most venerated by devotees of the Buddhist faith?

That is why in certain French provinces (in Poitou, for example) people still say *a'nuit* (tonight) instead of *aujourd'hui* (today). And that is why the English still speak of a *fortnight* when they mean two weeks (14 days). And, incidentally, that is also why the festivals of the Christian Saints are celebrated on the **eve** of the day dedicated to a particular saint instead of on the day itself.

With reference to the *Maya* and to several other Hindu gods, there is only one obvious explanation for the *eight* arms of their busts: the fact that they represent the eternal symbol of the Atlantic *Maia* with its *eight* legs or the Pelagian jellyfish with its *eight* thread-like tentacles. The figure *eight* had been the especially sacred number in the Atlantic universe, after which India inherited the basis of its spiritual life from the conquerors of the Western World.

Maya was the mother of *Agni*, the fire god, a fact of great importance with regard to the *Calends of May*. Apropos, Schliemann writes in his *Trojan Antiquities*: "No sooner has the feeble spark emerged from the breasts of the mother, than it takes on the name *child*. We find in the *Veda* hymns about this frail but divine creature, which has just made its appearance. The parents place the little child on the straw. By its side is the mystic cow, in other words a symbol of milk and butter. Before it is a holy minister representing the *vagu*. He is holding a little wand in the shape of a flag and he is waving it to activate this new life on the brink of extinction. Then the little child is carried to the altar. There he acquires a marvellous strength which passes the understanding of those adoring him. Everything around him lights up. The ineffable light proceeding from him dispels the darkness and reveals the world. The angels (*devas*) rejoice and, bowing down before him, sing a hymn in his honour. On the left is the rising sun, and on his right the full moon. How has this transfiguration of *Agni* taken place? The moment the priest places the young god on the altar, another pours on his head the sacred libation, the *soma*, after which he smears him with the sacrificial butter. And when the priest has spread this purified butter over Agni, he is called the *anointed one* (*akta*). The inflammable matter has made him grow. His flame leaps up gloriously. It shines from within a cloud of smoke which rises in a column up to the sky. Its light mingles with the light of the stars on high. The god of beautiful clarity unveils before men that which had been hidden ..."

It is the birth of the *Ion* of archaic Greece.

So this is how fire on earth was born, in the image of fire in the sky: heat and the spark which preside over every act of creation. Now we have almost reached the First of May!

What is the name in Sanskrit of the stick which everywhere in the world primitive man has inserted into the middle of the wooden cross to create a spark? It is called *pramatha*: in other words, *Prometheus*, 'father of men', he who elevated them to the dignity of **workers** (in India the word for work is *artha,* cognate with our word *art*).

Festival of the workman-artisan: this is what May 1st has been since time immemorial, because it was a festival celebrating the birth of fire – all kinds of fire.

We now see why Mars took his place beside Flora during these celebrations. Whatever men may say and however they may prevaricate, has not every kind of *artillery* always been the main purpose of his industry?

Although Prometheus is an allegorical figure, he nevertheless represents Nordic, Occidental man, because we know him to be a **Titan**. Furthermore, his son *Deucalion* is attached in turn to the isles of the ocean called *Decalidonus*, or the ocean which washes over the shores of Ancient Caledonia (Scotland).

When we read that during the thousand years when he was held in chains, Prometheus' liver was devoured daily by the eagle representing the Dynasty of the **Air** (the third dynasty, according to legend), this means that for a millennium (or thereabouts) his descendants (who were still fighting to protect the Dynasty of the **Ocean**) were fighting North of the *Pont-Euxin* (Black Sea), and up to the foothills of the Caucasus, to safeguard the copper, gold and silver mines which they had been working since time immemorial and for their own very great profit. According to ancient belief, it was in the liver that a man's hereditary or *agnatic* seed was lodged. Now we can understand the image better. It should also be borne in mind that the Greeks called bronze *kaltos*, a word which closely resembles *keltos* and meant *Celtic man*. It could easily have been the result of related concepts.

In short, the men who made a name for themselves in History with *iron and fire*, and who set other lands on fire, as much with their **creative** power as with their ability to **destroy**, came from the **Atlantic** and from the **North**.

"When the first invaders we know of, the Aryans, came down onto the plains of the Indus and the Ganges, they constructed a pantheon on the basis of their own reactions to nature," Mulk Raj Anand writes in a book entitled *Kama Kala*. "Fire, which had always played an essential part in their nomadic life, was elevated to the rank of the gods and became *Agni* (5).

The 'North' was, of course, *Iran* (Persia) and *Armenia* whence the ancient Atlantic civilisation shone forth in the direction of India. This civilisation had already been long established in all the old Pelasgian colonies of Thrace, the Middle East and Western Asia.

Where indeed, thinking logically, could the cult of Spring, of light from the sun, of heat from fire, of the awakening of nature and of a return to activity have been born other than in the countries of the North? It is not in places where the sun is forever shining brightly, or where the seasons come and go without a slow and deep period of transition that men could have good reason to rejoice on the First of May. It was in the North: in Ireland, which the Latins called *Hibernia, Invernia*, and even further north, in Scandinavia, where the sun abandons men for six months and where the night seems to last for an eternity.

In no other part than in Nordic or northern regions were so many allusions made in legends to fire in general, and in particular to the fire which men kept burning near them: initially, because there were abundant peat bogs, and because peat was the first source of fuel, before oil and coal. In the poem of *Fjoelsuinn*, which comes from the Icelandic *Edda*, one of the heroes asks, "What demon is it that tarries in the front yard and walks around the flame?" In another passage we hear of Rig: "Rig entered, and fire broke out on earth..."

And blacksmiths: where do we find them? Of course, Greek mythology tells us of *Hephaistos* whose talents the gods were very happy to make use of. Which didn't make it any easier for him to enter Olympos! In Greece the smiths are never locals: they come from the *nether regions* (the *western* kingdom of *death* and *night*). This is not at all surprising since Greece was never especially industrial.

On the other hand, the *Kalevala* never stops referring to powerful workmen. *Illmarinen*, the great hero, is the man who is eternally forging metal, never happier than when he is wielding his hammer and setting the blue teeth of his saw to work. In his smithy at *Phojola*, he forges the famous sword, *sampo*. And, are customs not curiously perennial? At the Swedish Art Exhibition in Paris in 1963, only one pictorial composition was exhibited on the walls. And what did it show? *Visit to the smithy at Ancre.* A smithy which glowed red like the sun does in those parts, a smithy which revealed a love of fire going back thousands of years. It evoked the flaming torches which the old Nordic warriors used to attach to their helmets to terrify their enemies and to light up their camps. Looking at this picture by Pers Hillerstrom, one could almost hear the voice of old *Vainamoinen*, boasting as he built his copper boat that no other creature on earth, no other boat builder anywhere in the whole wide world, could compete with him. So, "clang! clang!" went the hammer. "Jump to it!" muttered the smith.

That is why the Nordics celebrated May 1st with heart and soul, a day they always called *Kalendertag*. They did it with heart and soul, and with true religious fervour – as is right and proper.

This is a dual festival. According to the old traditions it comprised the day before, and the following morning. The day before was April 30th, *Walpurgis* night (Swedish, *Valborgsmasseaften*). The next day, the Festival of Artisans, was a May 1st one like ours, not at all revolutionary. But there again, the month of May is called *Maj* and is pronounced *Mai*. Certain words are so powerful – powerful because they surge up from the depths of the human heart – that they are truly imperishable.

On April 30th the elite academic youth seem to have the place of honour because it is especially in the university cities that the ceremonies take place, and more particularly in the oldest ones: at Lund and at Upsala, for example - speaking only of Sweden.

In the latter city, a veritable Mecca of the land, all the students congregate in the early afternoon outside the wall which surrounds the university. On the stroke of three o'clock, the whole body moves into the enclosure, uttering joyful cries and shouts, and the students' caps of white velvet fly into the air. Then a religious silence descends on all those present, and one of the professors appears on a raised platform to make a speech. It is time to cheer, it is *hogtidlighet*: that is to say, the moment when the miracle takes place for all to see. A pale green light starts to appear over the top of the birch trees (the famous green ray). It is a time of intense emotion. Each student realises that at this very instant it is his own destiny that is being played out, since he is to be part of the action. After a speech in which he is free to introduce a personal note, the speaker finishes in a ritual manner by announcing the arrival of Spring. The great event is greeted with four resounding 'hurrahs'.

At nightfall, bright fires are lit everywhere, preferably at the top of hills (*calans*, the Celts would have said - they too celebrated all their festivals on high places, **Meccas** in the strictest sense of the word). Fire is supposed to chase away the evil spirits of the night. Who would deny that night gives us nightmares?

The young people then assemble at the foot of the tower of the old castle of Upsala near which there stands an ancient wooden bell tower. Then they move in procession towards the town. Torches. Fireworks everywhere. Festivities usually last until sunrise.

Is it not easy to relive those ancient rites? Is it not easy to imagine how those intrepid ancestors of the Vikings were only waiting for this sign from the skies to shake off their long inertia in order to sail over the seas and conquer strange lands?

My word, what a **moving day** indeed!

Even in the person of the *May Queen*, the *fiancée of the white sun* (as opposed to the *red winter* sun), the *magic* month, in the true sense of the word, resuscitates a pagan rite. The young woman chosen for this role is dressed in a white robe, like a true bride. But only 50 years ago she and her symbolic husband were supposed to give themselves totally to the god or goddess of fertility, to the creative power of the two sexes, and they were forbidden to enter later into a human marriage. When in time no more candidates for such a sacrifice were forthcoming, the gods were compelled to accept a compromise, and today a May Queen can marry as she wishes. The festivities continue all around her, there is a procession of waggons decorated with birch branches. The young people wear garlands of flowers around their necks (this explains the term 'bandoliers' which May days in Poitou have maintained) and throw drum-major batons into the air from which long ribbons are suspended.

To conclude, it is in no way surprising that in our Latinised countries we exchange bouquets of lily-of-the-valley on May 1st, whereas the Russians, who have a good deal of Scythian blood in their veins (and remember: the Scythians also wore helmets with torches attached to them!), demonstrate an atavistic tendency to revert to type by holding a grand procession on that day, on the great *mail* of the Red Square – a procession of Migs, soldiers and tanks.

And yet lily-of-the-valley too is rich in symbolism. Its scientific name is *convallaria Majalis* (May-flower-of-the-valley). But this lily-of-the-valley is no less a member of the family of *lileaceae*, one of several forms of lily: brother of the marsh lily of the Ligurians and Franks, ancient symbol of fecundity like the lotus of the Orientals, but also ancient symbol of working men's freedoms [and later of the French monarchy - Translator]. As late as the 15th Century, in France, the liege offered his lord a lily (*flos ligis*), preferably on Midsummer's Day, and that was enough to enter into an agreement with him, or to prolong the existing one.

Such is the history men have passed down to us about the First of May. Ever a *moving-day* as well as a day on which fire came from the heavens and enabled *Maia* to give birth to a new world.

* * *

3

RED AND GREEN

It is possible that the first race to impose itself on the others in the way that the white race has imposed itself over the past few centuries, more or less all over the world, was the red race.

The fact that it has now almost died out militates in favour of the theory, because all things that have lived a long time, moved over the curve and then begun their descent, usually do die.

Furthermore, this question has already been at issue for a long time because Garasse, quoted by Lacurne, quotes in turn Roman legal experts as stating that, when they had run out of red ink, they needed to use black - *explicate rubro, veniamus ad nigram.* (The dictionary explains that legal documents normally had to be written in red).

It is very well recorded that, with reference to giants as well as to certain peoples of North and East Africa and of the Middle East, men were described by historians as *red*. This was perhaps a reference to the copper tint of their skin, or to their habit of daubing themselves with some kind of reddish paint.

Plato speaks of the *red race of giants*.

Herodotus tells us that the Libyans around Lake Triton (south of what is now Tunisia) used to dye their skins *bright red*.

Eritrea is derived from the Greek *eruthios*, a word which means *red*. That is why the ancient Sea of Eritrea has come to be known as the *Red Sea*, although the colour of the water is in no way involved. It was probably looked on as an ancient fief of the *red men*, which would, of course, be historically correct.

It would in fact be difficult to argue that references to *red men* in the oldest legends and documents had no validity, bearing in mind that the habit of dyeing the skin bright red (from a substance taken out of the red soil) is still practised today by certain tribes in East Africa, in the Gulf of Bengal, the Malaccan Peninsular, and in some of the Philippine Islands. And it cannot be pure coincidence that the *Gallas* who live between Lake Nyanza and the river Juba, East of Abyssinia, and who interbred in the 16th Century with natives of this region and also with blacks, are said to be a race of people with a copper coloured skin.

Finally – and this is not unimportant – in heraldry (a very ancient art) blood-red, called *gules*, is the most highly esteemed colour of all because it relates to the oldest race. "The colour red or vermilion is of good estate and dignity", we read in the Sicilian 'Armory of Colours' (*"La rouge couleur ou vermeille est de grand état et dignité": Blason des Couleurs*).

How can all this be explained?

It could be argued that the *red race of giants* has been included in the category of *red heads*, a term applied to men with copper coloured hair of Celtic origin who had invaded the Orient. But this hair colour, although it was very characteristic and important at a certain epoch (for example, in the ten millennia preceding our era (1)), fails to explain why the *skin* was dyed red. This custom must certainly have been connected with a cult of enormous antiquity, no doubt perpetuating the memory not of the giants of the Epoch of Gigantism but of the antediluvian giants: Atlantans, Titans, Cyclops, whose *red heads* and white skin showed them to be the successors of the 'Gigantics', with perhaps a few heirs as well.

It is undeniable that the idea of 'red' has always throughout Antiquity been associated with the Nordic and Celtic races, i.e. the men of the North Atlantic.

On Tibetan frescoes showing the *Four Kings of the Four Compass Points*, West is represented by a red figure holding in its hands a *chorten*, a small funerary monument. There can really be no mistake.

The three ancient British Isles (Ireland, Scotland and Wales) were looked on as *red* by the Greeks and Latins. Caesar, referring to Ancient Caledonia (Scotland), speaks of the *Rutilae Caldonae Comae* (red - tending to golden yellow – Caledonian hair). In his *Dictionary of Greek and Roman Geography*, Smith quotes an ancient text beginning with the words: *Rutilae Caledonium habitantium comae* (red hair of the Caledonian inhabitants). In passing, we should draw attention to the coherence of this whole story, illustrated by the fact that at the bottom of the Red Sea there is a *Promontorium Chaldonae* ('Headland of Caledonia') at the mouth of the Euphrates. It was from the shelter of this headland that the Atlantan giants invaded Mesopotamia.

In Irish epic poetry there is a cycle of songs constituting the *Cycle of the Red Branch*. In one of the more recent ballads of this country's folklore, *Cailte* (an incarnation of the Celt), on meeting St. Patrick, describes for him the beauty of Aran, resplendent with the purple of its rocks.

Runic steles, discovered in Scandinavia and in ancient Celtic lands, are decorated with motifs drawn against a background of red ochre (the usual colour for materials with which furniture in Brittany is still covered).

We know that the Gauls touched up the features of their dead with red. And, in Scandinavian countries, corpses were laid out inside a hollowed-out oak. The tannin could be relied on to preserve them – and no doubt also to tint them.

The Picts, originally from the Atlantic part of the Celtic area, were men who dyed their skins. History does not tell us whether they dyed themselves red, but there is every reason to believe it – unless they dyed themselves red and green, like certain Indian tribes.

The ancient capital of Denmark (up to the 5th Century) was the city of *Roskilde*, fief of the kings from the heroic family of the *Skjoldung*, descendants of *Skjold*, son of *Odin*. Roskilde, which in Christian times would become *Rosenkilde*, means in etymological terms *red race* or *red descendants*. But even when altered to '*race of the rose*', the word does not change its meaning since the rose had been in very ancient times, indeed since time immemorial, the symbol of the colour red (and thus of *material* fire but also of the fire of *love*), which was associated with this race of conquerors. Wherever the symbol would later be seen and reproduced, for example, throughout German lands, traces of the roots *reuss*, *roth* or *reuth* (the flaming colour of fire and of combat) would be found in the names of towns, rivers and valleys. Did not the family Rothschild (red shield) also carry out their conquests with this name? (NB: the many references to the *rose* in Christmas carols, for example, *Es ist ein' Ros' entsprungen*, translated into English as 'the noble stem of Jesse'. And many more. Translator.)

The roots *erit*, *erut* and *rut*, in so far as they are connected with the idea of *desire* and of sexual satisfaction, are also linked to the concept of the colour red. For example, the island of *Erytheia*, Kingdom of the Dead where Hercules landed after sailing on a misty and unfriendly sea, cannot be anything other than Ireland or an island situated in the same area. The men of yore placed *Erytheia* (the Red) in the *Hesperides*. Consequently, certain historians have attached the island to the Canaries, although this region bore absolutely no resemblance to any descriptions which had been given of it. It should be remembered that the term *Hesperides* was understood in Antiquity to mean all the islands which enclosed the area to the *West*, within the *espère: sphère*

(Eng. sphere) of the setting sun. And, of these islands, the British Isles were by far the most important.

There are many Irish folk tales about sailors fishing for the souls of the dead on the seashore. Smith, in his Dictionary, quotes Procopius who relates that, according to the inhabitants of Caledonia, the souls of the dead were taken to this spot. In every other respect they were governed by the Franks (so the Latin author tells us) and yet they never had to pay tribute. They said they were for all time exempted from this obligation because of a certain service they rendered (…). Each one of them was in turn required to conduct the souls of the deceased to their last resting place.

In the *Gaelic and English Dictionary* of MacLachlan and Stewart we see that *Car-hon*, whose name means *murmur of the waves*, was the *Ocean Chief*, as well as chief of the *Reutmatic Race*. It is beyond doubt that this *red* figure is identical with *Charon* who later, in Greek mythology, would become the ferryman of the Nether Regions.

Thus, the Island of *Erytheia*, guarded by *Eurythion*, was definitely situated in this region. In the Finnish *Kalevala* the *Isle of the Blessed* (Deceased) is called the Isle of *Manala* (land of *Mana*) which reminds us of the Isle of *Man*.

While we are on the subject of *red*, iron and fire, it is worth noting the interesting relationship between the French roots *fer* and *ver* from which we derive the word *vermilion*, a term still used to describe the colour with which several peoples dye their skin.

And does the French verb *vermiller* not mean 'to turn over the earth with a snout', in the same way that the famous rod of Prometheus burrows into the hole of the wooden cross to produce fire? In Old French, *vermillon* had a sexual connotation. We read in a letter of Chaulieu quoted by Littré: "It (my health) is not in an enviable condition, and the happy 'vermillon' (Eng. worm, sexual organ, 'prick') is very much faded". Also, in a rhyme by the poet Charles d'Orléans: "*Je rougis comme vermillon, aussi flambant qu'une étincelle*" (Eng. "I blush crimson, and glow like a spark").

The root meaning of *ver* (worm), in as much as it contains the idea of a point which is inserted and procreates, is confirmed by all the words which are derived from it more or less directly: *ver* (worm), the animal which burrows tirelessly; *verrat*, pig or wild boar which '*vermillonne la terre*' (Eng. '*turns over*' or '*burrows into the earth*'). See also *verrat paillard* (Eng. *boar*, and by extension a *rake* or *dirty old man*: cf. Littré). These references are so widely valid that the word *cramois* (scarlet/crimson), which comes to us from the East, is derived from Sanskrit *karmi,* which also means a *worm*.

In Gaelic, *verdh* means *root* (which *burrows* into the earth).

The French adjective *vert*, describing the colour of vegetation, also implies the idea of *pouring forth* and of *first birth*, since the word is not only applied to *colour* but to any concept of *novelty* or *renewal*; of *youth* and *freshness* – as in the expression *green* vegetables (even when describing fresh *carrots*); *verte vieillesse* (green – i.e. *healthy* old age), etc.

So, there has always been a close analogy between green and red. We find confirmation of this in an old Irish text, *The Calendar of Oengus*, in which the words *ross* and *ros* are used to signify a *wood* or *forest*. This is exactly similar to *celadon* (willow green), cognate with *Caledonia*, meaning a soft green colour; and also cognate with *caledon*, an old English term for 'wood', 'forest', 'green shelter'.

This helps us understand the anomaly of the name *Greenland*, three-fifths of which is covered in ice, and was so covered in the 10th Century when the Norwegian king, Eric the Red, colonised it. The name given to it by this king, or by which it was already known, must originally have meant: *first land, original land, land of the racial root*. In fact, we now know that this land has been occupied since very early times. And remember that the word *hver* is still the name by which the warm waters are known, and that its symbol resembles the ejaculation of seed, or sap.

In the Icelandic Edda it is said that although men call the land *land*, or *earth*, the giants called it v*erdant*: not verdant (*green*), as we have erroneously come to understand the word, but rather, verdant in its *ancient* sense.

It must be properly understood that when the civilised world was young, words had quasi-magical power. To one main syllable, corresponding to a *sound*, several closely related *concepts* became attached, as if by magnetism. Thus, *ogres*, the heirs of the giants, bore the name which was confused with *red ochre*.

In Provence, or to be more exact, in the valley of the Luberon, at a place called *Roussillon* because of its *red ochre* coloured soil, "a path runs up to the blazing red hill from the village square". And what is the name of the spot thus described by Maurice Pezet? (2) It is the *Giants' Causeway*. Incidentally, in the Celtic tongue, the words *ocri* and *ogri* both mean *prince* or *young king*: almost certainly because they refer to men of the most ancient race.

To conclude. Why have *ogres* and *giants*, the colour *red* and the *red* earth become so closely interconnected? There could be several reasons.

First of all, the giants were red … because they were green! In other words … because in the days of yore they were looked upon as the *first* race, or at least the *oldest* race to be remembered by men.

Secondly, the giants could have been known and renowned for having been born on the *red earth* of the Nordic and Celtic regions, rich in iron and copper. One could almost imagine that by exploiting these minerals, the Atlantans appeared to be red, just as a coal miner is blackened by the work he does.

It is also possible that, very long ago, the first men to live in these parts were still very close to their animal heritage and could, therefore, have had violent physical reactions. Quite simply, they could – like other species – have undergone by adaptation the phenomenon of mimesis, and their skin could have taken on a bronzed hue. Do not forget that, to this very day, people from these same regions get burnt *red* in the sun, but do not get a *brown* tan. Also, it is the *red* head who has most freckles (French '*taches de rousseur*'). Why should the skins of their ancestors, ten or twenty thousand years earlier, not have been red all over?

Another possibility is that the giant Nordic races *looked* red to the people of the Mediterranean because of the copper breastplates and helmets that they were the first to wear, or perhaps because they arrived from the West, where the sun 'catches fire' as it sets.

But there is yet another explanation, because Red Skins do in fact exist.

There are many authors who think that a cataclysm, pre-dating the last flood, cut the land between America and Africa in two. That could explain the existence in very ancient times of native Red Skins on our (European) continent. They could have survived along the coasts and on the islands of the Atlantic Ocean where they could eventually have created the ancient Atlantan empire governed by ten kings. Of these kings, legend tells us that they were forbidden by law to fight each other and that they could not condemn their fellow citizens to death: two things that would later also feature in the charter of the *Order of the Golden Fleece*, conceived by the descendants of the Atlantans in the Duchy of Burgundy.

In his book entitled '*Aux Sources de l'Atlantide*' (The Sources of Atlantis), Leonard de Saint-Michel notes that, in certain South

American schools, children are taught in history classes about *our ancestors the Atlantans* ...

It could also be argued that an ancient race of red giants, originating on the American continent, spilled over onto the other continents via the North Pole, since Asia, as well as Europe, has preserved in its legends memories of giants who had come down from the Northern regions.

What might swing the balance in favour of this argument is the fact that there is a correlation between the nature of a man and the milieu in which he lives. After all, there are enormous marine animals in the Northern seas, and America itself bears the mark of a form of gigantism – especially in our times, and in many aspects of its life. In America, Nature has developed on a scale quite different from that in the rest of the world. Could the human race not have experienced the same phenomenon in its infancy? Perhaps the influence of the soil and of the atmosphere is still of a kind to have made it possible for modern Americans to develop a biggest-in-the-world complex in everything they undertake? Are they not the first Whites to want to erect the tallest buildings (which, into the bargain, they have dubbed skyscrapers, a perfect replica of the Atlantan ambition to climb up to the sky)? And do they not make the largest bombs, when they are not growing the largest peaches and apricots?

Or is this just a resurgence of their ancestral character and of a tendency which, from the Atlantans to the last Goths, drove the Atlantan races and all other races that were their heirs, or were civilised by them, to create colossal works of art?

* * *

4

PHRYGIA AND PHOENICIA:
TWO COLONIES
OF THE
ATLANTIC WORLD

We are told that Phrygia was "an ancient country in the middle of Asia Minor that owed its name to the *Briges* of Macedonia, an offshoot of the Pelasgians of Thrace". In fact, Phrygia was quite a lot besides this because, following on an investigation undertaken by Herodotus in Greece and Egypt to establish what nation was the oldest in the 'world', the Egyptians agreed that the Phrygians were older than they were (1). It is not important to question the veracity of this anecdote, although it is actually quite explicit. What **is** important is that Herodotus, along with other historians, accepted it as true.

We know who the Pelasgians were: their gigantic constructions were always mentioned together with those erected by the Cyclops. They were the *Sea People* who came from the North West Atlantic and, according to the Sages of Antiquity, they were the first conquerors of Egypt and Greece.

Herodotus' opinion about the Phrygians reminds us that the first invasions from the North to the East were undertaken by land and river and took them to the Black Sea before other invaders came via the Pillars of Hercules and the Mediterranean.

The Pelasgians who settled in Thrace were extremely powerful and founded several empires on the territories of the Middle East and of Western Asia. Phrygia was one of them. Unfortunately, this civilisation, which was one of the most brilliant (like that of Armenia, with which it is often confused), had already sunk very low by the beginning of 'historic' times. Consequently, very few elements remain to enable us to make a fair judgement, since the evidence that we do have has been distorted by successive waves of conquerors.

It is generally agreed that the word *Phrygian*, throughout Antiquity, meant Trojan, and both terms were used equally to describe the Aegean world (2). Seneca speaks of the *Phryxeum mare* to identify the Aegean Sea. *Greater Phrygia* did in fact include Troy and some other fairly large cities (*Iconios, Abidon, Gordion*), and there was a time when Troy was the largest city in the whole Middle East.

With regard to its founding, the legends agree with each other and with History.

It all began with Electra: not the daughter of Agamemnon, but Electra of Atlantis (sister of Maia) (3), who by the grace of Heaven (or by the grace of Zeus, since it is the Greeks who are telling the story) gave birth to *Dardanus* who was no doubt present when the fate of the future *Dardanelles* was being settled. Wishing to extend his empire, Dardanus built Troy and founded the *Troad*. He had a son, *Erechtonios*, whose son was *Tros*, whose son was *Illus*, whose son was *Laomedon*. This Laomedon, who was king of the Phrygians, had to fight Hercules (Gk. *Herakles*): not the great mythical Hercules, the giant dressed in leaves and wielding a club, but *Alcides of Tiryns*, surnamed Hercules, who defeated him and destroyed his capital. Alcides, acting as a good prince should, finally returned the city to *Priam*, son of Laomedon, when he was old enough to govern it. But 60 years later, Troy was razed to the ground and burnt by the army of Agamemnon.

When it was at its peak Troy had, in this part of the world, dominated all art and every kind of industry. Its *mares* (horses) were famous, so too were its materials embroidered in gold, which were, incidentally, called *phrygiae*. And there were also its singing and its *Phrygian music* (music in the Phrygian mode).

The most ancient divinity to have left a trace in the ruins of Troy is the one that Schliemann, for want of a better name, called the *Illian Minerva*, probably because he assigned it to the future *palladium*, guardian of the city, but which is in fact closer to *Juno* than to *Pallas*. She first appears in archeology in the archaic shape of a small disc of baked mud, with a hole or a cone in its middle, to represent the navel of the world. When she evolves with the passage of time, this rough disc will change into an owl's head on a body whose only sculptured feature will, once again, be a navel – an enormous navel.

Some scholars place these figurines in the Neolithic epoch, and others of exactly the same sort have been found in Gaul and in the Scandinavian countries. They illustrate the Atlantan myth about the appearance of life on earth, such as it is presented in the Finnish *Kalevala* and reported by Plato in references to the island of Atlantis (4). It is from this mythical island, also called *hile* (navel or vital centre) that *Illus* and *Illion* get their name. Then, from Illus we get *Yul* and *Julius*, and it is with this title that Julius Caesar, with Aeneas as go-between, claimed Troy as his mother-country. In Sweden, *Yul* is still the name with which the festival of symbolic birth (*Noel* in France or *Christmas* in Protestant England) is celebrated. In Korea, *Yul* means Spring, the beginning of life.

What was the name of the goddess-with-a-navel whose archaic Trojan effigies date back approximately to the 7th Millennium before our era, according to Schliemann? Actually, we don't know: but probably it was she who gave her name to Phrygia. Could it, therefore, have been *Frig* or *Frigga*, an old Scandinavian goddess who seems to correspond to *Freia* of the *Kalevala*? She was goddess of love and fruitfulness, from whose name the modern French words *frai* and *frayer* are derived (noun: *spawning*, and verb: *to spawn*).

We read in the *Great Encyclopedia* that the first divinity of the Phrygians was a goddess-mother-of-all-things. "The most suitable name for her (according to the writer of the article) is *Ma* which the Latins translated as *Magna Mater* (Great Mother)". This corresponds to *Maia* and corroborates everything we have written elsewhere on this subject.

The same sources tell us that, in archaic sanctuaries, the goddess was sometimes represented by a black stone. One of these stones, "... an ancient and venerable image of the goddess, was transported to Rome with great pomp and ceremony in the year 204 before our era". It came from *Pessinonte*. But is this *black stone* not the *aetite* or *eagle stone* which, according to legend, fell from heaven "*with a hole like an eye in the middle*"? The eye (Fr. *oeil*) is a word which according to the naturalists corresponds to French *hile* (*hilum* in anatomical botany). Furthermore, the eagle (according to the same legend – a legend which was powerful enough to be recorded in the *Larousse* Dictionary) *used to take this stone to its nest to facilitate the laying of her eggs.*

These stones have also been found in ancient Celtic countries. We French call them *haches* (axes) but they are in fact sacred stones, *pointed,* and with a hole in them. There are many examples in the Carnac museum. It has been suggested that the holes were there to make it possible to wear these little axes round the neck, strung together to form a necklace. But in our opinion the holes were intended to symbolise in one and the same object the hermaphrodite character of the Creator and the union of the two sexes (that which penetrates and that which is penetrated), as a result of which the world was born. These holes are also found in much larger stones, with the same shape, which it would be impossible to wear around the neck.

Finally, one should just add that in Celtic *Venetia* these stones were known as *men-garun: stones of thunder* or *Jupiter* stones or, again, *eagle* stones. And in Celtic Venetia, as in the Orient, they are also supposed to have 'fallen from Heaven' (or from the sky); while at the beginning of the 20th Century they were still an object of veneration in country districts of France. But let us return to Phrygia.

The etymology of *Phryge* via *Frig* does not exclude the root *brig* from the name of the Pelasgian clan in Thrace from which the Phrygians are known to have been descended. Remember that the letters p, b, v and f often mutate. Thus *frig* can explain *brig* according to the laws of etymology, but also as a matter of hard fact. For example, St. Brigitta is the Patron Saint of Sweden, and St. Pelagius was Patron Saint of Crete, just as St. Denis (as an extension of Dionysos) was Patron Saint of the Frankish kings. In almost every case the names of Pagan gods, revered in any given place, became the names of Christian saints revered in the same spot. The same thing applies to objects of worship. It is never possible to start again from scratch: **the future must always be rooted in the past**. With reference to St. Patrick and his companions, we read in *l'Art Irlandais* by Françoise Henry: "They seem to have followed a policy similar to the one that Gregory the Great would recommend two centuries later to Mellitus when he sent him on a mission to the Saxons: *keep the pagan temples and destroy only the idols. Turn the temples into churches. Continue to observe the traditional holy days and allow the faithful to sacrifice cattle as was their custom, but dedicating the red* (!) *letter days to the holy martyrs whose relics now rest in the churches.*"

We also see that *brig*, in both Gallic and Scandinavian languages, has been assimilated into *brick* or *brigantine*, the boat that floats on the water. It has adopted the name of *Virgin of the Waters*, which is why the English always call their ships by female names to this day. Ships are referred to as *she*: they are *mait*, then *maid*, by derivation from *maia*. (Incidentally, the English cathedral *nave* is taken from the French *nef*, which also meant a ship, originally). It is also worth noting that in the Danish language *bric* means a *disc* and describes a circular plate made of wood or cork, floating on the water. Surely this must remind us of the island (*hilum*) or navel, symbolised by discs of baked earth, which in the most ancient city of Troy (as in the most ancient parts of Gaul) symbolised the oldest divinity worshiped by men? And should we forget the amber discs with a hole in the middle, found at Maiendorf? (Does not the name itself prove the point?) Not to mention the fact that in Gaelic *brigh* means not only the 'essential substance', but also the 'power and rank' that goes hand in glove with great age? (5)

Enough said about a subject which we could continue to discuss at great length. Just remember that with *Phryge* the dictionaries refer us to *Brige* - and let us proceed.

When Troy was destroyed by Agamemnon, all the sons of Priam, the princes of the *Troad* and their allies fled. Some went south and to the sea. Others went via the Black Sea and swept back to the West to the Atlantan territories where they had originally come from; or to the lands they had colonised in the course of their migrations. It was at this point that Europe was born, the Europe we have inherited and which they created by their dynamism, their already very advanced civilisation and the perfection of their weapons.

In the course of the last few millennia, all peoples of the Orient have had only one word, in various forms, to distinguish the Europeans. They were called *Frengi*, *Ferengi*, *Feringhee*, derived from *Phrygian* (our *Franks*). They thought of Western Europe as *Frangistan*. **This Europe was built partly in the hope of taking revenge on Greece.** Hence, the expedition of the Galatians in the 3rd Century before our era, and later, that of the Romans. The Galatians pillaged Delphos, whose treasures they had good reason to reclaim, and together with the Phrygians (the *contemporary* Phrygians) they occupied Paphlagonia (ancient Phrygia) up to Halys (6).

The Romans avenged Aeneas and the Galatians avenged Phryxos, the eponymous ancestor of the Franks.

We read in the *Memoirs relating the Genealogy of the House of Austria* by Ollivier de la Marche that, "when the Trojans abandoned Troy, one of them, a godchild (**sic**) of King Priam, moved with his followers to the land called Austria, conquered it and reigned there, and had several children there".

Simultaneously, Aeneas moved to Latium, and "Francio, son of the pious Hector, exiled and expelled from Troy, worked hard and to such good effect that he reached the noble country which is today called France, where he enlarged the fine city of Lutèce (Lutetia) and called it Paris, after his uncle Paris of Troy". According to Tacitus, it was this same Francio (sometimes called Franco) who built the city of Frankfurt in Germany, when he conquered that part of Gaul.

Ollivier de la Marche is a credible scholar who liked to present history 'undressed' or 'in the raw', an expression which in Celtic times referred to an *oral* tradition, the only *true* History.

One finds the same story in *Les Antiquités Gauloises* by Claude Fouchet. He writes that according to ancient traditions, preserved by the druids (a caste that survived till the 6th Century) "... part of the [Gaulish] people were natives of the country, although there were also people in distant towns and in the areas along the Rhine who had had to flee their homes because of wars and frequent floods by a *tumultuous sea, as well as men fleeing from the Greeks after the destruction of Troy."*

Most of the Phrygians who streamed back to the West settled on land which was named after them, for example, *Friesland*. Friesland is in fact the same as *Phrygia*. In the Middle Ages, Frisian wool was still known as *laine de Phrygie* (Phrygian wool) (7). In architecture, *Larousse* tells us that the word *frieze* comes from Latin *phrygium*, as does the Italian *fregio*. It is certainly not without good cause that the house of Eastern Frisians showed a *phoenix* with its feet in flames as the most important part of its escutcheon. Phoenicia, with origins similar to those of Phrygia, suffered the same fate and the same destruction of its homes by fire.

It seems almost certain that the Phrygians also conquered the Feroe Islands known to ancient geographers as *Frisland*. In Danish, *fri* and *frank* both mean *free*. And, in the same language, *fri* is also interchangeable with *freo*, which could explain the name *Feroe*, from which we have up to now derived the word *faar*, which was supposed to mean *sheep*.

Whatever the truth of all this may be, it is certainly from Friesland proper, and from its marshes, that the sons of the ancient Phrygians, refugees from the Asiatic coast, came down to conquer the Gauls. The iris of the marshes, the French *fleur de lys* (lily), the emblem of the Frankish *race* long before it became that of the absolute *monarchy*, was a symbol born in Eastern Phrygia – just like the famous Phrygian bonnet, (revolutionary) symbol of liberty. It was in fact the slaves, or rather, the weavers of this part of Asia Minor who pioneered the defence of working men's liberties. And it was also the weavers of Frankish origin who, in the 14th Century AD, in the weaving houses of Flanders and Normandy, would defend the same liberties, wearing the same Phrygian bonnet. Unbeknown to those who created it, but nevertheless sealed in blood by History, it was because the French were born of Frankish or Phrygian domination that the famous Phrygian bonnet now adorns the coin we call a *franc*, and that France has come to be known as the country of liberty.

In his *Dictionary of Greek and Roman Geography*, Smith tells us that the real name by which the *Frisei* or *Frisaie* were known in Antiquity was *Frisaevones*. Apparently, this word should be translated as *Ancestors of the Frisians* (or *Phrygians*), or even *The Eternally Free*.

Since a sense of tradition was extremely powerful at the time in question, it is reasonable to suppose that the Phrygians of the *Troad* and their brothers, the *Briges* of the Black Sea, settled in Northern Europe because these lands were their ancestral territory; and that they had only left several millennia earlier because they had been driven away by the floods and tidal waves of a *tumultuous sea*. What could in fact be simpler than to sail up the Rhine and down the Danube to the Black Sea, and make a new start?

Phoenicia.

What are the oldest objects that archeologists have suppressed when displaying the results of their diggings in the soil of the various Phoenician ports? Teeth of deer, ibex and bears, mixed up with crafted flint. Plus *dolmens, menhirs, cromlechs*. Menhirs with a hole pierced through them were still part of the cult worship of sterile women in the 19th Century of our era (8).

And what else? Discs similar to those found in Phrygia, sometimes decorated with a crescent moon in a triangle or with a lotus flower. But what is a *crescent moon* other than an image of the *fertile crescent*, described by the French as *creux, nef, cal* or *van* in their different countries of passage, eternal symbols of divine gestation and birth? And here the crescent overlaps with the *hilum* or *eye,* set in a triangle, specifically at the time of Ionian domination – the triangle being the *Ioni*.

And what else? Walls and ramparts made of enormous blocks of stone. Stones pierced through with a hole, stones decorated with a cone, cones pierced through with a hole: drawings of divinities, male, female and hermaphrodite, similar to those discovered in Phrygia, as well as in Celtic and Nordic lands. Shaped like an amphora or vase. And once again, the owl with the great navel. Ornaments with braids, crenellated ornaments, patterns of concentric circles, winged *orbs* (according to the archeologists) which are in fact winged *seeds*, duplicating (in an age when the Divinities of the Air were triumphant) the tadpole or the embryo with hair or axil appendage, and symbolising the first 'seeds' of a 'grain-like' sea, the name given in ancient days to the Atlantic. The very size of the discs, which are tiny compared to the other ornaments, make it obvious that these are **not** depictions of *globes* or *worlds*, as has been thought up to now.

And there is more: for want of temples (indeed, before there **were** temples) – a sacred clearing within the forest, or on a high place. Bodies laid out in wooden coffins. According to Ovid and Xenophon, this was the evidence of a *fish* cult – very many sacred fish. All this evidence, all these traces, indicate the Pelasgian origin of a civilisation whose development was related to that of Egypt and Assyria.

It is obvious that the Pelasgians who set foot on the Lebanese coast in order to establish a series of trading posts in that region, invaded the East via the Pillars of Hercules, and that they also settled in Egypt where they were called *Peluzians* rather than Pelasgians. We should therefore not be surprised to find traces of the Celts rather than of the Scandinavians in Phoenicia. Even in an epoch marked by the unity of an Atlantic paganism, there is a distinct nuance between the northern territories and those of the British Isles. They were all fine sailors, but the former were realists while the latter were poets. The former were extrovert and the latter introvert, as we would rather say today. It is the sign of the Twins (*Gemini*; *Jumala* in Finnish mythology; *Jumelles* in French [feminine form]): in other words, the union of strength and poetry which enabled the Atlantans to accomplish such great deeds and have so much influence over a wide area. The concept of *Atlantis* could be compared to the concept of *Europe* in the 19th Century AD. Like modern Europe, Ancient Atlantis grouped together peoples of different tribal backgrounds who, by ceaseless commercial and warrior contact, had attained more or less the same level of civilisation and who had, in a general way, developed the same view of the universe. That is why all the countries fertilised by Western genius in pre-historic times still carry the indelible stamp of their founders, a stamp which is immediately obvious.

Moreover, the colonization of this area by a civilisation of Atlantic origin is sufficiently evidenced by the fact that hero-gods like Tant and Cadmus must have been *sage philosophers* – like those of Ancient Assyria, or like the Druids of Ancient Gaul: and with such revealing names!

There is absolutely no doubt of this even although so few traces have remained, just as is the case in Phrygia and in Mesopotamia. The reasons are simple. First of all, the provinces in question are immensely old; and, secondly, the natives were Semites (probably few in number at the time), and when the Aryan domination went into decline, they reacted in the way all subject peoples do, namely, they destroyed in a blind rage all traces of the grandeur of their former masters (even when they had benefited from it). They then ridiculed what had been considered sacred, and spread lies about what had been destroyed in order to ruin the name of the civilisers before posterity. "I do not believe (writes Renan in his *Mission en Phénicie*) that any great city having played a leading role for centuries, could have left fewer traces of its existence than Tyre. Ezechiel was being truly prophetic when he said about *Sur*: 'They will seek you, but you will not be there'". But Renan was doubly mistaken. On the one hand, the cities that have suffered a similar fate are too numerous to mention (we need only recall Troy, Nineve and Babylon); and on the other hand, the words of Ezechiel were not so much prophetic as representative of a programme of action and *vengeance*. Renan must in fact have realised this himself since he adds: "Thus, Tyre represents the first revolt of *municipal republics* against oriental despotism. (...) The antipathy of the Jewish prophets for Tyre, their jealous fury when they saw it escape from the Assyrian scourge, is only comprehensible when we realise that it was fanned by fraternal hatred".

In our opinion it is a slight exaggeration to speak here of a 'fraternal' hatred. Renan was still the product of false historical data. It is perfectly true that in making this assertion we are casting no stones. We are all God's children, that is true, and it is reasonable to assert from a humanitarian point of view that all peoples on earth are of equal importance in the 'world order'. Nevertheless, it is equally true that the way in which those differences that distinguish one people from another survive over vast periods of time, represents an historical phenomenon, which the honest historian, who wishes to be worthy of the name, must always take into account.

The civilisations which emerged from the Atlantan World, Celtic or Scandinavian, have always distinguished themselves - whether it be in the exercise of their cults or in their approach to the sciences - by a philosophical turn of mind that was resolutely opposed to Oriental despotism and fanaticism. They were characterised right from the start by a form of government that some scholars have defined as an *aristocratic democracy*. This system was maintained by the Franks up to the accession of the Capetians, while the English and Nordics have maintained it up to the present day – albeit in a very degraded form.

But it is important to establish where Phoenicia got its name from. Perhaps from Phoenix, one of its kings? This provides no answer to a question which deserves careful consideration.

There is no language except Celtic that can give meaning to the root *phoen*. This root is apparently of very great antiquity and can still be seen in the written version of the king's name just mentioned, as well as in the name of the bird which is always reborn from its ashes. We also see it in the name given to a red colouring called *phoenine* (Middle Eng.; *fenix* from Old Fr.; from Latin *Phoenix*; from Greek *phoinix* = *phoenix* = Phoenician purple. Translator).

The word *foen,* (also *foehn*), is primarily used to describe the *west wind* in France. Around this basic concept several others have been grouped, including that of harpoon or trident, known in French as *fouêne*, a tool for fishing still used under this name in Brittany (cf. the old French word *fouesnant*).

But, whether we are speaking of the West Wind or the Trident, the name most certainly connected with these things must be that of an essentially *seafaring* people. This etymology also explains the *fish* cult practised by the Phrygians, and also the *winged orbs*, symbols of seaweed and seeds (*gregnor*) blown by the West Wind onto Oriental coasts.

The idea of *wind* is so dominant in this matter that the root *phoen*, changed to *phon* (sound), has given birth to terms used in linguistics (phon-etics), and we know that human language was itself associated in furthest Antiquity with the sound of the wind and the waves.

As stated before, relative to *Grimm's Law*, ph and f can mutate into v: in fact, this can happen quite frequently. So *foen*, having produced *fen*, gave *ven* and *vain* (in Old French), words which have become modern [French] *vent* (wind). And so too the name *Vénètes*, or *Vaniques*, contains the same root as the name *Phénicien* (cf. Fr. *Vénitien*). It is not therefore surprising that Bailly's Dictionary refers to *Finland* as a derivation of *Venedia* via *Feningia*, and there is even less cause for surprise when we see that the Latin words *Fenni* and *Fenici* were once used to describe both Phoenicians and Finns.

In short, the Phoenicians were the descendants of the *fils-du-vent* (sons of the wind); of the primeval wind - the *phoen* or Norwegian (i.e., northern) wind. La Villemarqué creates from Pelasgian a first name, which in Breton is pronounced *Morvan*: 'man of the sea'. The

Vans of the Celts and the Nordic *Vanir*, ancestors of the *Vénètes* and the *Vaniques* of Western Asia, were the founders of Phoenicia. It is, therefore, easy to understand why the Phoenicians, according to historians, observed a *wind* cult.

As for the city of *Tyre*, one should point out that Tyre was the name of a god spelled Tyr that we find together with *Thor* in the *Edda* mythology (9). Modern Icelanders think that the first inhabitants of their country were Irish monks who emigrated to those parts in the 8th Century AD. But *Thule* was already very well known to the Ancient Greeks. For example, Procopius, at the beginning of our era, notes that it was *ten times larger than Brittany*, to the north of which it lay. The name *Thule* was probably given in Antiquity to both Iceland and Greenland, because these two islands were joined together in very early times (when sea levels were very much lower. Translator). Together with Scotland and Ireland, and probably Norway too, Thule no doubt formed part of the ancient Atlantan bloc before its destruction, probably during the flood which, according to myth, precipitated the survivors – or the most valorous ones – towards countries in the South and the Middle East.

Because of their colonising and mercantile spirit, the ancient Phoenicians have been called the *English of Antiquity*. Certain words thrust themselves onto our attention as a matter of pure common sense.

All ports called *Portus Herculus*, says Renan, *should be considered colonies of the ancient Syrians* (10). Hercules was never a Greek hero, but a prototype of the Pelasgian hero, Western in origin.

Finally, we know that the Phoenicians had close ties with the islands of the western North Atlantic. Smith notes in his *Dictionary of Greek and Roman Geography* that it was they who informed the Greeks about the islands of the West, particularly Ireland. He tells us, too, that there were *obvious* contacts between Europe and Phoenicians and that the latter *even sailed into the Baltic*. This has been emphasised because Smith, like everyone else (it is repeated *ad nauseam!*), believed that the civilising influence came from *Central Asia*. But if that were so, one is entitled to ask why the first great empires of Central Asia should have been created for the greater glory of a white race with blond hair and blue eyes - azure blue, into the bargain!

Furthermore, it is not easy to accept that sailors from the delightful Mediterranean world should have taken it into their heads to venture into the misty, stormy, Nordic empire of Pluto. Whereas it is, on the contrary, very easy to believe that bold sailors from the rough seas, sons of an ocean that was supposed to encircle the world, should have been tempted to cross the narrow passage into a miserable little interior lake in order to make History in virgin and radiant territories.

* * *

5

THE KING'S HORN:
LA LICORNE

Such is the definition of the unicorn: the King's Horn. This is the true meaning of the word, which never described a *uni*-corn, except by corruption of the original. Incidentally, it does not make good etymological sense to try and derive *li* from *uni* in *uni-cornis*. Why complicate matters? *Li* is a Celtic word which meant *king*. Perhaps we may eventually be willing to accept that our ancestors knew how to speak before being conquered by the Romans, and that once the conquerors had left, they returned to their original idiom – which they had in any case never totally abandoned. This idiom was Celtic and Nordic, and was related to Pelasgian Greek. Nevertheless, it did often overlap with Latin which was, so to speak, a cousin via the Etruscans.

Lli, in Gallic, also meant: productive; which spreads out; fills; multiplies; overflows. The horn of the unicorn is, therefore, the prototype of the cornucopia, the horn of abundance. It was also royal because, throughout Antiquity, kings and heroes considered it to be a matter of duty and honour to spread their seed.

It is an incontrovertible fact that the unicorn of Heraldry has never existed anywhere as any animal we know. But, like the dragon, the jellyfish of legend, the chimera and other figures of fable, it did have a genuine point of departure with a genuine value as totem. And, in this form it was able to bequeath us an authentic history more clearly, and with a longer shelf-life than could have been possible in any 500 page volume written by some scholar or other. In the ages that preceded our era, men experienced creation in a way that we, unfortunately, no longer can. Their artistic concepts reflected the sacred character of their interpretations, although they were at the same time direct and showed penetrating insights. These men felt at one with the world, intellectually and emotionally. This was a source of wonder which we can no longer appreciate, for it operated at a time when reason was still not divorced from instinct but marched hand in hand with instinct in order to achieve wisdom, a virtue which has now disappeared from the world.

The unicorn is not, therefore, a creature of pure fantasy. The unicorn says exactly what it wants to say, with its narwhal horn planted on the forehead of a *hemione*, and it speaks in great detail (*hemione* = *dziggetai* = wild ass from Tartary).

The narwhal is a *cetacean* (related to the whale).* With good reason it is called a *monodon* or, alternatively, *sea unicorn*. It has a very long, straight *tooth*, fluted and spiral in shape, usually measuring two to three metres in length. It lives in the North Sea and rarely moves south of the Arctic Circle, although, on rare occasions, some have been seen on the northern coasts of England and Germany. It is the subject of many legends. *Strabo* and other authors of his time have spoken about it at length (1).

This tooth, or horn – the only one to be found in the whole animal kingdom that is so straight, so beautiful and so long – was deemed to be priceless in Antiquity. "The Emperor and the monarchs had richly ornamented scepters made of it. With these teeth the most precious bishop's crooks were made. In the 16th century four narwhal teeth were kept in the Bayreuth Archives at Plassenburg as a very rare collector's item. In 1559, the Venetians offered 30,000 sequins for the largest of them. In vain. The third was used medicinally for members of the Prince's family: it was considered to be such a precious object that it was only permitted to cut a piece off in the presence of representatives of the two princes" (2).

Feeble echoes of ancient grandeur!

Those who know about the art of symbolism, and about symbolism in Heraldry, understand that nothing is left to chance. It is absolutely certain that the narwhal tooth could only be the emblem of a **sea** people and of a **northern** people.

And, indeed, a perfect symbol.

The animal is a *cetacean*. It unites the marine world with life on land, because, although it lives in the water, it has lungs for breathing and, if its front fins are dissected with a scalpel, embryonic hands will be found. Finally, it lows like a cow and suckles its little ones. Speaking in human terms, it represents the junction of the Ocean Dynasty and that of the Air – those dynasties which are clearly mentioned in Greek Mythology and which followed on the Dynasty of the Night (the North). What a splendid version of Genesis in which the evolution of Man - or, more exactly, of his civilisation - is in tune with all creation, and in which each creature reflects in itself, from birth to death, the passing of the seasons.

As is true of most cetaceans, the narwhal was a gigantic animal, the equal in size and strength of the hyperborean giants who, according to most historians, set forth on their epic voyage from *Jottenheim* - although it has also been claimed that this was one of their last places of refuge on their return. The narwhal horn was, unlike that of land-based mammals, not a bony excrescence on the forehead. It was a tooth, fixed into the upper jaw of the animal. A tooth! Is this not the right moment to recall that the word *dan* (pronounced in French like *dent*) has always been the family name of the ancient kings of Denmark; that in Old French *dan* was a homonym of *dent*; that in the modern Danish language *dent* is *tand* and that *tant* was the corresponding Celtic word? The tooth, used as symbol, was a Nordic prerogative in furthest Antiquity, which would explain the famous *dragon teeth* at a time when the ancestors of the Vikings already had a dragon for their totem, as, indeed, the Vikings would have in due course. Remember, too, *Harald Blue Tooth* – but that is another story.

Finally, the narwhal tooth was *fluted* and *spiral* in shape. This is important because the spiral was the most significant geometric pattern in the pictorial art of the Atlantic peoples – not to mention the Atlantans.

In order to make quite clear the esoteric meaning of the unicorn's horn, or tooth, we should add that it is *cone-shaped* and *pointed*; that the cone in Antiquity was not only a symbol of the male's reproductive power (or virility), but symbolised as well the flowering of all the arts based on fire. The reason for this was because fire (as has been stated earlier) was originally produced by the action of a twist-drill, rotated vigorously and spirally inside a wooden cross, from which a flame would emerge.

In the Burgundian dialect the word for horn (*corne*) is *cone*, and in Breton *korn* or *kon*. It is the word from which *Kon* or *Kung* is derived, which in the Nordic languages means *king*, and is, of course, cognate with English *King* and German *Koenig*. The initial syllable (*kon*) became a vulgar swear word when the civilisation of the West was changed, but this did not happen, as is commonly believed, in the first centuries of our era, but with the Capetians (10th Century AD), and with them, the supremacy of the Catholic Church.

When the houses of Frankish origin finally reassumed, or decided to maintain, the narwhal horn as emblem of their origin (the Franks were pure Nordics who had 'come home' after a long stay in territories conquered in the Middle East), several millennia would have passed, and the kings of the Air Dynasty would have long since displaced the kings of the Ocean Dynasty ('the men of the sea', or 'Pelasgians'), who were their **ancestors** but, nevertheless, their **enemies**. Consequently, it would have been very wrong (at the time) to lay claim to the narwhal alone, since its ancient role may by then have been forgotten.

So the *royal horn* was attached to the Asiatic *hemione* (some called it *Anatolian*), a truly noble animal, although it was called an 'ass', and had served our heroes well.

The *hemione* is described as a 'wild ass', of a species that today has almost disappeared. However, if we break down its name into *hemi-onos*, we see that it is only *half-ass*. Indeed, it is quite probable that this word is a malformation of a name which could originally have been *he*r-*mione*. This is not because there were once in Scandinavia some tribes to whom Pomponius Mela gave the name *Hermiones* (3), but because the *hemiones* (a species of small wild horses) were the favourite mounts of the *Armenians* and Persians, and it is well known that Armenia has also been called *Herminie* (***h*** not pronounced in French). And, since these nations were the inveterate enemies of the Greeks and since the nature of men never changes over the centuries, it could be for this reason that the Greeks gave their traditional enemies a rude name (*half-ass*) in order to demean them in the eyes of future generations.

Be that as it may, the *hemione*, the genuine *hemione*, has played an important part in history. For example, the ancient Tibetans called this animal the '*mount-of-the-god-of-fire-and-of-war*', and it cannot be denied that this description has for several millennia fitted the Nordic race very well.

Naturalists describe the *hemione* as a well-bred animal, swift and fleet of foot, more beautiful than the mule, slim and elegant. It was considered to be untameable and very aggressive. "It is the most beautiful animal on earth," said Voltaire, "the strongest, the most terrifying and the most gentle" (4). The English scholar Raddle has written the following lines about the *hemione*: "For hours on end the young stallion will stand on the highest point of a sheer cliff, breasting the wind and looking out over the vast extent of the plain before him. His nostrils flared, his gaze roams over the emptiness below: he is waiting for a rival to appear. As soon as he catches sight of him, he rushes up and engages him in a furious battle so as to deprive him of his mares" (5). (Shades of Helen of Troy and the Sabine women!) All the stallions shot by Raddle were covered in scars, bearing eloquent testimony to their many combats.

It was to these 'asses', says Herodotus, that Darius was supposedly indebted for his victory over the Scythians. According to the Greek historian, Scythians knew nothing about the animal, and "every time it charged and an ass began to bray, the Scythian horses reared and started to bolt" (6). This legend, which is often repeated (with slight variations), certainly does have a basis in reality, but it is at this point that the enemies of the ass in question begin to show their true colours, since it is, of course, not easy to believe that mere vulgar donkeys could serve as mounts for such formidable warriors! However, the *hemiones* on which the Persians rode must have had other qualities than that of simply braying when they were taken into battle. Herodotus shows some prejudice in the matter. And not for the first time. His writings are very precious to us but did he not boast of knowing **nothing** about the Western universe, although it was before his time well known to the Cretans and to the Phoenicians? He even went so far as to state that he doubted whether it existed!

But, let us get on with the symbiosis of these two elements: the narwhal's horn and the *hemione*. The horn is royal and the *hemione* provides the foundation for all chivalry since it originated in Armenia, one of the noblest of all countries. It would take too long to deal with the matter here and now, but we shall do so a little later.

The *hemione* (with its horned forehead provided by the narwhal) which we call a *unicorn*, is a figure on a par with centaurs and hippo-centaurs. It is not the product of naïve minds, but rather an interpretation of the act of birth and of the bearing of arms which is both synthetic and imaginative.

Since time immemorial men have charged at their enemies on animals that were readily available to them, provided they were strong and could move quickly. Speed was of the essence – the *blitzkrieg* wasn't invented yesterday! It cannot be doubted that in prehistoric times the aurochs, or wild ox, and later the bull, were used for this purpose – to be followed by the camel, the horse and the elephant, and probably by the ostrich as well.

The combination of animal strength and warrior will-power metamorphosed the man and his mount into a kind of vibrant supernatural unit, the sight of which could be overpowering. People used to say that the two of them had become one. On seeing them rush up at full speed, the enemy – unprepared for such a novelty but quick to use his imagination – transformed man and beast into a kind of god-like figure, in the original meaning of the word: that of a hero who is, quite literally, larger than life.

In other words, centaurs and hippo-centaurs are not creatures of an infantile mind, but rather the mythical and artistic expression of a fact based on an element of reality. When, with the passage of time, witnesses of their reality and authenticity had passed away, then they became the stuff of fable – like ogres and giants.

The narwhal horn (emblem of the *Sea People*, heirs of the ancient heroes of Gigantism) with which the skull of the Asiatic *hemione* was decorated, united within a single symbol the Scandinavian ancestors with Persia and Armenia, provinces founded by them. What name have the Norwegians given the Narwhal? *Lughtal* (7). What name did the inhabitants of ancient Mesopotamia give to the exceptionally powerful and virile male? *Lugal* (8). But wasn't *Lug* a god greatly venerated by the Celts? *In legend, he was the good worker capable of carrying out any kind of task* – in other words, the artisan, the *Arsacid*, the illustrious descendant of Prometheus. *Carpenter, smith, poet, leader bearing the lance.* Who could wish for better?

Long, sharp edged and straight as it is, is the horn of the unicorn not a perfect reflection of the knight's lance?

The horn is, of course, not simply a decoration for the animal. Its strength lies in the horn - it is a combat weapon. Not only because of its shape and hard substance but because it serves the animal as an antenna, adding to its physical strength a psychic element which is not negligible.

When, in our totally decadent world, the horns of the bull are filed down before he is sent into the arena, this is not so much intended to spare the toreador a savage wound as to disorient the animal and thereby reduce his combativeness. In animal combat, all the senses contribute to defence. The tip of the horn is an antenna, which gives off signals and receives them. By virtue of the toreador's cheating in this way just before the start of the *corrida*, the bull is no longer sure of himself; he can no longer properly test the wind, smell danger or the enemy. He loses confidence in his weapon, and his means of defence are greatly diminished.

What image could therefore better describe the Armenian or Persian warriors - charging on the back of an *hemione*, lance at the ready - than the unicorn, which was created after the defeat in the Orient of our Western pioneers?

What image could tell us more clearly that the Ocean Dynasty had been the mother of the gods of the Air Dynasty, after it had itself been a daughter of the Dynasty of Darkness?

The symbol of the horn was born in the West, probably and primarily because it is in the West, rather than in the East, that there was an abundance of animals with horns on their heads. It was also in the West that the rite of the drinking horn continued longest, and it was in the West that the gods, heroes and mortals maintained the custom of wearing horns on their own heads. We need only mention Thor and Teutates, amongst many others and, of course, the Vikings and the Gauls. As a rite it was certainly no more absurd or 'barbarous' than the habit of generals today who wear oak leaves on their caps, a silent (and probably unconscious) tribute to Hercules and Apollo the shield-bearer.

Many great houses of Flanders and Brittany display the ox or the bull as a most honourable symbol on their escutcheons.

We read in the *Triumph of Petrarch*, translated by Baron Oppede, *"Doncq, quel proufit vint-il a l'humain gendre (genre) dessus son chief les cornes d'orgueil prendre?"* ("So how did it profit mankind to place the horns of pride on its head?") Is pride something to be ashamed of? The truth of the matter is that the whole Western world is drawn up behind these horns from which it receives its dangerous, but marvellous, dynamism and its old myths, brimful of knowledge and wisdom. That is why the horns were transferred to the devil as an act of derision, when our world fell back before the peoples of the East. What could be more logical?

Before being designated as Hell, the *Isle of the Blessed* (Empire of the Dead, lying in the Ocean at the ends of the earth, rocky and dark, enveloped eternally in mist) lay in the regions of the Atlantic and Nordic territories, inhabited by Celts and Scandinavians. This is no longer questioned by modern historians, and the most ancient legends, together with the writings of several Greek and Latin authors, are in accord on this point of human history. Does not Ptolemy mention the tribe of the *Damni* as being one of the nations of the Group called 'British'? And does not Caesar inform us in his *Commentaries* that, "... the Gauls, Aquitanians, Belgians and Celts boast of being the offspring of Pluto, an inheritance that has been handed down to them by the Druids"?

It was only after the triumph of Zeus and the destruction of the Ancient West that Tartaros would be transferred to the area around the Caucasus where the Ocean Dynasty had finally collapsed.

Archaic Greek art has often shown on the shield of Geryon (*the oldest man*) and on that of his son, *Eurythion* (guardian of the empire of the dead) the head of the *milk white* bull with magnificent horns, of which it was said in legend that its blood quenched the thirst of the dead souls. But the bull was there primarily because Geryon was a cattle king (cowherd: Russian *boyar*), as were all the kings and kinglets of the West - the paradise of the horned animal, literally and figuratively speaking. Such a man was Harold, the enemy of William the Conqueror. This gave some historians the idea that he was simply a plebeian – because in their opinion the cowherd is just a man who 'works' with animals. But we must not forget that Hercules himself crossed the whole of Europe with those magnificent beasts of Geryon, on the way to Asia, or at least up to the Black Sea.

If the horn ever came to be venerated in the East, this was achieved by the peoples of the North Atlantic, fathers of the great Oriental and Occidental civilisations. Atlantis is not a myth. It is the oldest empire still remembered by men, and ruled over by the Ten Kings who, up to the deluge, exported their populations and industry to every country on earth.

In the opinion of some, the horn was a lucky charm which brought good fortune to those who wore it. In France, this Pagan cult seems to have died out in time, but not before reaching its apogee with the custom of painting the horns of *fatkine* in gold. In other lands, the horn was regarded as a *sinister* symbol (*sinister* in Latin means *left* or *West*) and was, therefore, a token of evil and of shame. For the same reason, the idle child who neglected his studies had horns tied to his head – a curious extension of the *donkey* or dunce's cap, shaped like a cone and like the pointed hat of the Armenians. Have we now not turned full circle and returned to the *hemione*?

It's just one thing after another: high time to remind ourselves of this old truth! And, it is the same story with symbols, which men have always been attached to, to a greater or lesser degree.

We have all loved the unicorn. Without really knowing how it embodied the concept of nobility and chivalry with which the Frankish races created Europe, we have all sensed with our innermost being, when looking at it, that it came from afar and came from on high.

The unicorn which appears in the English coat of arms (a perfect image of the *seahorse*, sacred to the Atlantic peoples) and the one that decorates the 'curious' tapestries of Boussac, at present in the museum of Cluny, and about which we are told that "legend links it, certainly in error, with the Orient" (whereas, on the contrary, nothing is **certainly** more correct!), had, according to ancient tradition, *a white body, red head, and blue eyes*. Throughout the ages these three elements have always distinguished those whom the writers in ancient times have called *red heads* as opposed to the *black* heads, or heads with black hair. In an age when colours had a mystic meaning quite as powerful as that of words, red, white and blue referred to some of the Scythians, the Geti, the Ari, the Vanics – all of them descendants of Nordics and Celts who had created *chivalry*, and to whom the gods· of Ancient Persia, Chaldea and Armenia owed their lapis-lazuli eyes.

A curious anomaly amongst the signs of the Zodiac is the result of a corruption of the name by which the *unicorn* was linked to the sign of the *Virgin*. What the sign represented initially (cf. the atlas of *Flamsteed*) was the *supreme magistrate*. (In French, *virgin* is *vierge*, whereas *supreme magistrate* was *vierg* from Latin *virga* [Virga: the *rod* wielded by the magistrate]). We find the word *vierg* used for *supreme magistrate* in ancient chronicles, inter alia, for the supreme magistrate in the town of Autun. The *vierg* is the man with the *verge* (rod, cane), which is well represented by the horn of the unicorn. However, *vierge* is pronounced *verge* in the Provencal language, and so, in France, places known as *Sainte-Vierge* have now come to mean *Sainte-Vierge* (Holy *Virgin* instead of holy *rod*).

The new meaning has now taken root so firmly that in botany the *verge d'or* (golden rod, Latin *solidago virga aurea*) is described as a 'long spike (Fr. *épi*) of yellow flowers'. But *épi* is also the largest, most beautiful star in the constellation of *Virgo*.

The coupling of the terms *rod* and *virgin* need not shock us. The men who were the first to speak Indo-European languages believed that everything had its opposite and that both were contained in a single entity. They could, therefore, be called by the same name. So it came about that rod and virgin (*verge* and *vierge*) could be one or both faces of the same fertility myth.

The Zodiac sign of the Virgin has not changed since the days of ancient Chaldea. It is still the *sigma* of the Ionians, or the *san* of the Dorians (from which the word *saint* is derived), a symbol of rank like no other for the Persians, the Scythians and the first Greeks.

In most societies the rod ennobles, says Loisel. Here we mean the rod of authority.

The unicorn, which in Cluny places its two hoofs on the lady, is already far advanced in decadence: or shall we say sophistication? A far cry from the English unicorn, rampant like a lion, perfect incarnation of the idea of the medieval knight. Its secret has made us dream many dreams. But even so, fewer than its history would make us dream if we took the time to try.

* * *

*Translator's Note, p.46:

It is an arctic, aquatic animal/mammal *Monodon Monoceros,* or 'spotted pelt'. The male has a long tusk and is hunted for ivory and oil. Dutch *narwhal*, Danish *narhval*, Old Norse *nahvalr* ('corpse whale' because of whitish corpse-like colour), English 'toothed whale', family of the dolphin.

6

GONDOLA AND CANTILENA

No one would deny that a visit to Venice would be 'enchanting'. But remove the gondolas and replace them with any other boat, and Venice would lose much of its enchantment, both figuratively and literally speaking. Because, by its shape, name and powers of incantation, the gondola is a continuation of the *kantele*, that is, the first lyre invented by man, first of all to imitate the sound of the wind and the waters, and then to accompany his singing and his words.

The *kantele* was born in the North Atlantic. It was the instrument of the *Vanir*, or *Vanes*, or *Venetes*, ancestors of the Venetians. It was the sacred instrument of the eternal wanderer of the seas, the son of the giant Kaleva, the *old, imperturbable Vainamoinen*, master boat builder, but also master *runoia*, eternal singer and musician (1).

Let us take a look at the gondola. Does it not resemble a lyre? All boats called *cantiel* or *gondola*, up to the end of the Middle Ages, would have this shape, suggesting outstretched wings. And the prow? It looks just like the scroll of a violin, with pegs screwed into the wood.

The gondola of the Venetian canals keeps watch over the spirit of the magicians who planned the foundations of the city. It is right and proper that it should survive on the most beautiful canals in the world, in memory of those men who delighted in digging canals and surrounding their cities with them: cities which were almost always built on strips of land surrounded by lagoons, as a token of homage to the old fatherland – antediluvian Atlantis.

Every detail of the story is lovely.

Its loveliness is first of all expressed by the form of the words – which is logical, since the Kantele was the first instrument to give voice and measure to the words of the men who built our civilisations. To pluck the strings of the harp, these men used the *scald* (scale) of the fish – hence their *skaldic* or folk poetry, thus called because it was *scanned*. The Greek *scolies*, sisters of the skaldic poets, owed their name to the Pelasgians (peoples of the high seas) who had left their islands in the North Atlantic and taken their civilisation to the Orient, either by the southern passages, or through Thrace where, in the time of Herodotus, there were still a few of them left, known to each other as the *Scolotes*.

Littré tells us that *gond* (the root of gondola) comes from the Greek and means *hook* (or wedge). *Wedge* (or hook, peg) is also one of the meanings of the old French word *cantel*. Besides its usual meaning, *gond* is used as synonym for French *crosse*. But *crosse* can also mean violin *scroll*, as well as harpoon (Fr. *harpon*). Which is also cognate with French *harpe*.

At the same time *kant* (root of Kantele) had in Gallic languages the meaning of *series of numbers* or *harmony of numbers*, and this is the very essence of music. That is why all derivations from the old root *kant* or *cant* are principally related to religious song or to the spoken word, two things of equal importance in the thinking of the men who created our first civilisations. The origin of language, whatever may be said to the contrary, is more directly connected to the sacred than to the utilitarian domain. In Celtic vocabulary, *kan* or *can* could mean both *sing* and *speak*, and even *sign*, *weep*, *resound* or *echo*. What this syllable evoked right at the beginning of things was primarily the sound of the *waves*. It was what the intrepid *vagabonds* of the ocean heard all their life (the *gens vaga* of whom Posidonius spoke). It was what awakened them to the reality of music. *Vago*, in Danish, still means *to be seaworthy, to float on the water*.

How was the harp, or Kantele, born? Encyclopedias tell us that men first had the idea of making this instrument when they heard the twang of the bow string. This explanation is logical and probably correct. The only error would be to pretend that bow and harp originated in an area of the world to which they were in fact imported. Because of a deep-rooted orientational error, we have, since the beginning of our era, claimed that everything has come to us from the East, and yet it could not be less exact to state that the harp is of Eastern origin. The harp is the child of the Celts and of the North. The Atlantic peoples have taken it to Phoenicia, to Persia, to Egypt, to Chaldea, because it is they who placed these peoples on the road to High Culture. But it was not in these countries that the stringed instrument achieved the development that was to occur in the West. It is, incidentally, in Ireland where the harp continues to be a national instrument, and even a national emblem. And it is in the *Kalevala*, the epic of the Finnish peoples, that the origin of the lyre is mentioned. And in the following terms: one day when a pike tried to stop his boat, Vainamoinen, the eternal vagabond of the seas, and prototype of Scandinavian Man, killed the fish and made a *kantele* from its bones.

When Vainamoinen and his descendants one day no longer ruled the world – which corresponds both in Legend and in History with the arrival of the Christian Era and of the Virgin Marjetta – the old *runoia* (runic bard) would bequeath the *kantele* to his heirs as a *source of eternal joy*.

What does all this mean?

The pike is frequently mentioned in the *Kalevala*. Great importance is attached in this work to the *Tuoni* which is found in the region of the Isle of *Manala*, Empire of the Dead. It probably corresponds with the Isle of *Man*. Since the word *tonawg* meant in the Celtic tongue a **sea disturbed by a heavy ground swell**, or by large waves (3), it is more than likely that *Tuoni* was referring to the *cruel sea*, namely, Pluto's empire.

The pike is a very old fish. Its skeleton has been found in the Middle Tertiary. It was enormous at this time. Brehm tells us that some of these *fresh water sharks* (which, incidentally, could also live quite happily in sea water) weighed between 75 and 200 kilos. They had been captured off the coasts of England! One particular feature of the pike is that it has *perfectly cone-shaped* teeth in the lower jaw. Could these little bony cones have given the ancient Scandinavians a means of making the first Kantele? Since the basic principle of the harp consists of giving each string a different sound by altering the degree of tension, it is easy to understand the importance of the peg (or **cone, cant, gond**) in this matter.

But there is something else. The name of the pike (*hawki* in Finnish) could perfectly well have been given in earliest mythological times to some shark or dogfish which was not the same as our pike today. We can see in Brehm's book *Les Merveilles de la Nature* (The Wonders of Nature) a picture of the spinal column of one of these gristly fish of the *Hybodontes* group, which dates from the Tertiary Period and has died out completely today. The alignment of the fish's tendons reminds us of the shape of a kantele to an astonishing degree. It is quite certain that fish gut was used to make instrument strings, and History also refers to the use of tendons to make strings for bows.

Later, when the monster had disappeared from the waters (like the chimera which had also had a role to play in History), the river pike (well known to the Finns, and not so very different from the great sharks) was able to take the place of its noble ancestor. And, strange to relate, it too can boast of a connection with music and singing which goes back a long way.

In Old French, pike (*brochet*) was called *lus* or *luz*. At the same time, the lute (that is, the musical instrument) was also called in Old French *lut, leuth, lus, luz*. Thus, these two words, *lus* and *luz*, have both been used to translate pike (fish) and lute (musical instrument). The Latins called the pike *lucius*. They thought there was some connection between *lucius (*pike*)* and *lux* (light) – which is perhaps paralleled by the Old Finns who, in the *Kalevala*, said that the pike had *swallowed fire*. But *lus* and *luz* were also the words used to describe the **mud, slime** or **swampy ground** in which life is said to have originated. Thus, the word *lucina*, often applied to *Juno* (Goddess of Child Birth), is explained by the men of those days by the fact that this goddess was present at the birth of a child and kept watch over its *entry into the light of day*. These two interpretations of the word *luz* have survived into modern times in the expression *donner le jour* (literally, **give day light**), meaning *mettre au monde* (**bring into the world**), an action whereby the child emerges from the darkness of the mother's womb.

It is interesting to note that the word *lute* is common to all Nordic and Anglo-Saxon languages. We find *luit* in Dutch, *lute* in English, *luta* in Swedish, *lut* in Danish, *lhut* in High German.

But the parallel with *pike* goes further still. The word *hybodonte* (name of one of the oldest sharks, the one with a spinal column that resembles a lute) can be broken down into *hy – bodonte*. *Hy* is cognate with *Hyaea*, the Greek name of the letter Y (Cf. Freund: *Grand Dictionnaire de la Langue Latine*). *Hy* is also cognate with High German *Hay* which means *sacred grove*. This is also the symbolic meaning of the letter Y, corresponding with the Egyptian hieroglyph, which depicts a tuft of reeds growing out of fertile mud.

In German, the generic term for sharks and dogfish, but also the river pike, is *Hayfisch*, which literally means 'fish of the sacred mud'.

As for the *bodonte*, this is a very old term, in which one part (*donte*) is up to the present day the *name given by the luthiers to the belly of instruments such as the lute, the teorbe*, etc. Without doubt, the two parts together (*bodonte*) formed the basis of the words *bedon* and *bedaine* (paunch) in Old French. It is also possible that, at a certain stage of development, *hybodonte* changed to *hypodonte*, setting *donte* free, as it were, and leaving the prefix *hypo* where it still is today: suggesting a position not only *lower*, but even *subterranean* and, in the case under review, that position which represented the *belly* of the night (or north), where (according to the men of Antiquity) the dogfish and sharks came from.

Thus, we can clearly see the connection between the pike of Vainamoinen and the first musical instrument ever made by man. If we were to study the matter more closely, we could show that a very long time ago the 'pike' provided the Atlantans with a myth corresponding (as do all Western myths) with a reality – and in point of fact, a scientific reality: a myth which the Western peoples transplanted to Greece and to the Middle East together with their civilisation.

When we pursue this inquest a little further, we come up against the *orphie* (garfish), a variety of sea pike: and thereby hangs an interesting tale. In days long past, the tales men told were, sometimes, not too specific, and it is very possible that people spoke about the *brochet* when they meant *orphie*. This name is most revealing. But then, all scientific names of animal and plant species are of great historic interest. Derived from Greek or Latin, they correspond in general with a concept tested by time. As the *Kantele* is a source of melody and poetry, it would not be in any way surprising if the *orphie* (whose name reminds us of *Orpheus*) had also been associated with the *brochet* of the *Kalevala* in earliest Antiquity. The *orphie* is present in particularly large numbers around the coasts of the British Isles, and thereby hangs yet **another** interesting tale. Harps in the earliest days were triangular in shape. Now, up to the end of the 19th Century, the *orphie* was fished in a very particular way in the Ionian Sea. It was quite obviously an ancient custom. Brehm writes as follows, "For this kind of fishing a very curious construction is used. It consists of three sticks, arranged in a triangle and tied together. In the middle of the triangle a lateen sail is stretched. When the wind is blowing from the land, the fisherman stands on a rock overhanging the steep cliff face. He launches his strange contraption onto the water and lets it drift out as far as it will go on a long line he holds in his hand. To this line he has attached, usually about two paces apart, some cork floats which are in turn tied to baited hooks …"

Surely this manner of fishing the *orphie* by means of a floating lyre – or what appears to be a lyre – must have some connection with old Nordic legend? And what about this one?

Several authors have reported that the flesh of the *orphie* could be poisonous in certain unspecified circumstances. This remark relates to all fish that have served as symbols or totems for the ocean dynasty, the true breeding ground of a paganism with which both Imperial and

Christian Rome have had a problematical relationship. Incidentally, the flesh of the pike was said to be nauseating. In France it has never been eaten, although it is much enjoyed by the English.

Lutes and Lyres

The first lutes had *eight* strings.

The first lyres or Celtic harps had *five* strings. This is very important since the **five** and the **eight**, together with the **three**, were the most revered numbers in the North Atlantic West. And it is in fact the **eight**, the Celtic *ochd*, which became *og* or *oc* in the Mediterranean countries, that is the real root of our word *Occident*. *Cinq* (5) was the number most highly esteemed by the *Veneti*. That is why the Finnish *ecu* is covered in *cinqfoil*, and why in Latin the letter V was used to represent this number. Presumably it was basically thought of as a hand with five fingers. But long ago, the thumb was looked on as something apart from the fingers. It was, therefore, considered preferable to count 4 fingers plus one, rather than 5 fingers. But then, at a time when people counted on their fingers, they did not count *five* with the whole hand, as one might think, but only by raising the thumb and the little finger, while lowering the three middle fingers. And this would give us, roughly speaking, a letter V. So it is that there are **5** pegs on the primitive (or first) *kantele*, fixed into the scroll of the instrument; and there are **5** streamers which serve as banner for the modern Venetians.

Remember, too, that the roots *kant* and *quint* (pronounced roughly in the same way in French) are related, and that *quint* was the name given in the Middle Ages to the *pal, pieu, poteau* (pole), used in certain exercises of chivalry (called *quintaines*). The *pal* is, of course, still fixed in the water in front of Venetian *palais* (palaces), and gondolas are attached to it.

Closely associated with the Sea People, the ancient *kantele* (harp or lyre) was also the instrument of the Finnish *runoia* and of the Celtic bards – in a word, of the poets, the word-magicians.

And, it is at this point that History becomes immeasurably beautiful because it is the kantele which gave birth to the alphabet of the Aryan peoples. Depending on different kinds of harp or lyre, the strings are set at right angles to the sound board, or at varying angles – an accurate definition of what in anatomy is called the *lyre-of-the-brain*: "The lower surface of the dome with three supports where one can see two longtitudinal lines, crossed transversely or obliquely by other lines."

Ogham Alphabet

I II III IIII IIIII   *I II III IIII IIIII*   I II III IIII IIIII

The *ogham* system of writing is the oldest of all, and traces can still be found in Scandinavia, Celtic lands, the German territories, and even the confines of Ancient Troy. And is it not a system in which sticks (or staves) cross a horizontal line transversely and obliquely? We have all, when we were children, drawn similar lines in our school books until we had learnt how to make other signs which had, however, been developed over millennia.

Ogham evolved into various systems of writing: Oscan, Phoenician and Greek, all based on the principle of the angle and the staff.

The number of strings on a harp has also evolved, parallel with the number of letters in the alphabets. This tendency has progressed up to the excesses of today when the harp, having abandoned all original norms, can have as many as **one hundred** strings. Such is the triumph of the metric system, and we French can well understand why the British may be unwilling to adopt it!

To sum up: there is undeniably a link, **on the one hand**, between the letter V (capital letter of the Veneti) and the number *five*; and **on the other hand**, between the rune stick which is used to scratch *runes* on a flat surface (considered to be magic and secret) and the Finnish *runoia*: singer, Greek bard and magician, in every sense of the term. Perhaps this is the reason why Finland venerates the ability to read and write to such an extent. In this country, illiterates are, and almost always have been, unknown. It would perhaps also explain the country's innate love of the theatre, an art form which grew out of the bard's art. The word *Histrion* comes from *histrio*, which in Greek meant **flute-player**, **flautist**, **bard** or **strolling historian**.

We are, thus, led to believe that writing developed from a musical notation of the principal sounds produced by the throat. And it is because it was originally so closely related to singing and incantation – because, in a word, it was so *lyrical* in character – that the spoken word of Celtic and Nordic peoples was for so long linked to the power of magic, allied to the sound of wind, storm and water. It is also because a proper understanding of oracles was dependent on modulations of these sounds, if Destiny was to be correctly interpreted. So, by singing and chanting, these peoples believed themselves to be obeying the voice of the Great Regulator of the World: in other words, the Divine Logos.

In his presentation of the Finnish epic, Léouzon le Duc writes, "In this epic the spirit dominates matter, and of all the powers it can command, the most powerful by far is that of the Word [.....]. Possession of the Word implies knowledge and, thus, it is *only given to the few*, and is almost always passed down from generation to generation" (**New Testament:** In the beginning was the Word! **Or:** Many are called but few are chosen).

However, when Vainamoinen runs out of magic words, he goes to seek them in the Kingdom of *Manala* because it is the giant *Kaleva*, his (spiritual) father, who had been the first to reveal the sacred words to him when the Finnish hero had *forced open his breast*. This anecdote seems to indicate that the Nordics learnt the art of singing and writing from the Celts; that is, everything that has to do with the use and magic of the word. In the ancient days about which we are speaking, the Celts and the Scandinavians were constantly at war with each other – nation against nation or clan against clan – and each was conquered by the other in turn.

Whatever the origin of the *Vanir* may have been – Celtic or Scandinavian – it was certainly these *Vanir*, mentioned in the Kalevala, who gave birth to the *Veneti* of the Black Sea and of Western Asia, and also to the *Veneti* of both the Atlantic and the Mediterranean. There is no need to discuss here and now this point of History, which has been substantiated by many authors. Let us rather concentrate on the *Veneti* of Venice, related to the *Venetes* of the French town of *Vannes*. This tribe, in Caesar's day, occupied the whole southern coast of Brittany (4).

The Venetians and the *Veneti* had many characteristics in common. We need only draw attention to the famous *Venetian blond* with a touch of red, the glory of the people known in Antiquity as *red heads* because of the copper colour of their hair. We might also mention the Ancient Veneti custom, still practiced by the Venetians in the Middle Ages, of marrying off all girls in the city on the same day. Herodotus writes: "Of all Babylon's laws, the most sensible in my opinion was the following (still in force, so I have been told, with the *Veneti* of Illyria). In each village, once a year, all marriageable young women are assembled and taken to a place where the men are also assembled and waiting for them. Then an auction takes place. It starts with the best looking girl [.....]. The girls are sold only to be married [.....]. The money which is paid for the plain ones comes from the sale of those who are better looking, and so it is they who help to find a home for, and to marry off, those who are less advantaged. Unfortunately, since Babylon has been conquered and all her families are ruined, this excellent custom has practically disappeared" (5).

Once again we should recall that the colour *blue*, because of the blue eyes of the red-heads, was more or less sacred for the *Veneti* of Persia, Armenia and Chaldea, and that, up to the decline of Rome, the word *venetus* meant *azure blue*, while the *Venetiani* were the *blue team* in the circus games. The reason is that the colour azure or periwinkle blue (like *cinqfoil* blue) is an emblem of the *Aesir* (or Divinities of the Air) who followed the *Veneti* as masters of the world. They were, however, also the descendants of the *Veneti*. It would be interesting to study the *quinte essence*, personified by these two races throughout Antiquity: since *quintessence* (fifth essence, the essence *above* the others) was, according to Littré, in its origins an element of the fifth sphere called **azure** or **ether**.

On the other hand, the gondola is black, like the Breton boats and the Chaldean *vans*, because the *Vanir*, wherever they settled, introduced the technique of tarring their boats. They were the first to use tar in this way because of the forests and peat bogs from which it is obtained, and which abounded in the areas they originally came from.

Finally, we should not be surprised that the *cantilena* and the *gondola* should have been inseparable on the waters of Venice. And we should understand and marvel, while there is still time, that the latter should represent today a miraculous survival of the *kantele* from the dawn of creation, *source of eternal joy*, according to the words of the old bard.

For it is undeniable that the ancient world, despite its barbaric character (certainly no worse than our own, but without our hypocrisy) was genuinely infused with joy, a joy that drank deep from the Song of the Earth.

And if we further take note that in the Finnish language *sarana* means *gond*, and that this word is also cognate with Gaelic *sar*, meaning "hero shining like the star **ser**" (which is itself composed symbolically of *gonds* or *cones*, shining in every direction), we can, with the aid of the gondola, continue to dream endlessly of Venice, the most **ser**-*ene*, and also of the ancient adventure to which it owes this epithet.

And then we have not yet mentioned that the kings of *Denmark* have never borne any title other than that of **ser**-ene (Majesty).

* * *

7

THERE WAS ONCE
A KING
IN THULE

A remarkable king, this king of Myth. And his kingdom too was remarkable. It was one of those that, very probably, gave shape to Ancient Atlantis and which placed an ineradicable seal on ancient civilisations.

It seems as if a fanatical rationalism has for many centuries forced us to substitute unadorned intellectualism for any kind of traditional history, good sense or concrete facts. As a result, the point of departure of human migrations has been placed in the geometrical centre of their field of expansion. This is pure Cartesianism. And yet Dr. Kahn was quite right to point out in his *Livre de la Nature* (**Book of Nature**) that the political absurdity of a small island dominating the world temporarily is, nevertheless, a characteristic confirmed by History. For the spirit of adventure and the spirit of conquest are indeed the prerogatives of seafaring peoples (1).

When the world was young, human tribes were either pastoral or fishermen. The sea makes men sturdy and rough. Its limitless horizons and perpetual movement fire the imagination and urge us to seek out, not only what is material, but also what is spiritual. It is, therefore, perfectly natural that everything should have started in Atlantis rather than in Central Asia. By 'everything' we mean those civilisations of which an echo has reached us. And since the historians and sages of Antiquity are very much in agreement on this point, why not listen to them, why contradict them? And yet that is what we do.

For example, the Icelanders (whose mythological and historical sagas are unbelievably valuable) are quite happy to accept that their earliest ancestors were a handful of Irish monks in search of solitude on their windswept island, and that the Norwegians did the rest.

This is comparable to the claim that Gaul was civilised by the Romans!

But, thank God, the memory of poets is much longer. They can repair the twists and turns to which the truth about the generations preceding our era has been subjected by Western Man who has, quite literally, lost his way. The men of old were always careful to honour their ancestors, both in flesh and in spirit: when they rushed forward, their backs were covered.

However, Iceland has the greater claim to the name of *Thule*, a claim which certain historians would rather attribute to the Shetland Islands. Furthermore, it seems that in very ancient times this name included Greenland as well as Iceland, and perhaps the Shetlands as well, which could have formed part of the kingdom before it was torn apart by what we call **The Flood**, or by any other cataclysm that could have destroyed the Atlantan world.

We are told that Pytheas, a sailor from Marseilles, discovered the island of Thule in the 4th Century BC. No doubt in the same way that Christopher Columbus discovered America, i.e., after a long period of oblivion or engineered blackout. Even today, we are aware, or admit, that the Northern part of the American continent had been long known to the Nordics by the time that Christopher Columbus 'discovered' the 'New World'.

We have very little idea just how far Western Man has gone **backwards** in the course of the last few millennia. Today, we are just beginning to rediscover knowledge and truths that are age-old. Five thousand years before Julius Caesar, it was known that the world was round, but just three hundred years ago people who spoke of these things were burnt at the stake.

According to Smith (2), the island of Thule was known to the Ancient Greeks. What leads us to think that they considered Greenland to be Thule is the way in which they described it. They said that Thule was a very large island, ten times greater than the British Isles, on one side of which it extended over a considerable distance (3). The Latin author Procopius says in turn that, as far as anybody knew, Thule lay at the extreme northern end of the ocean (4).

This fits the adjective *ultima* (**furthest**) perfectly. *Ultima* is a word often used by Latin authors to describe Thule. One of them was Virgil: *Tibi serviat ultima Thule* (**may far-distant Thule have care of you**).

When the Atlantan empire finally disappeared, the survivors of the cataclysm found themselves stranded on the coasts and the islands of the Atlantic Ocean, on the land stretching from Scandinavia to the Atlas Mountains, which fixed its boundaries from north to south.

This *gens vaga* - this sea people - then spread southwards and eastwards to those areas around the Black Sea, the areas of gigantism, where many famous wars took place. But even earlier, during their

Golden Age, the Atlantans had certainly pushed down towards the countries of the Levant where we have found traces of their myths.

With regard to Thule, what has survived up to our times in Germanic song, is the cult of the *cup of gold*. Of course, numerous legends and numerous mythologies tell us of gods or heroes making libations on festival days. But it must be admitted that the use of a **sacred** cup has been the prerogative of Celto-Nordic peoples. It was only in Valhalla that the warrior had the right to empty the cup of hydromel (mead), which was the supreme reward; and it was in ancient Celtic lands that the rite of the marriage cup was practised originally.

The King of Thule, *under whose balcony the sea roared*, is the mirror image of King Uther, who is mentioned in *Merlin* as having before him *une moult bele coupe d'or* (a very beautiful golden cup).

This cup was the cup of oaths: oaths of chivalry and oaths of marriage.

In his *History of France* (*Histoire de France*) H. Martin writes as follows about *Gamma*, the great Gallic Priestess: "The nuptial moment arrives; she takes a golden cup, offers a libation to the god she serves, and holds out the cup to her fiancé...."

The custom of the nuptial cup is also found, the same author tells us, in the traditions of Marseilles (*Massalie*) and of *Gamma*, in Asia Minor – and this is, of course, not at all surprising since Asia Minor was colonised and civilised by the Summerians. Furthermore, the custom still lives on with the French and Spanish Basques, heirs – together with the Celts and the Scandinavians – of the ancient Atlantan kingdom.

At the same time, Mythology teaches us that *Iris* (whose name meant **rainbow**) '*drank from a golden cup the water of the Styx which was used for the oaths of the gods*'. And, of course, the Ancients always believed that the first human race, the race of the *arc* or *arch*, born from the rainbow (which fertilised the **Virgin of the Waters**), was the Nordic race, the *arctic* race (5). And it can only be for the same reason that the town of *Arques*, in France, has placed a cover over its bell tower in the shape of a pot, and that in days gone by a golden goblet was kept there from which the King drank as a gesture of honour when he passed that way.

The modern French word *godet* is not derived from the Latin *guttus* (narrow necked drinking vessel: also *gutus*) as is commonly believed. It has received its patents of nobility from the ancient lords of Iceland, known as *Godi*. Hercules was a Western hero who would one day exchange his original club for two other attributes: the bow (*arc* in French) and the drinking cup (*godet*).

With regard to the Styx, or river of the Empire of the Dead, about which we spoke when mentioning *Iris*, it was never in the most Ancient of Days situated anywhere other than in the islands of the North Atlantic. Virgil bears witness to this when he tells us in the *Aeneid* that Proserpina was the mother of the different Gallic peoples. Claudian, living in the 5th Century AD, says the same thing: "There is a place in these parts where the sea limits the extent of Gaul, on the shores of the Ocean. There, it is said, Ulysses, having shed the blood of the victims, called up the silent host of the dead".

The cup on which the oaths were sworn was so well associated with the peoples under discussion that the Franks and the Goths (their descendants) were always called *swearers of oaths* by their enemies. And eventually, at the Council of Constance, lay-persons who had previously been parties to the practice, were forbidden to participate in it any longer. It was considered to be a sacred practice, for the exclusive use of the Church.

In pagan times the rite of swearing an oath was widely practised by warlike peoples. The oldest oaths bound warriors to defend the clan or the tribe. The cult was still very much alive in Roman times, and it is interesting to note that in Gaelic the syllable *ser* indicates **hero** or **warrior**. And just as in the case of the Christian oath, the pagan oath presupposed a sacred character. However, no other people has had such a high regard as the Celts and Nordics for the spoken word, or evidenced so much faith in its power. One only has to read the *Kalevala* to be convinced of this.

Professor Sauvageot, in his study of the *Old Finns*, has an interesting tale to tell on this subject. It concerns the *Oath of the Father*, an old Nordic rite abolished by the Christians. In the case of a natural birth ('illegitimate'), all the men of the community were assembled, and the man who knew himself to be the father was called upon to swear an oath to this effect, so that the new born child could bear the name of his forefathers, which was considered very important.

But it is now time to enquire about where and how the idea took root that the cup should be given a sacred character, deemed able to authenticate an oath.

To find the answer, we must, of course, return to the cup used for religious libations. This rite is age-old since it is mentioned in Plato's *Timeas*, with reference to Atlantis. Plato tells us that the ten kings of this empire used to begin their meetings with the sacrifice of a bull whose blood was caught in a cup. This is the first reference to blood, shed for the renewal of life, and thereby imparting a sacred character to the vessel in which it is contained. The idea remained alive for thousands of years, and, after several variations in time and space, found its final Christian expression in the Holy Grail and the chalice of the Holy Sacrament. And although this concept gathered momentum in the East, it nevertheless started off in the West, and we need to pay a visit to the world of Joseph of Arimathea to explain how and why the Holy Grail is still in the possession of the Celts. Do not, however, forget that in Nordic languages the word *graal* means both **sacred cup** and **drop** or **tear** – which would seem to indicate that these two things have been associated since time immemorial in the mind-world of the North.

In our opinion the concept of the sacred cup goes back even further than the rite of the bull sacrifice – since this sacrifice was no more than an imitation by men of a natural phenomenon, and was, therefore, of divine origin. Such is after all the process from which most religious rites are derived.

What we French call *coupe* (cup) was once described by words such as *coppe*, *cuve* (vat) and *cave* (cellar). We also read in *du Cange* that *cavitas*, *tallea* or *talles* "were three synonymous terms which in the Middle Ages meant: *vasa offertoria* (offertory plates)". This is very important if we bear in mind that Ancient Thule was, by virtue of its singular geographical position, at the very heart of the *Talle* or *Talos* cult, and that the word *talle* is the Old French word for *taille* or *coupe*. This leads us on to most interesting conclusions from a historical point of view, since the *Talos* cult has made its mark not only on Crete and in Asia Minor, but also in all other regions where Atlantic peoples had spread their civilisation. Incidentally, Lewis Spence shared the opinion of Schliemann, discoverer of Troy, that Crete was most certainly a colony of Atlantis.

How then can the cult of the *talle* explain Thule, or vice-versa?

What is the most characteristic feature of Iceland? This must be its volcanic soil, and more especially its geysers: *geyzir* in the language of the land.

This word, now a common noun, was originally a proper noun used to describe one of the most impressive warm water springs in Iceland: the Great Geyser, or *Stori Geyzir*. It must have referred originally not only to the personification but to the deification of a very stunning phenomenon when one remembers that the boiling water emerged from soil which lay on the edge of the Arctic Circle.

Geyzir is a word of Norwegian derivation. That means that it is part of the oldest vocabulary of the Scandinavian languages. From this word numerous other terms are derived, all of them containing the idea of a violent and powerful eruption. Thus, the verb *geysa* means 'to erupt with fury'. The adjective *geysi* means 'enormous', 'excessive'. The adverb *geysiliga* and the noun *geysinger* both indicate an idea of impetuosity.

Geyzir as a common noun seems to have passed out of usage. Today, the Icelandic word describing a warm water spring is generally *hver*, which literally means *warm well*. In the Icelandic Edda, *Hvergelmer* is the name of the fountain in the middle of Niflheim, where the dragon Nid-Hug lives. Philologists have come to the conclusion that the term *geyzir* must be the product of a "pretty legend referring to the motion of springs when defiled with innocent blood" (7). It is certain that since the Great Geyzir was capricious, like all other geyzirs, primitive man might have had the idea of encouraging it to carry out its duties by sacrificing an animal to it. It is also certain that all sacrifices based on the outpouring of a reinvigorating life force (blood and water) started from this point. What better proof have we than the fact that the lance, which makes the victim's blood pour out of his side, is called by a name common to all Celto-Nordic peoples, and by all those peoples that have been fertilised by them. These names are variants of *gai*, *gesai*, *gesa* and *gesum*.

The above-mentioned philologists are, of course, quite sure of their interpretation, but in the case of the Geyzir we are not speaking of *pretty legend* but of a primordial myth of the Atlantan world: the myth describing the gushing forth of sap, the vital life force, which occurs every year in Spring time, and in all three living categories of the world: vegetable, animal and human.

In his book *Islande, Terre de Glace et de Feu* (**Iceland, Land of Ice and Fire**), Jean-Pierre Vernet relates a most remarkable anecdote (8): at the foot of the Great Geyzir (the principle tourist attraction of the country), the guide explains that, when necessary, the jet of hot water is forced out of the earth by pouring into the cavity (the spring's *belly*, as it were) two tons of soap. "Then", says the man, "the recalcitrant old goat agrees against his will to show his horns – I mean, his jet of water". This subconscious confusion of the *horn*, as symbol of fertilisation, with the water spout, demonstrates how deep rooted the geyser myth has become. The comparison with a recalcitrant old goat is most apt.

Is it really possible to imagine an image more grandiose, more direct, more eloquent to describe the ejection of seed than the powerful eruption of these enormous warm water columns? How could our pagan ancestors, with their very real concept of the nature of the Divine, have failed to revere the Great Geyser as a magnificent symbol? And how can we doubt that Thule was at the origin of the name *Talos* which, in Crete, embodied this myth, just as *Hesus* embodied it in Celtic lands where, quite possibly, it was a variation of *Gesus*: he who has been touched by the *Gesum* with a view to his redemption?

Before the arrival of *Minos* it was *Talos* who had guarded Crete. Talos was a giant, thus a descendant of the Atlantans. Talos is a mythical figure. Talos embodies a people, a civilisation, a view of the world. Which world? This man, according to myth, wore a bronze spur on his heel. When it was removed, the blood which poured out, watered the earth. It was the miracle of Spring, the renewal of nature. The symbol is really so obvious, and reminds us so clearly of the function of the Great Geyser, that it is unnecessary to labour the point.

What happened in Crete at a time such as this, we do not know. But we do know that in Celtic lands, at the same time of year and for the same reasons, the people celebrated the feast of the *Eyzies* (cf. the name *Esus*) in the course of which the *talle* or *taille* was performed. This religious rite consisted of cutting down (French *tailler*) the lowest branch (*talon*: heel) of the tree or shrub in order to liberate symbolically the *sap at ground level*, a very important part of the original rite.

The Cretan *Talos* is a copy of the Celtic *Taliesin*, son of *Koridwen* (Proserpina) who guards all knowledge in (*the Kingdom of*) the Night. He is the child of light whose forehead shines bright as day. He is the eruption of the forces underground into fresh air. It is certainly to *Taliesin* that allusion is made by the illuminated first letter of a page in the Book of Kells, a precious Irish manuscript. The **T** is traced in such a fashion as to show (in the centre of a very complicated design in the Celtic manner) a creature with an enormous *eye*, the forehead decorated with horns. With its arms, this creature is drawing towards itself an eagle (or falcon) whose one heel shows a trace of the sacred spur.

From the above we can, therefore, deduce that the word *geyzir* is probably cognate with the name describing the Scandinavian *Aesir*, the *Eyzies* near Lascaux, and also the term *Eyzir* which, in the Etruscan language, meant 'divinity'. Of this, more later.

We see, then, that Geysir was first 'assembled' as *word* from a **G**, plus the root *eis* or *eiz*, meaning *water which spurts out of the earth*. And, of course, *ge* (pronounced with a hard **g**) was the word for *earth*. Moreover, *eau* (in Old French) was written as *eiss* (as in the old name-form *Aix-la-Chapelle*), while all Scandinavian terms with the root *eis* contain by derivation the idea of an uncontrolable and violent movement: *eisar* means to rush through the waves; *eiskra* – means to 'roar', 'foam'; *eista* – means 'testicle', etc.

The root *eis* is equivalent to the root *is* in Old French in words such as *issoir* – *issir* – *issue* – *isard* (animal that jumps) – *isa* (arrow) – *issis* (little insect that jumps) – *isatis* (white or blue fox), *which for a long time was the only wild animal on Iceland*, and which reminds us of our old friend *Ysengrin* (**Brer Fox** in the Medieval *Roman du Renard*, and in the *Brer Rabbit* tales of the old American Deep South).

From the above we can deduce that the modern name *Iceland*, which has replaced *Thule*, must once have had, perhaps, the symbolic meaning of *land of waters – land from which life emerged – land of living waters* and that it lost its pagan associations because the root *iss* (which today still refers especially to *the ice on sea and on water*) must originally have been used to describe the ice *issant* (freezing) on the sea (in other words, the iceberg), and then ended up by describing, or referring to, the ice itself.

Isis, the Egyptian goddess who represented the resurrection of nature, gets her name from the root *is*. The very oldest *Isis*, the one we find right at the start of civilisation in the valley of the Nile, was called *Mait*, which to this day is the name of a certain area in the Shetland Islands. This name corresponded to the ancient *Mai* or *Maia* of whom we have already spoken, the first goddess of fertility who emerged from the depths of the northern sea, as the other had risen from the depths of the earth. It is probably because of this connection that we find certain other qualities attributed to Isis, for example, guardianship of mariners: which is why, every year, at the time of her main festival, a small ship was taken along the sea shore, as a token of honour, and then thrown into the waves. (10)

Isis, the very image of a powerful and fruitful nature, *warmed all living creatures against her bosom.* But here we meet up with a paradox, for where could the bosom of the earth ever be warmer than in Iceland, with its innumerable volcanoes and its 1,500 hot springs, often reaching 100 degrees [Celsius] – the only place on earth in which the temperature of the subsoil is so warm that it can be used to heat the towns, together with any number of greenhouses where, in closest proximity to the glaciers, all varieties of flowers and early vegetables are cultivated – even bananas!

Isis, goddess of life and death, was very often associated with Proserpina, queen of the Nether Regions, where Isis went to fetch *Osiris*. And it is rather amusing to note that the Lord and Master of Hades, the Christian Devil, is known to the Finns by the name of *Hiisi* – and that in the Icelandic *Edda* a certain *Hysi* proclaims himself to be *King of Death and of Eternal Cold*. There is every reason to believe that this is the same personage who has passed from one epoch to another, and from one country to another. Nor is it too far-fetched to summon up before the mind's eye that little imp we call a **Jack-in-the-box**, jumping up (*issant*) suddenly and impudently like the most violent and brutal of geysers. Today it is a simple little toy, but it has come a very long way before coming to rest on a shelf for jokes and tricks.

However, before symbolising the spirit of evil, the term *hiisi*, in Finnish, meant *sacred wood* (11) or grove (of alders, birch or water-willow) which gave birth to all animal life, according to the most ancient systems of cosmogony: Nordic, Egyptian, Archaic Greek – to name just a few.

In practical terms, Isis and Osiris personified the subterranean force which drove the water-willows upwards, out of the mud of the Nile Delta, where layers of sand had no doubt been accumulating since the famous Flood, and where Isis was especially revered. Does Littré not inform us that the French word *osier* (water-willow) translates *oseria*, *ouzilz*, *oseire, oisis*? The last word in this list (*oisis*), must certainly be cognate with our modern 'oasis', a desert spot where we find a well or source of springing water and, of course, some vegetation.

If Osiris was sometimes represented by an **eye** in the middle of a triangle or **delta**, it is because in Antiquity **eye** was gradually transformed into French *hile* (*ile*: island), where the miracle of first life took place.

And if *Horus*, the sparrow-hawk, constitutes a divine trinity with *Isis* and *Osiris*, it is because he represents the sun, like the eagle of the Finnish *Genesis* which laid its young in the tuft of reeds from which life on earth emerged. Do not forget that it is because of the old sagas that a sparrow-hawk (or vulture?) appears on the Icelandic coat of arms. But in the old sagas the vulture's name is *gammur* whereas the eagle's is more poetic, namely, *gamli*.

Is this not the right moment to recall that the **g** of *geyzir* is the equivalent of Greek *gamma*, which resembles our **y** and which is used to symbolise the syllable *iss* in coats of arms of towns such as *Issoire* and *Issoudun*? And as confirmation of what has just been suggested, is it not delightful to read the following lines in Jubinal, a 13th Century author: "*Plus que nule letre que j'oie, signifie G la goie qui par femme revient au monde?*" (12) (More than any other letter in my possession, G symbolises the joy that enters the world by woman). In French the letter G is pronounced like the English word *gay*. Thus, it has via mythology come to be the symbol for mother-earth, opening herself for the fertilising stream. *Gai, gai, marions-nous!* (Let us be merry, let us be married!).

* * *

Now we should reflect on the mystery of the town of *Ys*, or *Is*. The Celtic legend about the submerged city is well known. The basic structure of the legend, gilded in the course of the centuries and refashioned according to the changing mood of the time, tells of a fine city, ruled by King *Gradlon*, called *le Meur*, which could be translated as *the* Great, *the Powerful*, in today's parlance, but which probably meant '*man of the sea*' initially (*homme de la mer*). Which is more or less the same thing. This city disappeared under the waters after the gate of one of the dykes had burst open. No one knows for sure where this famous city stood. Some say it was in the Bay of Cardigan in Wales; others prefer the area around *Douarnenez*; a third preference is for the Bay of the Dead (*Baie des Trépassés*); while another possibility is at Lough Neagh in Ireland. The scope of the legend and the tenacity with which belief in it lives on, leads us to think that some historical event must lie at the bottom of it all.

It would be interesting to ascertain whether *Ys* was just some Celtic town destroyed, like so many others, by a normal tidal wave, or whether it was the victim of a gigantic cataclysm such as the World Flood. Or again, whether it was the capital of Atlantis, or even (why not?) Atlantis itself. This country, whose existence can no longer be thought doubtful, was not only surnamed *Ultima*, but was also called *Hyperborean*; and Spence, whose speciality this matter is, places it in the northern basin of the Atlantic (13).

Another question arises, this time concerning the name of the city of *Ys*. In Celtic languages the root *Is* is synonymous with a lower or even subterranean level (14). The submerged city in question could, therefore, very easily have been given the name *Ys* (or *Is*) after its destruction by the sea and it would thenceforth quite reasonably have been called *submerged*. But the submerged *city of Ys* could just as well have been the *island of Ys*, or indeed the *whole* of Atlantis, since the word *island* was used to describe the whole fief or area of land, and could, therefore, quite easily have been later, and by derivation, applied to the word *town* (Old English *tun*: meant enclosed space < homestead < village. Dutch *tuin* now means *garden*). The French word *ville*, we believe, is derived (via Latin *villa*: country house; seat; farm; villa – also *gathering place* for recruits; the census; other public business) from *hile* (or *ille* or *ile*), which meant *vital centre*.

Whatever the truth of all this may be, the legends and ballads which have come down to us indicate that *Is* was built according to the Atlantan plan, so characteristic and described in so much detail, that one can trace the descendants of the Atlantans through the many countries they colonised. The plan was as follows. A city or fortress was built on a natural or artificial hill, *surrounded by circles of earthworks and water communicating with each other by canals and gates*. This is how Atlantis, mother of all labyrinths, the ruins of which we have discovered, was described for us. This was the plan of the prehistoric forts on the isles of Aran, attributed to the giants. We find similar remains in Scotland, in Sardinia, at Mycenae, at Knossos, in Thessaly and in Asia Minor.

The *thalos-tholos-tholoi* temples of Archaic Greece where the *Talos* cult (already mentioned) was perpetuated, were also built according to this plan: for example, the one at Epidaurus, consisting of a central well or spring (Latin *tullium*), surrounded by concentric walls, each one with an opening giving access to the different rings around the sanctuary (15).

Need we be surprised that in the Norwegian language, which has maintained itself in Iceland, the word *tale* also has the meaning – **still** has the meaning – of a group of houses almost always built around or near a spring? Let us look further. The dictionaries tell us that the *Isis cult spread through Archaic Greece, Asia Minor, Gaul and Brittany. The Bretons were, it seems, remarkably receptive to outside influences.* But the story can be turned round.

There was also a town of *Ys*, eight days march from Babylon, in Mesopotamia, in the land of the Sumerians who, as their name indicates, originally came from the North. It is startling to reflect that the Asiatic town of *Is*, having at an earlier period been called *Aesopolis*, is today known as *Hit*. But in Norwegian the plural of *Hiisi* (cf. above) is *Hiidet*. Could this not indicate a link with the *Hittite* people? We shall come back to this point a little later. As Pasteur put it, good theories should be productive (16).

Meanwhile, it seems very reasonable to ask whether Iceland or the Land of *Ys* does not have a better claim to be called the centre of Ancient Atlantis than any other country. It is a land that constantly quakes, a land of lava and basalt, a land tunneled like no other by fiery subterranean channels, burning beneath an ice layer a thousand metres thick. All its geological characteristics bear witness to a truly gigantic cataclysm in the not-so-distant past. And is it not the most perfect symbol imaginable of the alliance between fire and water which has dominated all pagan cosmogonies since pre-history?

In Greek, the prefix *isos* means *equality*, in the sense of two masses or forms in equilibrium. This prefix is there for good reason: for very good reason. What better reason could there be than to be joined to the *is* of iceberg (perfectly stable in the water because of the balance **below** the sea-level and **above** it, in the air) and to the *is* of Isis, goddess both of life and of death, of the forces **beneath** the earth and **in the air** – the forces which create balance in the world? She has often been depicted with scales in her hand.

And what could be more suitable, if we recall that *Gradlon*, king of the city of *Ys*, bears a name whose root *Grad* (in Gaelic, *gradh*) means *root; the height* of love; *that which is rapid, warm, violent, vehement* (17) – and is also cognate (according to Littré) with *grael* and *Graal*?

There was once a king in Thule – who will certainly cause a great deal more ink to flow.

* * *

8

TONTAINE AND TONTON

Rome has planted many signposts in the territories she conquered. These signposts 'speak' to us symbolically in that they have confined our Western history for a very long period within a Latin universe. For example, in the case of language (and since language is a social factor, more important than any other, it is the best guide to follow in any kind of historical research), our ceaseless reference to Latin in matters of etymology has cast a veil over our relations with all other Indo-European languages. It has erected a barrier that no one has dared scale beyond a few timid steps towards Greek and Hebrew. And yet, quite often, the relationship of a French word with a Latin word is no more than one between cousins which is wrongly interpreted as representing a line of direct descent. On the other hand, Pelasgian Greek and Sanskrit, Norwegian and the Celtic languages explain numerous words in our vocabulary that Latin on its own cannot explain – or, at least, not in their truly original meaning. If we have doubts today about the use of studying dead languages, this is because we have ourselves sullied their sap with our blindness. The oldest languages are very much alive. To prove the truth of this claim we need only study them in the right way: that is, by grouping them around essential concepts, which have held almost universal dominion over men, or to be more precise, which have bound men together in their manner of behaving, loving, working and training themselves spiritually. If we did this, we would realise how closely related they are and we would have rock solid foundations upon which to instruct our youth how men have in the past given form to this Earth of ours.

The Celts of Antiquity, unfortunately, left us no texts describing their civilisation - just a few inscriptions. They were men of deep wisdom, convinced long before Plato about the truth of what he wrote on the subject of the god Thoth, suspected of having invented writing. Plato writes: "Writing will encourage forgetfulness in men's souls by causing them to neglect their memory [.....] What the disciples of the art of writing will learn, is to presume that they have acquired knowledge although they have not done so: for when they have read a great deal without learning, they will believe themselves wise – but will in fact only be boring clods, thinking that they know a great deal, but knowing nothing".

This point of view was allied to a very great respect for the spoken word. Of course, the spoken word is suffering at present from hyper-inflation like all the rest, and it is quite possible that the flood in which we are already drowning is a flood of words and printed paper. Is it a kind of prescience which causes young people all over the world to neglect with so much abandon their spelling and the culture which we have given them; to scorn letters and to worship sound, the pure magic of words; and to try to escape from a tradition of learning that is stale, cramped and utterly dishonest? It's possible – but dangerous when there is no hand to guide them.

The oldest documents we have about the old Celts only go back to the 11th Century of our era. It seems that, at this time, when Christian beliefs were winning the contest against the ancient Pagan gods, it was thought necessary to put down in writing the beliefs and traditions which had till then been transmitted orally and which now ran the risk of being totally forgotten. It is not difficult to imagine what gaps and adaptations occurred in the reports which were almost entirely composed by churchmen. They are certainly interesting enough, but if we want to learn something about the mysteries of pre-History, we must necessarily have recourse to the Greek texts. Provided we approach them without prejudice and study them methodically, we will discover to our very great surprise that they describe events of the greatest antiquity with complete clarity. We simply have to know how to read the texts and then, having stripped them of the inventions and distortions that have accumulated throughout the ages, to take a good look at those solid facts on which they are based.

How could we possibly think that the Greeks, astute and logical as they were, could ever have accepted a world view conceived on the basis of fables that would not be acceptable to the mind? The works they have left us – like those of the Celts and Nordics – were often the product of folklore, but were certainly not (as is often said) the silly tales of peasants – *pagani* – pagans. They represent, on the contrary, the only true repository for the deeds and chronicles of men through time and space. How could History ever be able to travel through the millennia without the contribution of men's imagination which makes it easier to recall them? The Frankish warriors considered any man who could read or write as being capable of treachery: but it is quite certain that the songs launched by the bards on the wings of the winds did not betray the truth more than the scribblings of all the serried ranks of churchmen.

Before the Roman occupation, the language of the Gauls was closely related to Pelasgian Greek. The inscriptions we have found relative to this time were all written in Greek characters. On the subject of the Druids, Caesar writes that "*in publicis privatisque rationibus graecis litteris utebantur*" (in public and private discourse they used Greek letters). In his *Histoire Générale du Dauphiné*, Nicolas Chorier writes in turn that, "[.....] the Gauls were passionately devoted to the Greek language [.....] The first assault on the Celtic language wounded it so badly that when the Romans again attacked it later, the Druids themselves stopped confiding their secrets to it (Celtic) and started confiding them instead to this foreign tongue (Greek)."

Of course, anyone who knows the Druids and the Celts would realise that there would have been no question of their regarding the Greek language as 'foreign'. When the Romans eventually ran out of steam, and their empire collapsed, the Gauls were quick to try and wipe out all trace of them and return, at least in part, and with delight, to their former vocabulary. And so they began once again to call Paris, *Paris* – and not Lutetia; and a *coq* (cock) a *ko*. The Frankish influence played a large part in this return to Celtic sources.

If Greek was closely related to the language of pre-Roman Gaul, this cannot be attributed (or at least, not wholly attributed) to the Greek colonies of Marseilles or to the wave of Trojans and their allies returning Westwards after the destruction of Troy. The real reason is that the Atlantan peoples (as we have seen earlier) were the fathers of the Pelasgians or, to be more exact, were themselves Pelasgians in the eyes of the Orientals.

There can be no mistake about the direction in which the first input occurred. In Greek mythology it was *Cadmos*, brother of Europe, who was said to have given the Greek alphabet to the West, but some scholars (including Chorier, quoted above) claim the contrary. "It is undeniable," he writes, "that the Gallic characters were similar to the Greek, but it was these illustrious liars who took the chance to claim that they were the authors [of the alphabet] and that it was from them that the Gauls received it. In fact, it was Cadmos who was the first to give the Greeks sixteen letters similar to those of the Gauls."

Since his opinion seems to be confirmed by History, we would agree with Chorier. For who, in fact, was *Cadmos*? According to Greek mythology, he was the son of a king of Phoenicia, the grandson of

Neptune and Io. He was, therefore, quite definitely a member of the Ocean Dynasty, which means he was of Western origin. Perhaps he was the hero called *Cod*, of Irish folklore, descendant of the mythical king *Ioruath* [from *Io*?], who had many adventures in Greece and Syria, and whose brother reigned over Greater Asia (2). And when Plato claims that the god *Thoth* or *Teuth* invented writing (3), then we should remember the Gallic god *Teutates* (*Teuth-ates* or *Teuth-antes*, that is: *God the Father*) and also the Danish word *Taet,* which means *tree*. We know that the great Regulator-God of the Celts was worshipped in the shape of an oak. It is, therefore, very possible that it was the Celtic *Teut* or the Danish *Taet* (also written as *Tuat*) that gave birth to the Egyptian *Thoth*. It could be argued that this is a gratuitous supposition, but that would not be so. Let us refer to Homer. We read in the *Iliad* that just before having to join in combat with the *giant* Achilles, Hector is dreaming beneath the walls of Troy about various ways of avoiding the combat. He could give back Helen to the Achaeans or share with them the treasures which Alexander carried off in his hollow vessels. "But," he asks himself, "what will I achieve by doing that? When all is said and done, this is not the time to tell old stories and to **return to the days of the oak and the rock**."

According to Homer's way of thinking, 'the days of the oak and the rock' were the remotest times in history – a concept which is valid to this day. When Italians speak of *una persona canuta*, they are referring to someone *white* because of his age. The word is derived from Latin *canutus* which means *oak* and is cognate with dog-Latin *casnus*. The French *chenu*, the equivalent of Italian *canuto*, comes from the same root, and Littré points out that in everyday parlance the word is used in the sense of excellent, strong, rich – because it suggests great *age*.

The *chenu* man of modern times is, therefore, certainly the understudy of the *canut*, the *man of oak* who, in the opinion of Homer and of all the ancients, was the very best of humanity.

Now it so happens that it was in Celtic Antiquity that the cult of the oak was continued for the longest period of time. Moreover, it was in Norway, Denmark and England that several kings were called *Canute* (or *Knut*), and this was most certainly a tradition with a very long ancestry (4).

In the Gaelic, oak is *tann*. (French) giants in days of yore lived in a *tanière* which was originally a vault of branches from a cluster of *oaks* before it eventually became (in English) a rock *lair*. *Tan* or *tanin* (*téné* in old Walloon), which right through Antiquity was used to prepare animal skins, was originally composed from an extract of *oak* bark (hence its name) and later of fir. In the Middle Ages, *tanière* (French: meaning either *oak grove* or *cavern*) was also written as *tesnière*. Ancient sites with names beginning in *téné* (such as *Ténédos*, *Ténériffe*, *Tenès*) are very interesting material for this kind of historical research, as is shown by *La Tène* in Switzerland.

With regard to *Danemark* (Denmark), whose kings were often called *Canute* (and were thus very estimable, since their name evoked the strength of the tree), the country's present name probably means 'country of the *Dans*', and might be derived from some ancient country of the *Tasnes* or *Tanns*, i.e. country of the *oak* or *fir* men – which comes to the same thing, since we find this root *tann* in the German word *Tanne* or *Tannenbaum* (fir). That *dan* and *tan* should also have described the object called *dent* (tooth) is explained by the form of the fir (Royal Tree), which is shaped like a *cone* (or *kan*), and which stands out against the sky.

At the time we are studying in this book, a language was only spoken. Its evolution and fluctuations were shaped only by the sound and not by the spelling, which did not exist. That is why we are not attempting to give a precise, grammatical etymology for words which have taken shape via a series of associations of ideas, lasting and developing over many thousands of years. Our guide is above all the living, mental and spiritual character of their evolution.

In the countries of the North, as in Gaul, the oak was the most sacred of all trees. In the 24th *runa* of the Finnish Kalevala it is called *divine*. We know that the very earliest Celts had no other temples in which to make sacrifices to their gods than those formed by the vaults of oak branches over their heads. Thus, we read in the 38th dissertation of Maxim of Tyre: "The Gauls worship Jupiter, but for them this god is represented by a very tall oak."

Etymologically, *druid* means *man-oak*. The word is derived from Welsh-Gallic *derw*, which also gives us *derviche* (dervish), which is in turn cognate with Welsh-Breton *doro* and Greek *druios*, having the same meaning.

No cult of this tree has existed anywhere other than in Ancient Celtic lands and in the Ancient North Atlantic, except of course (and with good reason) in Pelasgian Greece. It would, therefore, be difficult to deny, in the light of what has been said earlier, that the Celts were, *par excellence*, 'men of the oak'. Just think of *noix de Galle* if you need to be convinced. [*Galle* : gall (bot.), oak nut. **Also**: the English Folk Song refrain: *Hearts of Oak*.]

Now, there were ten kings of Atlantis. Ten (French *dix*) is in Danish *ti*. Were the *Ti-tans* perhaps originally (and mythologically, of course) the ten *Tans*, or ten first *men-oaks*, as the etymology of their name might suggest? *Dan*, the root of Danish, meant in ancient days any legendary king of this country (5). In the *Kalevala* we read that when *Illmarinen*, the Finnish *divine smith*, had to quit his country because he had committed a serious misdeed there, his mother advised him to hide himself on an island which he would reach *having crossed nine seas and half of the tenth* (6). Did each sea have its own king?

Be that as it may, Greek mythology informs us that men were born from the *ashes* of the Titans. This myth is astonishingly true to the most ancient Finnish legends. In the *Kalevala* we are actually told that at the beginning of the world, the oaks were so tall, so numerous and so dense, that they darkened the skies and stopped the sun from giving life to the earth. Vainamoinen then begs his mother to send him a hero capable of cutting down the trees. Thereupon a not very large creature appears and proclaims himself, without batting an eyelid, able to cut the trees down – which he does with three blows of his axe. The sun sets the dead wood on fire (continues the poem), *the wind fans the flames, and reduces everything to cinders*. The old, imperturbable Vainamoinen then takes seven seeds from his bag of marten and ermine skins, and sows them in the earth. Here again it seems right to grant priority to Nordic thought rather than to Greek because, as late as the 19th Century, it was widespread practice in Finland and in other Scandinavian countries to burn the fields on an immense scale before sowing seed in the ashes.

It is worth noting that it was the *men of the sea* who followed in the steps of the *men-of-oak* or *Titans*, and that they owed their superiority to their being armed with axes. It seems that they originated in Celtic Britain whose inhabitants had apparently been the first to exploit the minerals iron and copper. It is also worth noting that the *dent* (tooth) of the axe, which bit into the tree and opened up the earth to the sun, remained a sacred symbol for these peoples as, indeed, did the axe itself. In Greek art it would be the prerogative of the giants of the second category: the descendants of the Titans.

* * *

The undeniable relationship between East and West, which was evident in the millennia which preceded our era, can of course be interpreted in the reverse direction, which is indeed what has been done up to now by those who claim that Central Asia was the starting point for human migrations. But we remain convinced that the population shifts originally followed the pattern we have described.

It is possible that this *Drang nach Osten* (Urge to go East) coincided with a *Drang nach Westen* on the part of the Asiatic peoples, and that the two movements collided, fought and intermingled to a certain extent on the Middle Eastern turntable. But it was *in the home of the Atlantans that the gods were born* (according to Plato and Solon) and these authors knew what they were talking about because, when men speak of gods, they are talking *civilisation*.

In the minds of the Ancient Greeks, Atlantis remained the *island* or *navel* of the world where the rainbow had touched the earth and given birth to life. The icy Northern Ocean never had any other reason to be surnamed the *Arctic* – and if it had only been a question of the shape of the earth at this spot, the South Pole would never have had any cause to call itself *Ant*-arctic. Moreover, do the Scandinavians not call that period of the Quaternary (in which it is agreed that men first appeared on earth) the *arctic period*?

In the poem *The Feast of Aegger* (one of the songs of the Icelandic Edda) it is said that Thor was absent from a certain banquet of the gods *'because he was on an expedition to the* East' (7). In another passage it is Loki who advises the god Thor *never to speak to the mortals about his expedition to the East.*

No smoke without fire!

But let us return to Pelasgian Greek from which we have strayed. Pelasgian Greek, or *Argolid* Greek, lives on in the word *argot* (French for *slang*). If we call *argot* a *langue verte* (**green** language, in the sense explained in Chapter 3: Red and Green), this is done for the same reason that we gave for calling Greenland *green*. *Argot* (slang) is simply a left-over from the original language of the men known as the race of the *Arc*. And, if it became the secret language of the mendicant beggars, that is because it was the secret language of the implacable enemies of Rome – both Imperial and Christian: those men who were always pursued by the law, excommunicated, condemned to the galleys, and, therefore, taught it to the victims of 'common law'. It was to a large extent the 'jargon' of the first Protestants and of those who came before them in the cause of religious rebellion. It has remained the language of the French *caves* (cellars) because **Cawe** was the other name (no doubt a diminutive) of *Kalewa*, the giant, father of the *sea people* according to Finnish legend (8). **Cave** represents in the Kalewala a powerful, benevolent spirit – and incidentally, can also be seen as being cognate with Celtic **Cal.**

And is the *taulière* (*Madam* of the *House of Ill Repute*) not the person who carries on in a degraded manner the work of the woman who kept watch over the *tolos*, ancient sanctuary of love, where (during the **night of errors**, or **night of tolerance**) women formerly gave themselves to all who wanted them?

Many expressions, and phrases which are no longer in use, and whose origin (according to Littré) are unknown, can be traced back to Northern languages. For example, *donner un coup de fion* (to give a *shine* to something) is very possibly derived from *Fion* or *Fynn*, the great Celtic hero, the *shining* hero. Then there is the word *gueules* (*gules*: *red*), a term in heraldry, which comes from Icelandic *gull*, cognate with *gul persan* which, before describing gold, must have been used for *red.*

But let us now consider the word *tante.*

Littré has given up on the origin of this term while, nevertheless, admitting that it was extremely old. The problem was to explain the agglutination of the **t** before *ante*, since *tante* in Old French was spelled *ente* or *ante*, and meant *first mother*. However, in the Scandinavian languages (or at least in Danish) the same word *tante* is, strange to relate, used for *foster mother*, in the sense of *first* mother, or *blood* mother, since she is the sister of the father. This use of the word suggests a matriarchal view of the family.

The Scandinavian and French *tante* seem to be cognate with old *tan* (oak) which became *tant* (dent, *tooth*), meaning *great ancestor*. Moreover, all these words are cognate with Finnish *tonttu* and Swedish *tomte*, which today mean *domestic spirit – ancestor of the house.* Which, of course, must be the origin of the old French word *tonton* (familiar for *uncle*). *Teutates*, father of men, was also called *Tut-tat* (9), cognate too with the Nordic word *taet*, meaning *tree* in general, but also *toit* (French for *roof*), and everything that is dense, massive and solid.

What do we know about *tontine*? It was a collection of individuals who put all their possessions in common. The system was, it seems, introduced in the 17th Century by a Neapolitan called *Tonti*. He had been obliged to adopt a symbolic name, and his enterprise was very much like that of the famous *Compagnons*, who were themselves the heirs of the Free Masons, imbued with the traditions of which we are speaking in this book. Incidentally, the word *tontine* is probably the same as *tontaine* in our old songs, and we can well understand why the French sometimes refer to the *Mont-de-Piété* (*pawn shop*, lit. "*mountain of piety*") as *ma tante*. (Perhaps a favourite aunt who will always "help out" in a tight spot? Translator.)

We could of course continue our little journey into the complexities of philology much further because, in the Scandinavian languages, the great Pelagic fishes are all grouped under the name of *tantei*, fishes which are reputed to defend each other to the death, and were formally sacred to the tribes of the Atlantic, otherwise known as the Pelasgians.

The *tantes* were, therefore, originally comrades in arms, heroes of a fraternity which placed a special stamp on the mores of the Nordic warriors before spreading out to other parts of the world. A trace of this fraternity has survived to this day, especially in the Navy, and in the French practice of *amatelotage* (share-and-share-alike), which was especially favoured by pirates. The idea of share-and-share-alike was highly regarded in the Pagan world, even when it was taken too far. But this was not acceptable to the Christians – hence the modern pejorative meaning attached to the word *tante*.

* * *

9

FROM HERACLES TO QUEEN PEDAUQUE

Hercules belongs to us! Hercules is not a Greek hero. The Greeks made a hero of him, but that is not the same thing at all.

Herodotus seems to be acting very honestly when he makes a distinction between Hercules, the old god, and the hero Alcides of Tiryns, who had the same name, partly because of his courage, and partly because he belonged to the clan of the Alcmenoids.

When confusing the exploits of the old giants with those of Alcides, the Greeks of the classical period (the period which told us the story) took the lion's share for themselves. This did not make bigger liars of them than any other nation: each new civilisation has always considered it a matter of importance to make a clean sweep of all that has gone before.

The historian of Halicarnassos is of the opinion that the cult of Hercules is of Egyptian origin – which is tantamount to saying that it was of Atlantan origin. "The Egyptians must indeed have had a god by the name of Hercules," he tells us. "Incidentally, they believe that the twelve present gods - including Hercules - were born of the eight original gods, 17,000 years before the reign of Amasis".

Eight original gods? Isn't this the *ogdoad*? One thinks immediately of *och* (*oc* or *og*), i.e. of *eight*, the key-number of the *Occident* which, of course, gets its *name* from this number, a name, moreover, which by extension means 'region of the setting sun'. The Maia was the oldest, or one of the oldest, Pelasgian symbols because (quite exceptionally) it has *eight* legs like the *octopod* jellyfish, with its *eight* threadlike tentacles. And it is certainly for the same reason that Odin's horse also had *eight* legs (1).

Since Herodotus was very much interested in the question of Hercules' origin, he wanted to pursue the matter, and in order to hear the opinions of 'competent persons' he set off for Tyre, in Phoenicia, where the god's most famous sanctuary was situated. The other principle temples were in Thrace and in Asia Minor, at Rhodes and at Kos ... in fact, in every region that our Knights Errant had ever established themselves. At the sight of the Tyre sanctuary, Herodotus cried out, "I have seen it! It is truly magnificent". And he adds, while describing his itinerary, "I entered into discussion with the priests of the god and I asked them how long the temple had been in existence. 'Since the foundation of Tyre', they told me. This meant for 2,300 years, which clashes with Greek opinion. I also saw another sanctuary of Hercules at Tyre, that of Thasos, and I actually found a temple of Hercules built by the Phoenicians when they set out to discover Europe: and this places the foundation of the temple five generations before the birth of the Greek Hercules. My investigation has convinced me that Hercules is a very ancient god and I think it most sensible that two temples should have been built in Greece for two different Hercules figures; one is an immortal god and is called Olympian Hercules, while the other receives only those honours which are due to heroes (.....). As for the gods who do not come from Egypt", the historian continues, "they must have come to us from the Pelasgians" (2).

One of these gods, quoted by Herodotus, was *Mercury with an upraised staff*. Could this possibly be *Erech*, a true Atlantan hero if ever there was one, and father of all *Erics* from the North Atlantic?

Confirming the judgement of Herodotus, the Greeks are very embarrassed in their myths when they have to make only one hero of the two Hercules figures, which they almost always treated as one in their legends although they were separated in the temples. The confusion is particularly noticeable in the story of their births. We shall, therefore, pass over Alcides and confine ourselves to the Hercules in whose name the great deeds of the Atlantic world were done and whose very first contacts with the Orient were noted.

The hero, called Hercules by the Romans, was known as Heracles to the Greeks, and he was the son of *Hera* - although, at the same time, he was not! One day, when the goddess was feeding the child, some drops of milk fell from her breast onto the earth, so the legend tells us. The earth, thus fertilised by the *arc*, described by the jet of milk (symbol of the rainbow), gave birth to the first men, the *géants* or *gaians* (as the French still said in the Middle Ages) - *ge* or *gaea* meaning *earth*. In mythology, the giants were surnamed *sons of the sky and of the earth*. One can understand why.

This legend makes Hercules the father, or symbol, of the race called the race of the *arc* or *eye* (*oeil*, in French), or of the *Hyperborean giants*. For this reason Hellenic art will always show him wielding not just a club (a weapon called 'the weapon of the Finns' in the *Kalevala*), but a club covered in *eyes*. The vegetable eye (therefore, the animal and human ones too) was throughout Antiquity a symbol of the *hile* (hilum) or *ile*, the first *umbilicus* or *navel*, i.e. symbol of the aqueous area into which the sap of the nutritional canals flows. In botany, *hile* and *oeil* are still defined in the same way, and there is no other way to explain the importance of the symbol of the eye (*oeil*) throughout Antiquity than by studying this cosmogony. The same applies when trying to explain the famous eye of the Cyclops. The oldest texts make no mention anywhere of the single eye in this category of giants, of whom so much was said later. The error (committed on purpose, or by mistake) can be explained by the fact that they were also of the race of the *oeil*. This concept and cult of the *oeil* or 'navel' (the primordial sacred navel) helps us, too, to understand the contemplation of the navel, practised by the sages of India, the Brahmins and Buddhas.

A propos of the very crudest representation of the navel (i.e. by means of little circles of stone or clay pierced with a hole, or showing in their middle a slight lump), these little stones are found in their thousands in the ruins of ancient cities, but also in Celtic lands and in Scandinavia. They were apparently used for counting and for voting. This was perfectly normal since they were themselves an image of the principle of sexual duality, and indeed of that basic duality in accordance with which all life in the world is organised. It should be noted that the French word *nombril* (navel) contains the word *nombre* (number), and that in the French *calcul* (calculation) we find *cal*, the Celtic name for the little round stone.

In the West, the name *Hercules* has a totally *concrete* meaning: *Her, harra, herra* or *hari, herran* in Finnish; *here* in Swedish; *her* and *haer* in Breton; *heer* and *Herr* in Dutch and German respectively, are all words meaning *seigneur* in French and *lord* in English, or *héritier* in French or *heir* in English, or sometimes prince or king (3). As for the syllable *cule*, it is the equivalent of *cal* (pebble) or *cave* (cellar).

Ancient *Chaldonie* (Caledonia, Scotland) was also called *Caldee* or *Culdee*, and since every archaic root always meant both the thing and its opposite (because of the androgynous character of the creator), the root *cul* or *cal* could either mean *hollow* or *bulging, tender* or *hard*. These two meanings have been maintained in French: *cale* can be the wedge which is driven **in**, or *cal*, an **ex**-crescence or callosity.

Similarly, we have *cale de navire* (hold of a ship) or *culasse* (*breech* of a gun) etc. And then, because it is used to translate *hollow*, we find in old French the word *calais*, meaning *deep basket*, which is why, in the coat of arms of the *city* of Calais, we also see a hollow basket - usually mistaken for a crescent shaped moon!

In the refrains of the old French songs such as: "... I've had it once, Jeanette, I shall have it again, your pretty basket (*panier*), Jeanette," the allusion is quite clear, albeit expressed in poetic terms (4).

The name *Hercules* can, therefore, have three meanings: *Lord of the Deep* (or of the country of the Night, Dynasty of the Night); *hero of heroes* (*culmen principum*, highest of the high) or, again: *hardest of the hard* (*dur des durs*).

Thus, we find Mistral, in his *Poème du Rhône*, alluding to *un raco d'ome caloussado*, which he himself translates as '*race of men with strong muscles*' (English *calloused* or *hardened*). In another passage he recalls the days of the *colossus with the thick beard, large, corpulent, with limbs like an oak*. It goes without saying that the *colossal* size of the works constructed by the Pelasgians, the Cyclops and their heirs (pyramids, ziggurats or Gothic cathedrals) is part of an ancestral cult of gigantism which goes back to the giants of the Stone Age. *Calmach*, in the Celtic language, still means *power, enormous size*.

Here is another interesting story. We read in 'History of the Gauls' (taken from Greek authors) that *Iber*, a son of Hercules, was the brother of *Celtus*, father of the Celts. Heavens above! Why not believe these statements? They are, of course, too clear - too simple! *Iber* is said, naturally enough, to have founded *Iberia*, a province which in ancient days was so closely tied to Ireland that certain historians think that Ireland was colonised by the Iberians. We are more inclined to believe the opposite. Be that as it may, many Irish legends have references to black hair and to the 'pretty brown complexion' of the heroines. Auburn hair, very common among people in the British Isles and particularly in Ireland, must have been the result of a cross between brunette and Scandinavian blond. But the mythical *Iber* in question (who founded Iberia) could also be *Ymer*, father of the Nordic giants, whose name in modern German means *always* (*immer*), because he is said to have given birth to a race of men considered to be *immortal*. The fraternal bond between Iber and *Celtus* shows Hercules, their father, to have been Atlantic Man *par excellence*. And let us not forget that in Irish legend we shall in time hear of a certain *Her Culann*, Lord of Culann, in Ulster, who could quite easily - like some Alcides of Tiryns – be the continuator of a mythical hero. The coats of arms of Ulster do, after all, show a great black vat or cauldron in which we see a skeleton and a tower, which indubitably indicate that there is a strong connection with the *Empire of the Vasty Deep*, the empire in which *Orcus* reigned. What could be more clear?

For us, the oldest and most authentic etymology for Hercules is, of course, also the simplest. It is the one which relates this name to *Orcula* or *Orculi*, diminutive of *Orca* or *Orcu*. The roots *arc* and *orc* have coincided, and indicate *that which concerns the Arctic or Sumerian regions*, i.e. the regions whence the giants of the earliest days of the world would start on their travels. Which, in turn, explains why these roots remained linked to the idea of gigantism. The Portuguese call the whale and several other cetaceans that are giant animals *orca*. The Corsicans in their dialect still use two related words, *orcu* and *orcu balenu*, to describe, on the one hand, the *ogre*, and on the other, the *rainbow*. It is, therefore, not unreasonable to think that the original meaning of Hercules was *the young giant*. This is an interpretation, moreover, which relates to those we have just mentioned and which, in their turn, simply show an evolution of the term through the millennia.

We read under the heading of Hercules in the *Grande Encyclopédie* that "When Graeco-Roman polytheism spread over the West there was no (hero) who could better be identified with the divinities of the Celtic or Germanic peoples".

We should have been surprised to hear anything to the contrary.

From whichever angle we examine the matter, Hercules seems to have represented for the Greeks the prototype of a hero in the ancient Atlantic empire, the prototype of animal vitality, the virile *genius* of the Latins. At Rome, only men were admitted to his temple. By his primitive nature (symbolised by his loin 'cloth' made of *oak* leaves), he symbolised, as is well known, the power of the animal - good, or at least without malice: a characteristic, no doubt, of the giants from the Dynasty of the Night.

We find a reference to these giants in the Prediction of *Wala*, at the beginning of the Icelandic *Edda*: "I recall the giants born at the dawn of our days, the giants who once taught me wisdom ..." In the same work, *Jottenheim* is said to be the principal dwelling of these men. The *Jotes*, former inhabitants of the North, are the ancestors of the *Getes* and of the *Goths*. According to an old saga, the Jotes were the first inhabitants of the North. That is why the Goths, the Getes and all their descendants would say, and as all their legends and as History would relate, that their race was immortal. We should just add that they produced so many children who settled in the four corners of the earth, that today there is no nation anywhere that could not make the same claim!

Smith (5) rejects the testimony of authors such as Procopius, Jerome and Uopiscus, but especially that of Jordanes, who all claimed that the *long-haired* Goths of Scandinavia were one and the same people. We, however, agree with these old authors, and even with Paulus Diaconus, who believed the Lombards to have been of Scandinavian descent.

Our era of prissy humility has classified the image of the primitive Hercules, as it survives in heraldry to this day, as 'savage'. And yet the kingdom of Denmark and several old Norman families have kept it on their coat of arms - while Greece, too, knows very well what it owes to this 'savage' ancestor.

And now we come to the *Labours*, generally presented in an order differing from the original. Moreover, it was only from the 4th Century that we have spoken of *twelve* labours - adding, incidentally, many episodes to the story which never appeared in the original tradition.

Just as in the case of his origins, the achievements and heroic deeds of Hercules (which were probably spread over several generations - the eight *years* mentioned by Diodorus of Sicily could well have been eight *centuries* ... or even eight millennia!), prove decisively that the Pillars of Hercules were crossed in a direction different to the accepted one – at least, as regards the first crossing. In line with Pre-History, the Giants moved from the Atlantic Ocean to the Mediterranean, and not vice-versa. If the opposite were true, it would be difficult to explain why the old ocean *Okeinos* should finally have come to be called the *Atlantic*, since the syllables *at, aet, ath* have always (like *ant*) had the meaning of *ancestral*. *Aet* (in modern Danish) still means *origin, lineage*; *athach* (in Gaelic) means *giant*; *athair* means *ancestor*; *Aethan* (changing to *Aedan*) finally ended up as *Adam*. *Athi* (in the Finnish Kalevala) is the *old man of the sea with grass-green beard, king of the waves*; and if the first vertebra of the neck is called the *atlas*, this is because it supports the head, the most important part of the body, just like the Atlantan people bore the weight of the world on its shoulders at a certain period in time.

That Hercules should have hunted the hind in the Hyperborean regions and that he should have slain the *Erymanthan* boar in *Arcadia* (altered from the original French *Oechalie*); that he should have overcome the *Nemean* lion (near Argolis) and the *Cretan* bull is not in dispute. But what is really interesting is that he should have become a legend for founding *Alesia* (Gaul); for killing the *Lernaean Hydra* (near Argos) and draining the marshes; for cleansing the *Augean* stables and, finally, for leading *Geryon's* cattle to Thrace. The Golden Apples of the Hesperides deserve a chapter of their own, since this episode (like a few others) seems to belong to a much later period than the first labours.

We must now open that eye. Hellenistic Greece appropriated the heroes of the great dynasties that had preceded its own, but History must now return them to us.

The Lernaean Hydra is, in fact, the hydra of *Erne* or *Loch Erne*, a lake in Ireland corresponding with the sea. This monstrous 'sea serpent' is said to have been the son of *Echidna*; the great, mythical, Atlantic sea-spider. Is it not in these regions (the Northern British Isles) that we find, more than anywhere else, the giant *octopus* (or squid) and the monstrous *crabs* (brothers and sons of the Maia)? Are they not always ready (according to the old legends) to help the Hydra and the gorgons? And **where** is it that the *Loch Ness* monster appears from time to time - either in the water or in the imagination of the people?

As for the Augean Stables, we should lay a hundred to one that they were situated in France's valley of the *Auge*. We should point out that if Charles the Simple 'offered' Normandy to Rollo (although at the time it was regarded as the richest province in Europe), this was because Rollo had shown that his claim went back a very long way and that this region had been part of the northern conquerors' domain since time immemorial - just like the coast of Flanders and Poitou, which had long since served as landing stages on the way to Iberia and Barbary, in Africa.

Where do we find kings whose first name is *Ogier* (or *Augeas*)? Where else than in the North, and mainly in Denmark - for example, *Ogier-the-Dane*, whose statue stands in an underground chamber of Elsinor, where an angel announces on each Christmas Eve that he may sleep on in peace till the day when the *Dans* should once again have need of him.

The land of Augeas had so many herds, the legend says, that the *excrement of the animals was making the soil sterile*. Has anyone ever seen in the East herds of cattle so large? The cleansing of these 'stables' no doubt took place at a time when the civilising giant already knew how to use the plough. Augeas reigned over the *Eleans*. *Elis*, in the Peloponnese, belonged to the dynasty of the *Achaeans*, who were of Pelasgian origin. *Achaia*, like Achaean, is cognate with *Og* and *Aug*, just as *aqua* is cognate with *auge*. Once again, this is a province baptised with the name of a mother province, like Arcadia and so many others. For example, French Brittany (*Bretagne*) has a name borrowed from an older 'relative', Paris as well. Pausanias derives *Augeas* from *Eleinos*, another name for *Okeinos*, meaning *ocean*. The root *ell* or *oel* abounds in place names along the North Atlantic where *Ellen* has replaced *Helen*, and where the name *Hell* was given to the abode of the *dead*, i.e. the *illustrious forefathers*. In Gaelic, *eilean* means *island* and *eile-anach* means *of good birth*. Once again, everything agrees with, and confirms, our point of view.

If we pursue this line of investigation, no more doubt is possible. Truth emerges from the lie. According to legend, Augeas, angered by having to give nine-tenths of his herds to Hercules (because of the Labour he had undertaken), sent him off to King *Dexamenos*, a relative, asking him to dispose of young Erythion who wanted to marry his daughter.

This must have been a neighbour. And who was this Dexamenos? He was King of the Realm of the Night (*Dex* in old French meant *night*), or the tenth great king of the Atlantic (*dekmnos* in Gaelic could possibly mean *the tenth*) (6). We read in Varende: "The mother of Arlette (mother of William the Conqueror) could have been *Dode* or *Duixa* or even *Deixa*, daughter of a deceased king of England" (7) – a curious reminder in those parts of the legendary *Dexamenos*.

Now we come to *Erythion* who reigned over the island of *Erytheia* (island of the Dead) and who is described by one source as the *guardian of Geryon's cattle*. He was either the son or nephew of the latter.

Geryon, *that veteran of the Western World*, was thought by the Greeks to be the *oldest of men*. His mother was *Calliroe* (a name that could be translated as *queen of the Celts*, even *pretty queen* or *daughter of the Illustrious Ocean*).

Without doubt, Geryon's empire, of which *Erytheia* (the red) was part, lay at the *uttermost limits* of the earth and was also known as the *blessed isle* or 'land of the dead'. And, according to the legend, it was to the countries of the Far North that Apollo and Artemis disappeared periodically, where in Greenland the firework display of the Aurora Borealis is still called the *Dead at Play*.

There is yet another proof that Erytheia was situated in the North Atlantic. With reference to the wall separating Scotland from the country of the Angles, the Latin author Procopius notes that it is impossible to cross it without dying *because of the atmosphere* *prevailing at this spot.* This reminds us of what Herodotus wrote about the *Plutonium* (the sanctuary of Hades or of Pluto at Hieropolis): "The Plutonium has a narrow opening [.....] extremely deep [.....]. The hole is filled with a dense and misty vapour. Any animal entering into it is killed outright but the *Galles ennuques** can go in without any ill effect" (8).

The ancient writers also mentioned the *Cassitérides* (tin islands) which they imagined to have been probably located nearby the England of today. It is thought that these were the Scilly Isles (Sorlingues). But the adjective *cassitérides* could also have been applied to other areas considered by them to be islands: Ireland, Scotland and Wales. The *Cassiteride* islands were strictly speaking those lands where tin (*étain*: Old French *stan* or *estaing*) was extracted. This metal, considered in Homer's time to be a precious metal, still constituted an important commercial commodity in the Middle Ages. In its natural state tin oxide is still called *cassiterite*. We know that when it comes into contact with air, *stannic* chloride gives off dense fumes. This fact could have caused the men of that time to think that there were very good reasons for regarding this area as the future *satanic* empire. The more so when Zeus and the Dynasty of the Air would later triumph, since anything and everything to do with the dynasties of the Night and of the Ocean (whose kingdoms were in the West) would then become *sinister* and *baneful*. There are no other reasons for believing the *left hand* to be unlucky (Latin *sinister*: left).

The parallel is taken further throughout Greek mythology between Geryon and the Kingdom of Hades. According to legend, Geryon had three heads and three bodies, making one single body (9). Apollodorus of Athens notes that "these three bodies were joined at the stomach and separated again from the side and the thighs". We are here reminded of *Cerberus*, the dog from the infernal regions with three heads, a replica of the dog *Orthos,* guardian of the empire of Geryon which Hercules had to overcome and which also had three heads.

There can be no doubt that Ireland has, over a long period of time, had excellent pasturage which could have been a source of great wealth to Geryon. A large number of Irish epic poems deals with the cattle raids that took place on its soil and, on the shield of *the oldest man*, as described in Greek art, there is the head of a fine white ox, not seen on any other hero's shield. Another source has also shown a connection between these oxen, symbols of Geryon's wealth, and the animals which, according to myth, slaked the thirst of the dead souls in Hades with their blood. It is obvious how the myth began.

The famous steers were taken by Hercules, so the myths tell us, *right across Europe into Sicily and Thrace*, two provinces which were, at one and the same time, Pelasgian colonies and two important points of entry for all conquerors from the North West. And this is how we know that Hercules is certainly the Ancestor of the Scythians *with their blue eyes and red hair* who, for this reason, never failed to call themselves, in their turn, part of the *immortal race*. Herodotus writes: "Hercules, driving Geryon's cattle before him, is said to have arrived in a country that was empty at the time but is now inhabited by the Scythians. [.....] Geryon lived a very long way from the Black Sea, on an island which the Greeks called Erytrea, beyond the Pillars of Hercules (10). [.....] Hercules then set off in the direction of the Levant and arrived in what is now called Scythia".

There, the Historian continues, the hero fell asleep, and while he slept, his mares galloped off. On awaking, he began to look for them, and while he was searching, he came to a cavern in which there was a creature, *half woman and half serpent*, who said she would return his property to him if he rewarded her with a very well defined service. The hero performed this service and the gentle creature conceived three children. "Now then," she asked the father, "before you leave, tell me what I must do when they have grown up." "When your sons have become men," Hercules replied, "follow my instructions and you will have no cause to regret it. Give your kingdom without fear to the one who draws his bow thus and puts on his belt as I do."

Hercules then gave to the woman the two objects in question. "The belt's buckle," Herodotus continues, "was shaped like a cup. It is from one of Hercules' sons that the Scythians of today are said to be descended, and it is in memory of the belt buckle that all their men now wear a cup at their belt" (11). We already know all about the story of the cup, and now we see that Hercules was also the spiritual father of the scouts! This is yet another idea which did not come to us from the East.

In this story, Herodotus speaks of *mares* and *cattle* which would seem to indicate that he was confusing two epochs. Confirmation of this supposition is provided by the fact that the *giant-father* of the Scythians is a giant who has evolved considerably: the hero who personifies him is no longer armed just with a club but also with a bow. Furthermore, since he has a cup or goblet with him, this demonstrates that he comes from the *Sea People* who have already conquered the darkness and know how to forge metals.

This Hercules is a brother of the previous one, his twin: the *good animal*, which he overcame *in honourable combat* and in a *fatal struggle*, according to the bards of Ireland who preserved an echo of the tale in their songs.

It explains why, in the Hercules legend, there has always been a reference to a brother, or a half-brother, in which the Greeks opted in favour of Alcides of Tiryns. That is also the origin of the ancient myth of the twins (*Gemini*). On Flamsteed's atlas, one of them is carrying a lyre and an arrow, the other has the primitive club. The name *Gemini*, or *Twins*, is derived from Finnish *Jumala* (Fr. *jumeaux*), a term which in the *Kalevala* refers to a divinity, part good and part bad. The Greek Twins, *Castor* and *Pollux*, were born very much later and were the brothers of *Helen*, and are, therefore, only a new version of the ancient Nordic myth. Incidentally, their mother is *Leda* (which is perhaps a corruption of the Northern *eider*), and Zeus, in order to seduce her, had to change into a swan, which is very significant.

Gemini correspond with the Roman *Dioscuri*, usually translated as *sons of Jupiter*: which could in fact be true. *Dios* in Greek means *god* (genitive) plus *kouroi* (plural of *kouros*) meaning *boys*. However, *dis* or *dies* in Latin means *day*, and *oscurus* means *what is dark or obscure*, i.e. the *night*. So, by a contraction of the terms, the *dioscuri* have come to represent the characteristics of *brute* force and *creative* force - the union (and duality) of day and night, of light and shadow, i.e. the principle of a world in *equilibrium*, so dear to the Atlantans.

The constellation of Hercules shines in the Northern Hemisphere, between the *Lyre*, the *Serpent* and the *Dragon*.

But it is at this stage that the plot thickens, with regard to Geryon's cattle. The Isle of Man, religious 'mecca' of the Celts (which probably constitutes part of the *Manala* in the sacred book of the Finns) still carries in its coat of arms the *trika* or *treskeles*, a heraldic emblem composed of *three bent legs emerging from the centre of the shield like the spokes of a wheel*, which corresponds in every point with the description of Geryon and his *three bodies meeting at the centre and separating again from the trunk and the thighs*. Now, the Isle of Man's *trika* also appears in the coat of arms of Sicily and on the shield of *Encelades*, the illustrious giant of mythology of whom we are told that he symbolised all the inhabitants of the islands *encircling* the earth (that is, those of a *Baltic* sea). Finally, it constitutes the armoury of the

Alcmenoids who gave birth to Alcides of Tiryns, also known as Hercules.

There is a definite connection between the three joints of the *trika* (sometimes shown as three legs of a spider and sometimes as three human legs) and the three toes of the *auk* (of the genus of the *alcidae*, web-footed arctic birds which include the wild goose, the penguin and the puffin) which is to be found in especially large numbers in Scotland and Iceland (Norwegian *alk* or *alka*, Old Norse *alka*).

It is a particular characteristic of this animal genus, bound to an ancient human family by its use as a totem, that since time immemorial it is considered *elegant* and *dignified* to walk slowly, with feet pointing *outwards*. This was the way that Charlemagne's mother walked (perhaps a sign of affection). She was *Queen Pedauque* (that is, with the feet (Latin *pedes*) of an *alque*, *auque* or *auk*). It might, of course, also be possible that her toes were *webbed* so that she had only three, instead of five, but the first explanation seems more probable to us..... unless this queen came from a family having the *trika* in its coat of arms, which is also quite possible.

Be that as it may, this heraldic emblem, one of the oldest in the world and, furthermore, very often to be seen on megalithic monuments in Gaul, deserves our full attention and needs a whole chapter to itself.

* * *

*Translator's note p.95:

See *ennuques* in *Information for General Interest*.

10

THE GREAT FAMILY
OF THE
THREE-LEGGED

The family of the *Alcmenoids*, one of the two hundred in Antiquity, was believed by historians to have originated in *Messenia*, in the Peloponnese. Would this not have been a province colonised by the Sicilian *Gallas* who were themselves allied to the kings of the Isle of the Blessed? There could have been a connection between this province and *Messenia*. Be that as it may, the *Messenians* were *Achaeans* and, therefore, descendants of the race of giants. *Alcmion*, their forefather, claimed to be the son of Nestor, son of *Neleus*, son of Poseidon; that is, son of *Okeinos* or *Olkeinos* or *Oleinos* - name of the ancient ocean which encircled the earth and which was spelled in these three ways (1). It seems, therefore, that they were all entitled to claim the *treskeles* for their own, since they were all descended through one of the gods, known as Hercules, from *Geryon*, the oldest and strongest of men with whom Hesiod, when describing winter, compares his contemporaries: "[They are] like the old man with three legs, for they [walk] through the world, their backs bent and their foreheads bowed to the ground" (2). Earlier in the poem he speaks of the old man in these terms: "It is winter and the octopus without bones gnaws at his foot". There can be no mistake: the *geryonie*, we read in Larousse, *is a medusa or jellyfish, very similar in appearance to the octopus*. And what name did the Latins give to Ireland? Was it not *Hibernia* or *Ivernia*? (Fr. *hiver*, winter - cf. English, to *hibernate*).

So what was the meaning of this sign: *three bent legs pointing outwards from the centre*? Perhaps it was the origin of the three-headed gods of the Ancient Celts - unless the figures with the three faces were, in fact, representations of their great ancestor: *Geryon* for the Greeks; and *Orcus* for the Celts, ruler of the Nether Regions - the god who would later become the mighty *Dispater* of the Gauls, judge and ruler of the quick and the dead.

If we break down the word *treskeles*, we find *tre-skeles*, which in Greek means *three legs* or *limbs*. But the Gaelic word *Aran* also means *member* or *root*. We believe that Geryon was represented as having *three bodies and three heads* because his empire consisted of *three* kingdoms which pointed in different directions but were joined together at a central point which could have been the *Isle of Man*, to this day still theoretically a kingdom. In the time of the Latin author *Procopius*, *Brittia* had a *tripartite* structure. Smith translates a passage from his work as follows, "Three very numerous nations possess Brittia over which a king presides" (3).

The three members, roots or directions symbolised by the *trika* would thus have represented in the eyes of the Ancients *Ireland*, *Scotland* and *Wales*, which have always followed a very different path from that of England. Do we not read about Ireland in the *Great Encyclopedia* that it is an *old and exhausted land, older than England and contemporaneous with the Highlands of Scotland and with Wales? And that, in geological terms, it dates from the carboniferous age*?

Having deciphered History, we find that it is corroborated by Geology.

As almost always happens with the passage of time, the legends were distorted and ended up by describing Geryon as having many arms which looked like snakes and tentacles. There is no reason not to believe that this multiplicity of the most ancient of men's *arms* came to be seen as a multiplicity of *conquests* by the most ancient of peoples - the Atlantans. This is where we come back to the hydra of *Lerne* (or *Erne*), the *medusa-jellyfish* and the sea spider known in French as the *arine* or *érine*.

The *Erinyes*, which would later become the *Eumenides*, trace their origin back to the red *Erin* of the Giants. They were *daughters of the heavens and of the earth*: in other words, they were of gigantic stature. In Irish legend they are daughters of *Orcus*, the Western Hades. They lived in Tartarus, the kingdom of the dead. Snakes coiled out from their heads, which made them look like the *érines* (**sea-spiders**), or so we learn from Mythology. In one hand they held a torch, the ancient ferule of Prometheus, and in the other a dagger: this was a bronze weapon forged by the Cyclops. It would be impossible to describe their background more clearly.

The three legs of the *trika* are very carefully folded. They thereby conform exactly with the natural movement of the *érine*'s feet and with the folded leg of the sea god who one day exposed his knee above the water so as to give life to the world, as described in the cosmogony of the *Kalevala*. It should be noted that the joints in the feet resemble the joints in the wooden cross known as the *swastika*. Need this surprise us? According to the Larousse dictionary, the word *arani* described the wooden tool used to light the sacred fire - that is, the swastika.

The study of symbols is quite frankly untrammelled delight for the spirit.

Ancient Sicily, which preserved the *treskeles* in its coat of arms, was called *Trinacria*. The symbolic iron claw with its three branches, which was once used as an anchor and is described as a *trinacria*, was also called an *erine*. As an emblem it is used like a *trika*.

Very long ago, the *trika* had precedence over the trefoil or clover, also known as *shamrock*, which was Ireland's national plant and probably corresponded with the *trescalan* of Provence, mentioned but not described in detail by Charles Galtier, although he noted that *red oil* was extracted from it (4). The shamrock is now attached to a legend concerning St. Patrick, but there can be no doubt that the Church has in this case, as in so many others, adapted with the greatest discretion a pagan tradition, or rather cult, for its own teaching.

It was the Celtic trefoil (the ancient, authentic trefoil, the one that probably corresponds with the red clover, formerly called *hare's foot* because of the triangular imprint made by the paws of this animal) which became the trefoil in architecture. This trefoil is composed of *three circles which intersect and whose respective centres are positioned on each corner of an equilateral triangle*. We see, then, also the origin of the famous three points of the *ioni* which were developed from the trefoil and which are still to this day well known to certain men - men who were already putting their secret sign on coins in the workshops of Rennes and Nantes only a millennium ago. At the intersection of the three feet or three legs (whose long history culminates on the bonnet of the Mercedes!), the three points of the triangle appear without any particular emphasis. But their message is clear to initiates, and that is certainly the reason why the *treskeles* would later be called *triquèdre*, meaning *three angles*.

The concept of the *sacred angle* must certainly, at some time or other, have been a part of Celtic thought. Perhaps it alone can explain the shape of the *trihedral nose* which is so characteristic of archaic sculptured figures. One may be permitted to surmise that the *Angles*, the future English (in the Celtic tongue *engach* means *angular*), did not get their name (as is commonly believed) from a foreign Germanic people by whom they were conquered in the 5th Century, but that the name is very much older. *Procopius*, quoted by Smith, notes that the islands of Heligoland and of Rugen were inhabited by *Frisians* and *Angles*.

In what epoch did the three *legs* of the God of the Underworld give way to the three *toes* of the *Alcidae*? No doubt this happened when the *Aesir* (or gods of the air) triumphed over the *Uans*, or *Uanir*, gods of the underworld. The principle that had to be maintained was that of the three initial branches, and what creatures of the air were better suited (speaking symbolically) to carry on the tradition than the *Alcidae* in general and the puffin in particular? This bird of the northern seas is singularly endowed with a red beak and feet - Brehm says *cinnabar red* (5), that is to say, vermilion or the colour of sulphur. And let us not forget that the root of the word *cinder* is also part of *cinnabar*. Could there be any clearer indication than this double sign that it plunges into the very depths of the earth and, therefore, into the Empire of the Dead?

Furthermore, the *Alcidae* or *Alcae* or *Alques* are called *Larventaucher* in German (grub-divers): they dive in order to catch grubs..... or else, ghosts? There are many Irish tales telling of sailors sitting on the seashore, fishing for the souls of those who have drowned.

French dictionaries tell us that *puffin* is translated by *macareux*. These are Pelagian birds of the North Sea, and even of the Arctic, where large numbers are found, as in Iceland. They are marvellous hunters and can dive down thirty fathoms, remaining more than three minutes under the water.

The English puffin can go one better that this, and fly with quite remarkable virtuosity and speed. He seems to be tireless, always on the move, and able to survive all storms. It is easy to understand why a nation of sailors should have chosen this bird for its mascot.

It is interesting to note that the King of the Triple Feet (whose name, *Puffin*, adopted in Iceland, contains a suggestion of *wind*) is certainly allied to the composition of the heraldic *phoenix* (the *phoenix* of the *Phoenicians* or men-of-the-wind (6)). Just as in the case of the unicorn, this emblem has changed somewhat in the course of time and, in the East, the phoenix sometimes appears decked out in the feathers of the paradise bird. Nevertheless, this heraldic figure, which could still be seen in the 15th Century on the coat of arms of the *Oostfriese* (East Frisians) with its red beak and feet, leaves us in no doubt as to its origins. The wood pile on which the red feet are resting is usually (according to Littré) called *immortality*. Is this not confirmation of the fact that we are dealing here with a race that has always claimed to be immortal? Has it not been asserted that, having dived into the Empire of the Dead and of the Night, and having burnt its claws in the red-hot cinders, the bird reappears every time in the open air and flies off into the heavens? Is this not a perfect symbol of the resurrection of the ancient Titans from the ashes?

The goose, which also belongs to the *Alcidae*, is certainly held sacred on account of its three toes, but also because the wild goose, which is a migrating bird, flies in a perfect triangular formation - a triangle at the head of which there is **either a male or a female**. This was important in a world where the female was the equal of the male and where the *supreme god* was considered to be androgynous (hermaphrodite) in essence. In addition, the wild goose incubates its eggs with its webbed foot (7), just like the legendary eagle when the world began. It abounds in the *Feroe* Islands and throughout Scandinavia. It played an important role in History. We know that it was sacred to Juno and no one will forget the famous geese on the Roman Capitol. The game of snakes and ladders (French *jeu de l'oie*: 'the goose game') reminds us of a drawing which appears frequently on ancient Scandinavian steles. This and *Tales of Mother Goose* give us reason to believe that the fame of the bird goes back a very long way in History.

The goose was greatly favoured in Gaul. Its flesh, much sought after by gourmets, was especially prized by kings. *Charlemagne ordered in his capitularia that all his country houses should have them in good supply* (8). Was this to honour his mother? On several Medieval monuments we see women with feet like those of a goose. Was this Queen Bertha? And then there is Rabelais who tells us, "... the feet were turned slightly outwards, like those of the auk queen (*Reine Pédauque*) in Tholose" (9).

Buffon praises the goose very highly and says that it is extremely intelligent - which, of course, contradicts what we say today! Then, in Christian times, the goose became a symbol of the modest young woman: for it is beyond dispute that the goose, especially the wild goose, of which there were very great numbers along the Atlantic coasts, was indeed the fiercest of birds. Whereas for the Pagans it represented on the contrary the principle of fecundity!

In memory of Juno (who presided over births) we eat a goose at Christmas. The Scandinavians, for their part, eat it at Martinmas. *Martin* is the saint who replaced *Mars* by becoming his antithesis and renouncing the use of weapons. However, the warrior remains *martial*, and the *martinet* is a human instrument of discipline. In etymology, *Mart* is the Latin root of *Mars*. And it is significant that *Martin* in France should be the name given to the bear which ancient Nordics called *Otto*, a name derived from *Uther*, god of darkness and of *war* in the territories of the Celts. These inter-connections are rather curious when we remember that Saint Martin was born in Pannonia and that the festival held in his honour by the Nordics begins with a soup made of blood.

In our opinion, the goose is associated with the festival because of its order of flight: a perfect triangle. Was not the triangle the Franks' order of march and, long before them, probably of the ancient Nordic warriors' as well? Remember the song: "Pharamond! Pharamond! We have fought sword in hand. The foreheads of the warriors were wet with sweat and it ran down their arms. The eagles and *the birds with yellow feet* uttered joyous cries" (10).

Now we understand the origins of the *goose step*.

And we should not forget that geese were also called *chens*.

* * *

11

COME BACK, BOOMERANG!

Legend has it that the Atlantan capital was surrounded by concentric circles of earth works and water joined together by canals. This is a city plan which has been so popular throughout the world that it is worth looking at it again. In French, the Atlantan capital was called *Trézène*, and this name is not so much cognate with *three* (Fr. *trois*) or *thirteen* (Fr. *treize*) as with *braid* (French *tresse*) or *tracery* (*treza* in Provencal and *trenza* in Spanish). *Trézène* is like the flower of the *labyrinthine dream*, which was a characteristic of Atlantan thought. This term was coined by Françoise Henry who applies it to Irish art, since she finds it impossible to find any other suitable definition for its complex, meandering style, which can seem to be so disturbing (1).

How did this dream come about? It was probably a resurgent memory of the most ancient Atlantis. We can imagine it to have been rather like modern Finland with its 30,000 islands lying off its coasts and 60,000 lakes strewn with grassy mounds encircled by countless arms of water reflecting countless images of the first island where life was born, according to the Finnish genesis. It was this island that the Greeks in time would confuse with Atlantis itself.

Nowhere, except in Irish legend, have we seen so many 'Knights of the Lake'. Wasn't *Lochlin* (or *Locharn*) the name given by the inhabitants of Ancient Caledonia to the Scandinavian countries (2)? *Loch*, we know, meant 'lake'. We read in *Erec et Enide*, the novel by Chrétien de Troyes, "My name is Erec, son of King Lake; this is what the Bretons call me." And who cannot recall the song sung by the expiatory victim to the god *Hu* (or *Hy*) just before his death: "It is the festival which is related to the two lakes. One lake encircles me and encircles the circle; the circle and another circle enclose deep moats …" etc. Another legend, related by La Villemarqué, tells us that *Hu-Gudarn*, chief of the Ancient Bretons, had built his dwelling on the banks of a lake called 'the lake of lakes' which, in spite of the dykes, threatened to flood the land. Is this a memory of the town of Ys? It is in any case a memory of the *Deluge*, since it was there that the worthy *Nevez naf Neivion* had built the ship which was to save the world, according to Celtic legend.

Lug, the god who has given his name to many French towns, could perfectly well be related to some ancient god, *Lake*. In Irish legend, Lug is described as the *wise man*, the man who practises all the arts and who can handle the lance (3). He was still held in such honour during the Roman occupation that, in Gallic territories, the day on which his festival was celebrated (the calends of the eighth month) became the day of the Emperor's festival. From *Lug* (*Log* or *Loch*) it seemed quite natural to celebrate the *august* emperor of the Romans in the eighth month of the year. *

It was certainly the cult of the god *Lake* and of the ancient Atlantan *Trézène* which in Celtic lands gave a sacred character to *tresses* in matters of hair style. Tressing the hair, consisting of three elements already sacred in themselves, continually criss-crossing in an endless figure-of-eight chain, corresponded exactly with the idea that the Celts had about the perpetual interaction of the forces in the universe: for example, of earth and water. From this concept there also emerged the sacred character of all kinds of twisting patterns (French: *lac-et*) in matters of **ornamentation**; and this then led in turn to the sacred character of any kind of 'lacing-up', fishing or hunting **net**: and, of course, to the famous *magic net*. In old French, 'to lace up' (French *lacer*) meant 'to make a *mesh* net'. In this way the mesh itself achieved, in the shape of a rhombus or a diamond, a most important place in the art of the Atlantan peoples, eventually appearing in their coats of arms.

The magic net will go on its way. But when it turns up with the Greeks, it will still be an attribute of the heroes of the Empire of the Night. When those of the Dynasty of the Air use it in their combats, they will do so in order to try and be invisible: like their enemies, or like ghosts. In the Finnish *Kalevala*, the magic net spun by the sons of Tuoni (Empire of the Dead) is used to fish out *Vainamoinen*. We should note in passing that the Aztecs too have a *sacred lake* in their legends, and they also have a *golden net*, which they attach to a flag pole as if it were a flag (4). But then they claim descent from *a blond god with blue eyes*, as do the Mongols! One could almost believe that everything started up in the Arctic regions (5).

There is another form that took shape in the Atlantan mind and has dominated the whole of Western art: namely, the *spiral*, sister or cousin of the labyrinth.

The Celts believed, as Heraclitus would later state, that *all things flow, everything moves like a river*; and that *everything changes continually, nothing ever stands still*: The river is a son of the Ocean, with which it was even confused, since the Ancients believed that the Ocean flowed around the earth. "Old man River who just keeps rolling along" was, therefore, an essential symbol of the never-ending movement of things.

The way in which *Trézène* and other great capitals, built in the same way, were constructed (*inter alia*, Troy, Mycenae and Babylon), was to produce, in one particular point of the globe, not only the very first island, but also a general configuration of the world (or more exactly of the sphere, of the *infinite and intellectual sphere, whose centre is everywhere*) about which Rabelais spoke so ironically.

The Celts had divided the heavens into imaginary circles, thus creating an order of *spherical* reference markers (*espères* was a word still in use in France up to the 16th Century).

These imaginary markers were ranged around the globe forming *spirals*. In this way the *spiral* became one of the first esoteric symbols of the Celts. The *trika* (or *treskeles*), with its triangle drawn between the angles of the three legs (base lines), contains (as we have seen) the idea of the spiral with three centres, or of the *infinite* spiral.

Starting out from this symbol, everything falls into place. The reason that funereal birds decorate Geryon's shield is not only because their black plumage symbolises the Empire of the Night (which is **his** empire) but because these birds are *flying in an upward spiral*.

In the same way, snakes were sacred to the Celtic peoples: not only because they change their skins every year (thereby embodying the myth of divine metamorphosis), nor because they emerge from the entrails of the earth and go back whence they came; but also because they *coil themselves, climb up and down in a spiral*, and copulate by wrapping themselves around each other. When Greece and the Orient later came to granting snakes a mystical meaning, the symbol of the spiral, although it would remain, would be dominated by another: that of the large amounts of sticky substance left behind by this animal after copulation. In this period, happiness would not be directed toward death but toward life; not toward the night but toward the day. People would no longer place too much faith in the survival of the soul in the upper spheres but, instead, they turned to the light, to physical love and to the joy of uniting and producing offspring. This became of paramount importance. The Celts, for their part, continued to be plagued by the Cosmos and by the life of the spirit, and the spiral was without any doubt the single most significant geometric pattern in their eyes. Right up to the late Middle Ages it would remain the dominant motif of all artistic expression - in Gallic lands, in Scandinavian countries and in the British Isles. It would decorate swords, jewellery, belt buckles, sculptures and illuminated manuscripts.

What we call *Greek* is in fact the *Celtic* spiral reviewed and corrected by the spirit of the *Hellenes*. It is found on the most archaic specimens of their art.

The Celtic double spiral is expressed by the sign appearing in the Zodiac in the form of the Atlantic crab ⧢ , a double zero [00] or figure eight [8].

It is with this sign that the learned men of our time still indicate infinity. The sign follows the head-to-foot principle, which is another characteristic of Celtic art. There is no other explanation for the predilection of this nation for images of animals in this (diametrically opposite) position or for its habit of showing in the walls of buildings two amphoras arranged in the same way. And, since the amphora was itself a symbol of the liquid element, the Celts were placing their houses simultaneously under the sign of abundance and of fecundity.

In this double and so expressive form, the spiral has buried itself deep in the spiritual world of the Celts, not only with regard to celestial bodies (which, as they thought, turned this way and then that, since the stars rise and fall by turns in the heavens) but also as a result of watching the ebb and flow of the Ocean. This produced the idea, so dear to them, of *cyclic time*, perpetually turning back on itself under the influence of the movements of the stars, which order and regulate its course. This idea was expressed by the followers of innumerable sects and was in direct contradiction to the belief of the Roman Catholics for whom *time has been moving forwards irreversibly since the Creation towards the end of the universe*.

It is not immediately apparent why these two ideas should conflict.

The spiral simply resembles the *trika*, in that this sign (because of the revolving movement prescribed by its shape) itself resembles the *swastika* in the rotational movement which man gives it when making fire: a movement which will finally transform this cross into a symbol of the *wheel of life*.

It is curious to note that the inverted spiral placed vertically gives us the figure eight [8], a number which is sacred to all Celts; a sign which is found in the original egg; a sign peculiar to the Atlantic race; and one which in the Gallic tongue is called *ochd* (6). This number would be regarded with pride by all those peoples which this race, the mother race, would have raised from childhood and rescued from chaos. Later, for reasons which have remained undiscovered, it would be the guiding hand directing the octagonal plan of the first Protestant churches, but also of the first Ethiopian or Chaldean Christian churches to be directly influenced by Western thought. The oceanic origin of the spiral also explains why a curly beard and curly hair were regarded throughout Antiquity as a sign of virility, of wisdom and of good lineage. Furthermore, it explains why sea waves in primitive art, and right up to our Medieval art, were always shown in the form of curls.

The French word for *tacking* or *going about* (*virer*) which, together with its derivations, is used to describe a circular movement, is still more or less restricted to maritime vocabulary, but with special reference to the wind and to navigation. It is easy to understand why. As for *vireton* in our old French songs (now *viredon*), it was a kind of crossbow whose bolt turned back on itself in the air - a cousin of the boomerang!

* * *

*Translator's note, page 106:

Lat. *Augustus*: venerable. Hence Italian *Agosto* and French *Août*, for the *venerable* eighth month of the year.

12

"HOLY MAKREL!"

The study of totems is an excellent way to approach pre-history. We have foolishly ignored them up to now. They give expression to a certain mentality, a way of life and of action.

Totems born in the ocean are found in great number in the art of Pelasgian Greece – which is the most natural thing in the world. First, we have the jellyfish – the adventurous *Pelagie* and the famous *Maia*; then the dolphin (smaller version of the whale); finally, the mackerel and various other fish.

Maia is an inexhaustible subject. The *maia squinade* of the naturalists (which the Danes call *skal berende* – "wearing scales", in other words, the sea spider) belongs in scientific terms to the genus *maianées*. It is from this creature that the sea surrounding Crete will get its name *mare delle sapienze* in memory of the sea peoples who regarded it as a totem. Besides possessing astute camouflage allowing it to travel safely beneath marine plant life, it was also wise enough never to engage in any kind of combat while shedding its shell every spring. The Ancients tell us all kinds of wonderful stories about it and they held it in such high esteem that they hung it around the neck of *Diana of Ephesus.* (Its connection **specifically** with Diana and with Ephesus is important to note.) We also find images of it on coins from the Pelasgian cities.

Amongst the *maianées* there is one very special kind, namely, the *inachis* (German *Freikrabben*). These crustaceans have a *triangular* shell, retractable eyes on each side of the point of the triangle, and extremely long, slender legs. They wander over the muddy depths of the sea and are found along the European and American coasts of the North Atlantic. Another of their characteristics is that they never rest on anything but continually "hang" in the water.

In this connection one cannot help thinking of Finnish peasants, mindful of their traditions, who for a long time recited the *Kalevala* seated astride a bench and swaying back and forth, which they certainly did for a good reason. If it is true that, since time immemorial and in very many parts of the world, sacred texts have been recited in this way to help scan the rhythm, it is possible to surmise that long, long ago this movement was copied from the motions of the boatman, since we know that the **Word** was born from the sound of the sea and of the wind. And the boatman's rhythm was itself, perhaps, copied from the continually oscillating motion of the *maianée*, but also from the coming and going of the waves which, at the beginning of *History*, bore aloft old *Vainamoinen*, the very epitome of a vagabond of the seas. The spider, called *faucheux* by the French (probably because it imitates the back-and-forth movements of the *faux,* or **scythe**) and which the English call *daddy-long-legs*, is an exact replica of the general appearance of the *maianée* in question, having a small body and very long legs with angular joints. It is, therefore, very possible that the popular name *daddy*, given to it by the British, is very old indeed and was inspired by their habit of referring to the sea spider as a symbol of the Father of Mankind, in the person of *Vainamoinen*, or his Celtic equivalent.

Be that as it may, there is obviously a connection between the movement of the narrator's body and the name *skaldic poetry*, which was given to the songs of the ancient Scandinavian bards: either because the rhythm of the poem imitated the movement of the *skal berende* or (and we favour the alternative hypothesis) because the bard set the rhythm for the delivery of the text by accompanying himself on the lyre or the harp, whose strings he plucked with a fish scale – *skal*.

On most Cretan vases we find images of fish. These are Pelagian fish, vagabonds of the sea, who regularly come down into the Mediterranean from the North. Among these great *Pelagianer* we also find the *tantei*, about which we have already spoken: *mackerel, tuna* and *whales*.

The mackerel (*makrel* in **Nordic** languages, *macrell* in **Kimri-Celtic** and *maquerel* in old French) is a fish which must have had such a reputation at a certain moment in History (before its name took on a pejorative connotation for a reason already stated) that Littré quotes an ancient proverb about it: "One has never seen sheep turning into Mackerel". This seems to imply that either the animal itself, or the ancient races which it symbolised, possessed qualities of courage not shared by sheep.

For what reason could Atlantan tribes attribute such importance to the mackerel? First of all, it is because of its habits. We read in Brehm that this fish spends the winter in the North, its place of origin: "In the spring it swims past Iceland, Scotland, Ireland, then plunges into the Atlantic where one column goes round Portugal and Spain and enters the Mediterranean, while another column moves into the English

Channel where it appears in May along the coasts of France and England before reaching the Dutch coats in June. When this second column arrives at the coast of Jutland in July, one half enters the Baltic while the other one continues on to Norway and returns to the North"(1).

Is this not almost a carbon copy of the life led by our Nordic conquerors? The more so since we have seen mackerel roaming as far south as the Canaries to which their empire extended. Once again, man and beast proved to be close companions.

Finally, the mackerel hibernates (like Apollo and *Artemis*) for six months of the year behind the White Mountain. It is in the muddy depths of the North Atlantic, called *barachouas* (**sandbars**), that these fish hide during the winter and it is here that they "bury their heads and the top part of their bodies to a depth of about one decimetre, holding their tails straight up from the silt. They can be found in their thousands covering, as it were, the bottom of the sea with their tails standing up like bristles" (2).

Today, the sacred character of the mackerel in ancient times may seem surprising, but the expression in modern English *Holy Mackerel!* certainly does seem to confirm this.

The Latins called the fish *scomber* or *scombrus*. Aristotle, quoted by Cuvier, claims that this *travelling fish* emerged from the *Pont Euxin* (Black Sea) and returned to it. It is interesting to find it in a sea and in a region which played so important a part in the penetration of the Nordics into the Middle East. Several authors have made many references to it, amongst them Pliny the naturalist, Perse and Martial. *Garum*, a dish prepared by the ancients, was made from the entrails and blood of mackerel. Martial sings the praises of this "precious garum, prepared from the purest blood of the still breathing mackerel…" *Garum*, also very much appreciated in Carthage, was in fact a sauce made of putrefied fish, but, says Pliny, "apart from perfumes there is no liquid substance which is more expensive or highly regarded. *Garum* is greatly appreciated by everyone".

The fact that only the *tuna*, another pelagian, should have been added to the same sauce as the mackerel shows that there must have been some bond between the two fish, having probably sacred origins. Didn't the Phoenicians also worship these fish?

The Latins called tuna *orcynus*, a name very close to *Orcus* and *orca*, names given to the Celtic god of the underworld, and in Portugal to the whale. In general, the root *orc* (the equivalent of *arc*) indicated, by extension, anything that was connected with giants.

We can appreciate what the standing of the tuna was in ancient times when we remember that, as late as the 19th Century, this fish was still caught under the aegis of a saint and under the command of a master-fisherman bearing the title *reis* (king) (3). Mistral gives us some idea of this kind of fishing expedition in *Calendal* where we read: "Before the end of the fifteenth (hour?), oh miraculous Vespers! The air is filled with a distant dull and intense sound: the wind falls ... Through the shivering water above which great humps appear, I catch sight of an innumerable company of tuna! They fill the sea. They form a triangle, which seems to grow larger like the scales of a pine cone, and rushes through the azure blue liquid with a perfectly synchronised momentum. And the strongest is their guide".

All the great symbols are there: the triangle, the scaly pine cone, the leader at the point of the triangle, as in the marine and aerial groups of all migratory creatures. It is as if the poem is describing a fleet of 'Men of the Sea', arriving before our eyes. Can we not recognise our own *human* Pelasgians in these *marine* pelagians, these wanderers?

As for the whale, it must have been the most venerated of all our ancestors because of its gigantic size and the *geyser* which spouted from its blowhole. In the Icelandic language, the spot where the water emerges is still to this day called *vent*. Originally, the word was *van*, which explains our French word *vanne*, also written as *venne* (*vanne* means **sluice gate; valve; cock**).

The Greenland whale is called *balena mysticetus* by the experts. In Iceland, it is still commonly known as *the cow*. It is quite certain that, very long ago, and also later, as was the case with the medusa and the sea spider, it was seen as a symbol of the birth of life on earth because it also raises up its back like an *arch* over the waves and because its skin is covered in algae crawling with parasites.

Must we offer proof of what we claim? There are still numerous traces of Atlantic Celtism in Corsica. Well, in the old counting rhymes of that country, the rainbow (French *arc-en-ciel*, literally 'bow-in-the-sky') is called *orcu balenu*. But, *orcu* can also mean *ogre*, which was a giant in ancient days. The connection is obvious. *Orca* is the name given by the Portuguese to the whale which the Italians call *balena*. No other creature but the *orcu balenu* of the counting rhyme provides a better illustration of the link between the concept of the *whale* as mother of the world (according to the most ancient Atlantan myths) and that of the *rainbow of milk* with which *Juno* fertilized the earth and gave birth to the race of giants, of whom Hercules was one (according to the myth of Classical Greece).

Balenas was also the name given to the genital member of the male whale. The female is *lady and mistress of all other fish*, according to a 12th Century poem, quoted by Littré.

Our Northern ancestors must also have been struck by another characteristic of this animal. Although they have lungs with which to breathe, cetaceans die as soon as they wash up on the shore. This strange circumstance reminds us of those Celtic legends in which we are told that giants could no longer live after setting foot on land. This was the case with Fynn, one of the great Irish heroes.

The Atlantans looked on the whale as an enemy to be reckoned with. We read in the *Kalevala* that Hymer, "captain of the ship" and father of the giants, killed two of them with one shot of the harpoon. By what atavistic phenomenon does a whale-hunt to this day lead, in Iceland and Greenland, to veritable scenes of carnage whose vibrant frenzy must date back to the beginning of time, when fishermen dismembered the not-yet dead animal? Such scenes are probably an extension of a primitive desire to absorb the flesh of a creature, which seemed almost god-like, thereby acquiring its strength and being able to communicate through it with the creator of the world.

In the Icelandic Edda, we meet the *cow Audumba*, whose udders produce four torrents of milk (4). In Celtic mysticism, it was also the cow which pre-existed everything: but doubtless it was a marine cow. In the Walloon language, a cow is not *vache* (French) but *vag*. It is certain that our French word *vague* (wave), describing water ruffled by the wind, is cognate with the word for cow (*vache*), wandering over the waves in the darkness before time began. It was the Cimmerians and the Celts to whom the term *gens vaga* was applied by Posidonius (5). For the same reason, the first syllable of the name *Vainamoinen* is at the root of the word *voyageur* (*vaina* means French *vent*; English *wind*; Sanskrit *vaia*; and Gothic *vajan*), just as *van* is at the root of the English word *wander* (German **wandern**).

In Nordic languages *baleine* was a *whal*, and in English a *whale*. It must have been *whal* that produced ***baleine***, since **b** and **v** are frequently interchangeable. In the languages of Norway, the root *whal* is found in many terms belonging to the sacred world, for example: *Wala* (name of an ancient prophetess) and *Whalala* (home for warriors killed in battle), etc. It is not at all unlikely that the old god *Bal* or

Baal, of the Egyptians, Phoenicians and Assyrians, (who is the same as the *Bal*, *Bel* or *Bellenus* of the Celts and Gauls, who in turn was the god of life-giving rain and fruitfulness) was merely an anthropomorphic concept of the primordial divinity incarnate in ancient times in the whale or the sea cow (*Baleno* in Italian means 'the lightening flash preceding the rain').

In the West, we find images of the whale in Norway on flat slabs of rock. The images are few and far between because the cult of this animal goes back to a time when art as such had not yet been born. But all sacred hillocks, which still exist in Scandinavian countries, in the British Isles and in the Atlantic provinces, are a homage to the whale, to the medusa and to the knee of the *Maia* – eternal symbols of the First Island.

This myth of the *knee* is worth studying for its own sake, since it has a connection with the French word *genisse*, meaning 'the cow which is still untouched' (**virgin** – for we can never get away from the **virgin of the waters**) with whom everything began. The fact that *genisse* is translated by *junix* in Latin and by *gionesca* in *Come* country reminds us strangely of *Juno*. It is also possible that the *thick rich milk* of our childhood wetnurses is no more than a dim memory of our first grandmother, the mythical *vache* or *vage* in whose *vagina* life began. The Italians still call a wet nurse a *balia* – and, just like the English say *Holy Mackerel!* they say *Holy Cow!* But, let us return to the fish on the Cretan vases.

Besides those fish already mentioned, there was probably the parrot-fish, called Cretan parrot-fish. It had beautiful purple colouring. It could speak and sing (hence its other name **sea-parrot**) and, what is more, it could ruminate – which establishes a connection between it and the bovids, so dear to Westerners. Numerous authors have told us about parrot-fish: from Pliny to Aristotle, including Suetonius, Ovid and a few others. But all these men were born too late (and in an age which was already too reasonable) to be able to understand the great mysteries which this fish had embodied. However, Brehm quotes in his work the famous verse of *Epicharmus* which tells us that "the gods themselves did not dare to throw out the excrement of the parrot-fish" – which tells us a good deal!

If some people think that these ideas are purely hypothetical or too far-fetched, I would suggest that they have been too influenced by our mechanical age to be able to conceive how life was lived at a time when man was still 'unspoiled'. Life and Death were for him something grandiose, both marvellous and simple, although he had a very realistic appraisal of it. Thus, the idea of poetic *sirens* was the product of observing marine mammals approaching the coast, struggling onto dry land and taking a few halting steps along the shore. They were at home in the water but had a yearning for life on land. Were these animals not crossing over from a purely maritime universe to a universe of the air, from the Ocean Dynasty to the Dynasty of the Air? What better shape could be given to this bivalent desire than to place a human body on the tail of a fish?

So, what about the algae, another symbolic ornament of archaic or Pelasgian Greek pottery? It, too, was very important: on the one hand because it served as a shield for the sacred spider and, on the other, because it was in the algae's greenery that the eagle had made its nest at the beginning of the Nordic genesis. Apart from which, its name is related to that of the *alkis* or *achlys*, a variety of the *annelid*, which, according to Pliny, live exclusively on the coasts of the British Isles. The *Great Encyclopedia* informs us, however, that in certain cosmogonies the *alkis* meant 'eternal night', which establishes beyond doubt that the habitat of this animal was *at the ends of the earth*, in the Atlantic. Hesiod placed the *alkis* on the shield of Hercules – which is very interesting because it leads us back to the *Alcidae* that gave their name to *Hercules of Tiryns*. It was, no doubt, believed that the *alkis*, like the *puffin*, could dive into the *depths of darkness*.

It is equally possible that the *alcys*, which is normally included within the family of the *Alcyopides* (molluscs with a transparent body), could have owed its symbolic value (or, at least, part of it) to the fact that it possessed (and, no doubt, still possesses) *two large red eyes, specially well organised*, according to the experts (6). We see in the Poems of Ossian (written, of course, by MacPherson but which nevertheless draw their inspiration from the old Celtic legends) that *Car-hon*, the 'Cul-hal of heroes', "has two red eyes which roll in wrathful pride". Is it asking too much to make, in this case, a comparison with the astonishing and magnificent jewels of the Swedish National Treasure House which were exhibited in Paris at the Louvre Museum? Amongst the 7th Century exhibits, there was one showing the stylised head of an *alcys* with its two bulging eyes represented by two rubies. Could this piece have any other meaning than the one we are attributing to it?

The whole of archaic Crete reminds us of the Celtic Atlantic. Not only do we see Cnossos, or Gnossos, which was the temple of the

Gnostics or of the druidic magi's philosophy, flourishing at the same time in Western Asia: but we also see the *Hagia Triada* of which the *Hagia Sophia* in Byzantium would one day be a tardy echo. The motifs which most frequently decorate these works of art are – besides those already mentioned – the rosette, the spiral, the carbuncle with **eight** rays and the horn of a bull: the horn out of which (from the most ancient of days) the people of the North used to drink, and which decorated the helmets of the Vikings after having decorated the head of Teutates. Sacred animals not of marine origin are the bull, the stag, the boar, the hedgehog – all of them held sacred in the West as well. Later there would also be marsh birds.

The metal clasp still worn by the Scottish Highlanders and that was so cherished by the Nordics that it was buried with them in their graves (as it also was in the graves of the Franks) was similarly the chief ornamentation of the Cretan loin cloth. On their vases the warriors are represented wearing a helmet, *scaled armour* and a shield shaped like the figure **eight** [8]. Finally, we also see scales used in Crete in the representation of the rocky tumulus which was certainly a souvenir of the ancient, fabulous Atlantan capital, *built on a rocky bluff by an oceanic dynasty*.

Here we need to insert a long parenthesis relative to scales.

In tales about 'gigantism', which have come down to us from ancient Greek authors, giants are shown to be men of stature inferior to that of the Titans or Cyclops, their ancestors – and yet still *monstrous* and *prodigiously strong*, compared to those they have to fight. Furthermore, they are shown carrying *shining weapons*, with *enormous lances* in their hands, their *legs covered in scales* and *wearing their hair long*.

The scales tell us something important. They inform us peremptorily that these giants were indeed sons of the Ocean, of the Atlantic peoples. They also suggest a phonetic association between the *skeles* (leg or foot of the spider which appears on their shields) and the *écaille* (*skala* in Danish, *scalja* in Gothic), a word which in 13th Century French was still written as *escale*. It cannot be doubted that this same word is cognate with *eschele* or *eschiel* (*skala* in modern Danish), describing the tool with which one climbs into trees (English: *ladder*), as well as the maritime colony or port of call (*escale*), or the *Eschelles du Levant*. Moreover, in English, one also *scales* a ladder, and the musician is encouraged by his teacher to practise his *scales* (finger exercises which go *up and down* the piano, violin or cello, analogous to climbing a *ladder*. In Dutch too, *scales* are called toon*schaal*.)

This confirms the etymology given earlier for the word *Scandinavia*. The term *Scandinavia* (which appears for the first time in a text of Pliny (8)) is a corruption or transposition of *Scaldia* or *Scaldinavia*. It is said that there were several places called *Scandia* in the Aegean Sea, on the coasts of Phoenicia. Thucydides mentions this. The more *echelles* (ladders) we can trace back to the Sea Peoples, the more grist to our mill! We know that the inhabitants of the British Isles and the Nordics were better acquainted with the Phoenicians and the Iberians than they ever were with the Athenian Greeks.

Wherever we turn, we face a question: or rather, we no longer need to face it! Excavations in Scandinavia have revealed *tumuli* (barrows) of *scales* or *shells* of oysters (*skal* in Danish) where they are seen to overlap like tiles on a roof or scales on a fish. Specialists in the subject of pre-history have considered this to be *household rubbish*. The ghosts of our noble ancestors must have trembled on hearing such comments. Would it in fact not be more reasonable to think that they could have been very old constructions of a symbolic and sacred nature, perhaps even temples in which the shell reigned supreme in matters of decoration, since the shell or scale, which gave its name to modern Scandinavia, was the distinctive sign of the giants who came from the same regions? In the tale of *The Little Siren* (which, before soaring up into the heavens "attaches eight large oyster shells to its tail so as to bear witness to its elevated rank"), Hans Christian Andersen tells us that the castle of the King of the Sea is covered over with a **roof of shells**. Poets are inspired by an ancestral memory which they retain in their subconscious and that is why those who are merely gifted with the spirit of *geometry* are often further away from the truth than the poets.

The ancient temples, or *tumuli*, covered with *scales* (doubtless the predecessors of French *tuiles* and English *tiles* derived from *tholos*, which in turn is cognate with *talus*, meaning **mound**, **hillock** or **tumulus**) would also explain the mysterious heaps of oyster shells found on the banks of the Niger whither the Ancient Atlantan world is known to have expanded via Egypt and Ethiopia.

The scale as a symbol of the **man-of-the-sea** was certainly of primordial importance at this time. It taught the race of conquerors, who everywhere overcame their enemies with fire and sword, how to invent the breastplate and, before that, the vest onto which metal strips or scales were sewn to protect life and limb.

Is it generally known that primitive fish had a distinctive protective covering of shiny, bony scales coated with enamel, which was very much like armour-plating for the animal (9)? Richard Owen notes that one of them looked like a "French dragoon with a sturdy helmet and heavy breastplate" (10). Perhaps it was from observing these ancient animal shapes that warriors hit upon the idea of protecting themselves with armour against their enemy because, strange to relate, it was in the waters of the North Sea (Scandinavian and British) that species, which have died out or are on the way to extinction, lived the longest. And, according to the specialists, these creatures belonged to the **carboniferous** era.

Originally, the aquatic animals, which served as emblems or totems for the royal clans of the great sea peoples, were real creatures and not phantasmagoric. Each of them was chosen for a specific trait of appearance or of habit. And this symbolised the appearance, the habits, the ideals, indeed the **idea**, of a world-picture for the people who adopted it. In the Icelandic *Edda*, the eel (whose head adorned so many archaic *rhytons* – drinking cup, shaped like an animal head) symbolised the sea for the giants. The reason is obvious. The eel prefers to live in the fruitful mud and, incidentally, for six months of the year it remains plunged in semi-slumber, only waking up in the spring – thereby following the rhythm of the Nordic countries whose magic has spread over all the earth. It should also be remembered that it emigrates at the moment of fertilisation by swimming up the courses of rivers which flow into other seas. Furthermore, it moves like a snake, i.e. by twisting its body, which is a reflection of the twisting paths that life follows, a principle that was so dear to Celtic and Scandinavian thought that the ornamentation of the oldest *steles* found in the countries of these two races was inspired by it.

The essential characteristics of the eel are expressed in a 13th Century wooden sculpture on the Swedish ship *Vasa*, which sank on its first voyage and was recently salvaged from the waters. We see a human face, described as that of a dead sailor. But another interpretation springs to mind: **we** see *Okeinos*, the Ocean, defined by the giants as "the dwelling of the eels" in the Icelandic Edda. And, indeed, an eel goes in at the mouth, comes out of a nostril, goes back through one eye and reappears from the other: a perfect symbol of the creative force which penetrates and moves.

Here we can close the parenthesis. When they later cease to appear in Greek art with the *tail of a sea monster* (as in archaic art), the giants, and **only** the giants, will be shown with their *arms and legs covered in scales*. Surely this proves that they were greatly concerned with this characteristic?

Let us state it once again: there can be no doubt that these were the people to whom Plato alluded when he mentions an invasion of Greece and Egypt, right at the beginning of their history, by a Sea People coming from the West. Need we be surprised? "The whole of Scandinavian mythology tells of struggle", writes Léouzon le Duc. And then, with reference to *Frithiof*, he continues, "He is a national type. He embodies the great Scandinavian nation with its vast ranges of thought, its noble sentiments, its indomitable passions, its infinite aspirations. Frithiof is certainly the son of the kings of the sea who looked on the world as their domain".

* * *

13

TOM THUMB

When Zeus took over the Dynasties of the Night and of the Ocean, he was reborn in Crete. But he was certainly said to be of the same race as his predecessors – indeed, he boasted about it. On the coins of the island-mother, the "Great Bovid called Zeus" (as such he is described on his epitaph) is a young god: smart, beardless, sitting on a tree-trunk, his hand resting on a *cock*. He is the Zeus of *Velchanos*, very close to the Zeus of Phaestos and to Zeus-Amon in Libya, whose head is adorned with ram's horns.

Zeus thus took over the place of his older brothers in all the Pelasgian sanctuaries, as was right and proper. Outside Crete, the most important of these sanctuaries were those of *Dodona* and *Olympos*. We no longer know today which one was the older. Be that as it may, the great primitive deity of *Dodona* had been *Dione*, daughter of *Okeinos*, the Ocean. She was worshiped near a *spring* and she herself was seated at the foot of a sacred *oak*. According to legend, the waters of this spring had the supernatural power to extinguish burning torches and to relight torches that had been extinguished. This miracle made excellent propaganda for Zeus since the torches in question were the sun, dying every six months in the Northern regions and every day in the West. But where do we find the myth of the sun-torch? We find it in the Icelandic Edda. Once again, Thor asks Allvis what is the name given to the sun, and the dwarf answers that the *giants* call it the *sacred fire-brand*. It is the *ferule of Prometheus*.

And by the way, who was *Dione*? Some call her a daughter of the Ocean, others say she is a Titan, a daughter of Atlas. Is this not proof sufficient that, whether she came from the Atlantic or whether she was an Atlantan, Dione was an *Occidental*? And does legend not add that the sanctuary of Dodona was visited by *Deucalion*, son of Prometheus who, as we know, was none other than a descendant of *Decalidones*, ancient King of British Caledonia? And how were oracles delivered in the sanctuary of Dodona? The prophet lived in the *hollow of an oak*, a sacred oak which is shown with a *dove* in its branches. Too many legends concerning this place relate that the dove had come from Egypt for the story not to be at least partly true. Dodona's dove was said to be a sister of Amon's dove. But where else, other than in the Celtic or Scandinavian provinces, did the virgin priestess have the name *dove*?

Dodona grew up in *Hellopos*, famous for its flocks. On the stones of ruins found there, together with the dove and the oak, we see *Eleinos* (son of *Deucalion*), called the *divine woodman*, following in the steps of *Talos*, in Crete. But, again, where have we seen the woodman at work since the earliest days of the world other than in the songs of the Nordic epic, and especially in the *Kalevala*? At the festivals of the Calends of May it was always, and still is, the *woodmen* and the *smiths* who are honoured in the Scandinavian countries. The *Peliades*, or local priestesses, interpreted at Dodona the *rustling of the oak* or the *sound of the wind* in a bronze cup (the famous cauldron of sacred bronze, so typically Atlantan) which was supposed to contain the wisdom and the mysteries of the world, because it was an image of the earth's belly.

As for the sanctuary of Olympos, it was originally dedicated to *Uranos* and to *Gaia*, father and mother of the Titans *who were so difficult for Zeus to conquer*, according to legend.

What could be more obvious?

But it was not on the shores of the Mediterranean that Zeus defeated the giants. The Western Paladins died in a veritably titanic struggle when they ran up against the Orient between the *Black Sea* and the *Caucasus*. Prometheus had been their incarnation in legend and this is where he died.

Prometheus was a Titan. We know where he came from. He stole fire from Heaven to give to mankind. It must have been *heavenly fire*, for it seems logical that this element must have appeared on earth for the first time in the shape of fire released by lightning, by excessive heat from the sun or from flames pouring out of volcanoes. Many historians think that men captured these flames and kept them alive for as long as possible so as not to lose their substance. However, they may now have **had** fire, but they could not **produce** it. The Heavens jealously withheld it from them. This was when, according to Aeschylus, men lived a frightful life: "they had eyes but could not see, they had ears but could not hear", etc.

This was also when Prometheus, *the most cunning of the demi-gods,* had *the idea of trapping the shining rays of the sun in a ferule*. Let us be clear about this. In our modern French dictionaries, the word **férule** still means, *inter alia*, the two planks of wood of an *attelle* (splint). There is certainly a connection between the French word *férule* in this sense and the adjective *féru*, which means ' to be smitten by' or 'to burn for'. The legendary ferule is the stick one revolved in the central hole of the wooden cross in order to produce the swiftest possible rotation of the two *attelles* (splints), thereby finally creating fire. Much has been said of the two **flints** with which early man produced sparks. And yet ancient history makes few references to this practice, whereas we often hear of *boring* with a rod or ferule into the ligneous cavity (as with a gimlet), and of rotating two pieces of crossed wood. This way of lighting a fire is still practised today by primitive peoples who do not have matches or tinder boxes.

It is important to be certain about the origin of fire because it is at the heart of the myth concerning the *wheel of life*, so dear to the Celts and Hindus. According to Littré, the name *Prometheus* comes from Sanskrit *pramatha*, the name of the stick we rub in the hole to obtain fire. We need not argue about the exact meaning of the term initially. However, the ferule of Prometheus, which replaced the spear of the sun, reminds us very much of the Irish *gesa* or *gai*: that is the *lance* which, with its penetrating power, could cause blood to spurt out like the ferule produced fire. Fire: called *agni* by the Hindus (1).

The production of fire with the aid of a gimlet no doubt spread very quickly throughout a world in which men, mostly nomads, were perpetually in touch with one another, contrary to what we may think. However, it cannot be denied that someone somewhere must have been the first to hit on the idea. Prometheus was a brother of Atlas. Now, the Atlantans of Legend knew how to forge metals and, therefore, how to make fire. The Greeks called Deucalion, son of Prometheus, the *father of men* – as, indeed, they had called Prometheus himself. They had their reasons for this and they support our claim: the more so, because the word *danner* in Danish means 'procreator', while the verb *danne* (cognate with *to do* in English and with *tun* in German) means **to create, to produce, to forge** – and **to instruct**. And, if these words are etymologically related to German *Donner* (thunder), it is because everything in the thought processes of the Ancients was logically inter-connected.

As soon as he could make fire, Man made a prodigious leap forward through all the other arts. It was then that he learnt to extract and to forge metals and, as progress in one direction led to progress in another, he invented numbers and letters, and he started to till the earth and to tame animals, which he was finally able to dominate. To cut a long story short, he was now ready to explore the world and the secrets of the Almighty. The Almighty gets angry, we are told, and wants to be avenged: *'from a mixture of earth and water He creates Pandora, woman, source of all human afflictions'*.

We suspect that this legend dates from the *Hellenistic* Age, at the start of an era of *dogmatic* religions when there is already a faint whiff of *original sin*.

However that may be, the Ancients never invented stories that were entirely devoid of good sense. For them, the eternal *feminine* had begun with the eternal *masculine* (because these two faces of the world had been one in the beginning) and had always been a source of joy for them. The misogyny inherent in the fable that assigns to woman the role of an impure and perverse creature does not seem to us to correspond with the Celtic or Aegean spirit. It is more likely to have been a **foreign** import, probably Semitic.

In any event, it was during the Iron or the Bronze Age that Greek mythology introduced us to the **Deluge**. Zeus, angered by men's audacity, unleashes the floods: but Prometheus advises his son Deucalion to build a boat in which men will be able to take refuge. Having drifted about on the waters for nine days and nine nights, they reach *Parnassus*, according to one tradition, or *Orthrys*, according to another. In the version told by the Greek authors, the Deluge fits in well with the history of Atlantis, also destroyed as a punishment from God. The myth of Prometheus rounds the story off. The latter's death symbolises the agony of the first Atlantan race, to be followed by that of the giants who will, in turn, be vanquished by Zeus. Why does the eagle devour the **liver** of the Titan Prometheus and not some other organ? It should not be forgotten that, according to Ancient belief, the hereditary genes *on the male side* were found in the liver (and in the spleen). If the liver of Prometheus was restored every **night**, that means that for one thousand years (the mythical duration of the time he was chained to the rock) the Orient was invaded by successive waves of giants from the North and from the West. The route for those coming from the North passed through Thrace, south of Scythia and north of the Black Sea, not far from the Caucasus where they were stopped. The last river they followed, the *Danube*, must have taken its name from this tribe, the *Dans*. The reason for it's also being called *Isther* is because it is, *par excellence*, an especially historic river.

After the Deluge, which probably put an end to the great Atlantic kingdom, the survivors of this race, living on the coasts and islands of the Atlantic, set off once more to conquer the peoples of the South and of the East. The Irish verse chronicle entitled 'The Battle of Moytirra'

(2) (the latter word means **East-West**) could be a distant echo (certainly altered and reduced during the Christian Era to the dimensions of Ireland alone) of the gigantic combat which took place by the *Black Sea* and, more especially, in the marshes of the *Maotis*. Here, the *Maetae*, the *Gelons* and the *Dacians* had already settled for a long period before merging into one another to form the peoples of the West. Commenting on this mythological tale, Gerard Murphy writes: "It is reminiscent of Greek traditions concerning the defeat inflicted on Chronos and his Titans by Zeus and the Olympian gods, or of Scandinavian traditions concerning wars between Aesir and Vanir".

Greek mythology is formal on this point: Before he could establish his power, Zeus had to fight the previous gods several times (3). These *previous gods* (Hades and Poseidon – in other words, **Night** and the **Ocean**) could only be the gods of the Atlantic peoples who had multiplied and lengthened their tentacles right into this part of the world. When Zeus finally triumphed, an immense coalition must have united several younger branches, each with its own kingdom, against the ceaseless flow of the **mother race**, which was held responsible for the anger of the gods. The cataclysm of the Deluge had been appalling: "Suddenly", Hesiod writes, recalling this event, "the immense sea and the vast earth resounds with a frightful noise ... The sky shakes and groans ... the earth burns and trembles ... Everything boils, the whole earth and the currents of the Ocean ...", etc.

It is not difficult to understand that, after such a shattering experience, the survivors should have tried at all costs to triumph over the *darkness* (the *tène* or *oak* era), sister of the accursed *Ocean*. So they burnt what they had adored. From now on they would believe only in life's joys, a calm blue sky, the triumphant heavens, the sun reappearing every day; and in the white silt put down by the receding waters in which life began once more to flourish. The *Orient* had triumphed and, with it, the **right** hand. Everything that comes from the *West* or from the **left** is **sinister**: literally and figuratively speaking. "The captives of rock and wave ... unable to sleep but endlessly busy dreaming, are banished for ever to the island in the dark sea, with their violence, their anguish" (4). God becomes Greek. God becomes Zeus. The future is now Olympian.

But let us not forget that Zeus will claim to be the brother of the previous divinities, and that is why our Northern **giants** will play out their epic tale in the Hellenic Peninsula in the person of ... **Tom Thumb**! Incredible but true. The name *Tom Thumb* means, strictly speaking, *the finger separated from the hand*. We read in the Finnish *Kalevala* that *a finger is never named*. For what reason, if not for this one? We recall that the Vanir considered the thumb (*Maia's* claw) to be a separate finger. In the Icelandic Edda, when Loki advises Thor *never to speak to mortals about his expeditions to the East*, he adds: *When you hid in the thumb of the gauntlet, you no longer believed you were Thor*. Is this a reference to the fact that, when the ancient Nordic divinity finally believed himself to have been vanquished for ever, *he bequeathed his lightning to Zeus of his own free will*? Is the famous *separate finger* not the sacred **cock spur** which, since that time, has distinguished the clan of the *Argolids*, also known as the *Aegeans*, the first dynasty to take over the reins from that of the Pelasgians? The Aegeans would be very proud to decorate the back of their breaches with this **cock spur**, and they would deify all animals adorned with the symbolic spur – beginning with the cock.

What do we learn from Mythology? It tells us that after the Deluge *Deucalion* and *Pyrrha*, both of them children of Prometheus, climbed into a boat and saved the race. *Then they re-peopled the world by throwing out pebbles behind them* (5). Reworked in the course of time, the tale of *Tom Thumb* emphasises that these were *white pebbles* (and no longer **red** like the *red sandstones* of Scotland and Ireland, or *black* like the **eagle stone**). They were intended to help the child (or the young **shoot**) to escape from the wicked *ogre* and find his family which, thanks to him, would *greatly prosper*.

This child, in the old story, is *Erechtonios* or *Eleinos*, eponymous ancestor of *Greece*.

One race had just died and another had been born. Such is the tragedy of Fynn in the Irish legend. When he returns home after a long absence in the lands of the East, neither he nor the men he finds there can now *lift up the stones*. Fynn no longer recognises these men. They have become very small compared to what they had been. He himself suddenly feels very old. He loses his hair, his beard … And that is the end of the giants of the West.

Pursuing a career which was still very far from finished, the illustrious *torch of Prometheus* had just passed into the hands of the Orient. But it was no less the torch of Prometheus, for all that.

* * *

The Pelasgian universe, of which Crete had been a part, included ancient Thrace, Thessalonika, Phrygia, Lydia, Caria, Phoenicia, Epirus and Illyria, and it extended as far as the Samnites and the Oscans. This should be noted. It was with these same provinces that the Gauls would be dealing in the last millennium BC. It was there that they would again settle on several occasions. When the kings of the Peloponnese, of Argos and Mycenae in particular, were disputing at Troy the question of supremacy, all the aforementioned peoples joined together with the ancient *city of Neptune* in a defensive alliance. When it finally collapsed, it was to the lands of their ancestors – along the Danube, in the North and in the Celtic areas – that the vanquished returned. It was there that, bringing new life back to their old Celtic homelands, they would build new empires, creating Europe.

In the Aegean archipelago, Cretan supremacy came to an end around the year 1500 BC, about the same time that Troy had fallen. Mycenae then took over the lead: Achaean Mycenae. The Achaeans, or Aegeans, who are identified with the Pelasgians (from whom they are indeed descended) were also a *sea people*. The etymology of the word *Aegean* confirms this. In modern Danish the word *eg* (from ancient *og*) means **oak** but also **specific** or **true to type.** *Egentlik* means **essential**, **primordial**, **central** or **principal**. Incidentally, *ägäisch* (which in German means *Aegean*) corresponds to Danish *agaik*, which means **gigantic**.

Aegean, therefore, can be seen to mean 'essential' or 'primordial' as to race, as well as 'man-of-the-sea' and 'giant'.

The same root *eg* (which we find in Latin *ego*) gives us *aeg* and *eje*: *egg* in Danish and in English, *ei* in German (a word related to *Eiche* which, in the same language, means *oak*), *ek* in Swedish and *eike* in Dutch.

In legend, *Achaeus*, eponymous ancestor of the Achaeans, was born in Thessalonika, an ancient Pelasgian colony. The men of the oak had as their main secondary divinity the *divine woodman* (whatever his name may have been) who practised the rite of the *Talle* and whose tool was the *axe* (*acha* in Portuguese, *Hacke* or *Axt* in German, *hache* in French and *hatchet* in English). This is not far removed from *Achaean*, just as *pelekos* (*axe* in Greek) is not far from *Pelasgian*. Were the Greeks not fond of saying: *He has the axe of Tenes*, to describe a man equipped with great tenacity? And does this not, once again, tie in the principal use of this tool or weapon with the very ancient race of the *man-of-the-oak*?

These thoughts are further confirmed by the fact that in heraldry, when an axe comes into the story, it is always a *Danish axe*.

Historians are of the opinion that the same ancient dynasties reigned over Crete and Egypt. This need not surprise us. There was a time when, in Europe, the reigning princes were all more or less related, and all of them (which is the most important aspect of the matter) were descendants of the people we are speaking of. Most of the wars in ancient times were to do with settling accounts between *people-at-the-centre-of-things*, but again, in the correct sense of the word, that is: people from the *eye* or *navel* of the world, as seen by the Atlantan Island.

The races of the North Atlantic were certainly the first races who (with the help of the natives, to be sure, and thanks to them) took the Middle Eastern countries towards the summit of their civilization. So even when Zeus finally triumphed over the giants, and when Athena triumphed with him, she gave to *Erechtonios* (now *Eleinos* and ancestor-apparent of the new dynasty) *two drops of blood from Medusa who lived beyond the illustrious Ocean at the extremities of the earth, near the Night and the Hesperides with the thunderous voices* (6) And yet she had fought the Medusa with all her might and main.

This is true but Athena still had to legitimise her position and organise for the new *people-king* a bond with some very distant and venerable ancestors whom the people had not yet forgotten. However, **she** would write its history – **her** history – taking good care to present **herself** as the be-all-and-end-all of everything, while throwing a discreet veil over whatever had come from the *West*.

In fact, there is no agreement about the origin of *Erechtonios*, entrusted to Athena in the presence of *Cecrops*. Be that as it may, the root of the name is Celtic. To be convinced of this one has only to think of *Erech*, son of *King Lake*; all the *Erics* of the North and the West; and even of the sacred *hedgehog* known as *eureuchin* (or *erechin*) – not forgetting also the Gaelic verb *eirich*, which means 'to climb', 'to ascend' or 'to take off'. Some people claim that *Erechtonios* came from Egypt. Others think he is the son of *Hephaistos*, the divine smith. Others again call him the son of *Deucalion*. All these theories are in agreement. By some father or other he extended the lineage of the giants. Cecrops, who was present at his birth, was himself a giant. On antique vases he (*Erechtonios*) was never depicted without the tail of a *Triton*, which refers, without any possible doubt, to his Atlantic origin. History relates that he reigned over the capital of Attica before this region adopted this (new) name. *Inter alia*, the foundation of the *Mysteries of Eleusis* is attributed to him. This is all very coherent.

Then, when Cecrops subsequently relinquished his powers to his successor, according to legend, *Poseidon retreated everywhere, abandoning Egina, Delphi and Naxos to the Hellenes.* What could be more clear?

Athena, favourite daughter of Zeus, who has sprung fully armed from his **head** and is, therefore, essentially **rational**, immediately takes over History with a verve that stupefies the rest of the world, and makes herself the very incarnation of *lucidity*.

To achieve this result (and it must be said) she had stripped the **skin** off the giant Pallas (from which she made a shield) and taken the head of the Gorgon, cut off by Perseus. (It should be noted that the skin of Pallas is *scaly*.) The head of the Gorgon is proudly displayed by Athena on her *gorgonaion* (8) (also with a *scaly* base) and sometimes in the middle of the shield, in order to make use of its *magic* qualities. But, with the passage of time, when the horrible appearance with which it had initially been described (in order to impress the people and exalt Athena's victory) were no longer needed*, Medusa's head would change (in official propaganda) and become very attractive. Athena would encourage friendship with her former enemy and even compete with her in a beauty contest. We should not forget that *Eleinos* had Athena's blood in her veins, only **two** out of the three drops, but nevertheless **two** drops – and it is wise not to offend one's cousins who might in time seek retribution. What is the use of being the embodiment of *lucidity* if one is not *lucid*?*

So when Athena triumphed over Zeus, Medusa was finished. She had been one of the three Gorgon sisters to whom the natives of the Aegean Archipelago had been enslaved for millennia. Athena could now combat "obscurantism" at her leisure, deifying reason and deifying the light, the light of the Attic sky, purer and more like that of the diamond than any other in the world. There can never be enough reflection on this phenomenon, unique in the history of Antiquity, and there can never be enough written about it.

Nevertheless, even with a rampantly triumphant Athena, Celtic faith in an afterlife, in the immortality of the soul, in never-ending resurrections and in light through the darkness, would continue to make its way through the Asian lands it had also fertilised. Kept alive by a succession of ephemeral sects, interconnected by a long Ariadne-like thread, a spiritual current, born of intuitive knowledge, would continue to wind and to unwind its spirals as imperturbably as old

Okeinos piles up and unleashes his waves and his tides. It is this current that would explain all the great civilisations of Western Asia.

* * *

To wind up this short commentary on Greece, let us for a moment reflect on its present name: *Grèce*, in French. It is known to have been given the name by the Romans who extended to the *country* the epithet *graecus* with which they described the Hellenic *people*. Why this epithet?

In old French, the modern adjective *grec* was translated by *grieux* or *griès* (meaning **gravel**) and *grès* (**clay earth**).

The chain of mountains which the French call *Alpes Grèes, Graies, Graize* or *Grès* (all these spellings are known) are the same as the *Alpes Grecques* mentioned by Caesar.

In the minds of the Romans the word *Greece* must, therefore, have been able to mean *earth-mother*, in the sense of *initial silt*. It could also have been a reference to the *gravel* (pebbles) sown by Deucalion and Pyrrha, symbols of the offshoots of the Hellenic race. It is also possible that the two ideas could have been confused. In the poem of the dwarf Allvis, which is part of the *Edda* of Saemund the Wise, Allvis says to Thor, who has asked him about the name given to the earth: "The *Vanir* call it *path* and the Giants call it the *lush pasture*; the Alfar call it the *fruitful*, and the gods say the *august stones* (*gravier* means **gravel**)". The Alfes, or Alves, or Alfar are the *elves*, spirits of the air and of the light, whose Celtic name is *Elles*, a name which is strangely reminiscent of Hellenes, or *Ellenes* (in Greek). Not forgetting that the Celtic *Elles* also describes the *alders* in areas of swamps and marshes – in other words *rich and fruitful* areas. There is a real connection between the French words *grasse* (**rich** or **fruitful**) and *Grèce* – not, of course, because of an idle play on words but because the *Ellide* has always been described as a land that was especially *rich* and *fruitful**. The best proof of this connection can be found in an expression which has survived to this day when we speak in France of a *plaisanterie grasse et graveleuse*, which can be translated as a *dirty* or *smutty story*. The dictionaries explain the term *graveleux* by suggesting that a *plaisanterie grasse* offends polite society *comme le ferait un caillou qu'on recevrait sur la peau* (**as it would be by a pebble** [*caillou* or *gravier*] **by which one was struck on the skin**). We do not accept this

132

interpretation and suggest the origin for the expression mentioned above.

What is more surprising is to note that the word *grès* which initially refers to a *silt-covered earth-mother* (and which in this context could be translated as *sandstone*) also describes *gum which is scaly ... and the large teeth of the boar* which adorned the mouth of the *dragon*. Schliemann writes in his notes that he had found a certain number of boar's teeth in the ruins of Troy. They must have been held sacred, a question we shall be returning to.

*Translator's note, P.131:

> When all its work is done, the Lie shall rot:
> The Truth is great, and shall prevail –
> When none cares whether it prevail or not.
>   [Coventry Patmore]

*Translator's note, p132:

In his book on Greece before and after the Santorini catastrophe of circa 1200 BC (Das enträtselte Atlantis), Jürgen Spanuth reminds us that the oldest Greek myths describe sylvan scenes – trees, flowers and brooks. Men ate meat – beef. However, Classical and post-classical writing, and the evidence of our eyes, show the dry, hot, scorched country we know today. Fish is plentiful but beef has more or less disappeared from the menu.

* * *

14

THE BLUE COUNTRY
OF THE
CHIMERA (CHIMAERA)

To understand what follows, or to be more exact, the other phases of the Atlantic adventure in the East, and to admit with Jordanès that the *Scandinavian countries were the womb of the peoples* (1), it would be useful to look more closely at the manner in which the *Medusa* perished, and how she was related to the *Chimera* and to the *Dragon*, the other implacable enemies of Greece.

When Perseus descended on her with the aid of Athena, she was no longer the wandering, peaceful jellyfish of the early Pelasgian days. She was now *a frightful gorgon*, she had become the incarnation of an old dynasty of conquerors that several younger branches were trying to topple. She had sinned in their eyes by remaining *very powerful* and by monopolising the exploitation of the mines (gold, silver, copper and iron) whose principal melting pot was situated in Thrace and on the northern and eastern shores of the Black Sea. Nevertheless, this dynasty belonged to the eternal race, and this is why its enemies would admit before History that although the Medusa's sisters (the other two gorgons) were immortal and very beautiful, the one they were fighting was ugly and very much deserved to die.

Telling us that she was beheaded is the same as revealing to us that she would be destroyed on her own hearth, that all the sovereigns belonging to her house would be struck down and that nothing of her kingdom would be spared. Thus do the glories of this world pass away.

Where was the nest of this gigantic power that Zeus had so much trouble conquering? History does not tell us exactly. It only tells us that Perseus, in order to confront the Medusa, *had to travel to far-distant regions* and that, to overcome her, he needed to procure for himself the weapons belonging to the people of the Kingdom of the Night: the veil that could make one invisible and the harp or axe of the sinister harpies (2).

However, everything points to the fact that the fighting had taken place in the regions of *Tartarus*. But we have also seen earlier that, although the Athenian Tartarus was situated towards the *Caucasus*, the older Empire of the Dead lay in the **West**. We need not be surprised by this change of location or by the arrow which was shot at the Atlantic world. This is the oldest trick in the history books. And, by the way, it is the reason why *Kronos* devoured his own children. The Western World of which we are speaking was perfectly well known to the Orient 5000 or 3000 years ago, and yet Herodotus knew nothing of it. With reference to his voyages he wrote: "As for the boundaries of Europe beyond the setting sun, I know nothing about them with any certainty. Not for a moment do I believe in the existence of this river *Eridanus* which is what the Barbarians call it and which is supposed to flow into the Northern Sea, where we are supposed to get our amber. I know just as little about the *Cassiterid* islands where we are supposed to get our tin. To start with, the name *Eridanus* is obviously Greek and not a barbarian word: no doubt some poet or other invented it. And as for *Cassiterid islands*, I've asked everyone I've met anywhere: in vain. I've met no one who has seen with his own eyes this sea which is said to exist on the very edge of Europe. But it is nevertheless a fact that we do get our amber and tin at the ends of the earth" (3).

In the same way, the Azores, which were very well known to the Ancients, were then so totally forgotten at a time when it was convenient to sever all links with pagan Antiquity, that they had to be 'discovered' in the 15th Century AD! The same can, of course, be said about America.

But let us return to the Medusa. We know that just after she was beheaded by Perseus, the horse *Pegasus*, and *Chrysaor* its rider, were seen to emerge from the trunk of her body and *fly away to the Elysian Fields*, that is, towards the **West**. And let us just recall at this moment that a certain *Chrysaor* was the father of the three-headed Geryon. Symbolically, this name meant all that *shines* and *flashes*, like all precious metals and *all shining blades*. As we can read in a poem of Ossian's, the *Glassamore* of Irish legend describes him and his descendant *Fingall* as 'the dazzling son of brightness' whose sword 'never sought a second stroke'. *Chrysaor* is the symbolic name of those people (or that dynasty) that exploited the mines of the ancient *Chersonese*. The later (more recent) term is almost certainly a corruption of *Chrysonese*, or *vice versa*. The *tauric Chersonese* gave us the *Crimea*; *Croesus* was the richest of men, etc. Modern geographers quote four main *Chersonese* place-names: one north of the Black Sea, another in Thrace, another in Jutland and a fourth whose exact location is uncertain. Now, both Thrace and the Black Sea region were at that time dominated by the so-called Pelasgian races, and we also find three places with the name *Chersonese* in ancient Crete, and two others in *Cyrenaica* (4).

It can be assumed that, having been defeated in the eastern territories, or rather, in the colonies whose mineral wealth he was exploiting, *Chrysaor* (whose name, it should be repeated, symbolised the sons of Prometheus – great industrialists of the time) fled with his followers back to his native land where he was annihilated by the enemy at his heels. This head-over-heels retreat would normally have taken place on the backs of Thracian horses, which were famous for the speed at which they could run, and it must have made a great impression on those witnessing it. It should not be forgotten that Chrysaor's horse was Pegasus and that Pegasus had been born together with Chrysaor when Medusa had been beheaded. What connection could there have been between the destruction of a great industrial power and a horse, the steed of poets? It was a really moving bond: *The songs of those who are most desperate are the most beautiful songs.*

The old Irish legend which recounts the exploits of *Fynn* (the brilliant, the *dazzling*), who had set off on his horse towards the East and returned to his own land only to die on setting foot on the shore and finding his whole race reduced to nothing, was perhaps inspired by the story of Chrysaor, a hero who also possessed a *dazzling weapon*. This massacre (reminiscent of *Ronceveau*), having become **the** great source of inspiration for the bards of the Atlantic, the Thracian courser could for this reason have been transformed into the horse *that would give wings to the poets' flights of fancy whenever they recited their tales of woe.*

In all legends of the oldest Celtic countries we find this horse flying over land and sea. His image still appears on Gallic medallions in pre-Roman times, sometimes with a *lyre* between his hoofs, at other times, with a rider poised above the back of his mount as if to show that he was in fact flying rather than galloping (5). In our opinion it was the sculptor Carl Milles who gave the best interpretation of the myth of Pegasus and his rider. This sculpture can be seen in Stockholm. Never has the fervour with which man and beast chased after some inaccessible dream been expressed in such a troubling form. The appearance of two forces, so intimately bound together that they become one when they rush forward, is at the heart of the ancient idea of the *centaur* and of the *hippo-centaur*. Legend tells us that these creatures lived mostly in Thrace and Thessalonica. This need not surprise us because it was precisely in these two countries that the swiftest horses were bred.

Another proof that Perseus went to the West to deal the death blow to his enemy is provided by the fact that, according to Mythology, the combat took place in Tartarus, in a country *as far from the ends of the earth as the earth is from the sky*; a country that is always covered in dark clouds (6). Furthermore, Perseus, *on the way home*, stopped off in *Ethiopia*, an itinerary that is inexplicable if he was coming from the Black Sea,

In Ethiopia, Perseus had to destroy the *Chimera*, brought up by the King of *Caria*, a province on the coasts of Syria, founded by the Pelasgians. This Chimera was the offspring of the giant *Typhoeus* and of *Echidna*, daughter of Poseidon, the Ocean. Pure Atlantan lineage on both sides of the family. *Echidna the Divine, Echidna*, whose name meant the 'bristly one' and who had been the ancient and peaceful *jellyfish*, had now become a redoubtable figure. *The upper part of her body was that of a nymph of gentle appearance, with beautiful features; while the lower part of her body was that of an enormous snake covered in scales.* Her children were: the *Chimera*, the *Gorgons*, the *Hydra* of Lerne, the dog *Cerberus*, the *Sphynx* and the *Dragon* – in short, everything that was Athena's enemy, but for no other reason than this: they belonged to the ancient Western dynasties, *born of the entrails of the earth and of the waters.*

What could be more clear? And again, we have to admire the astonishing science of the Ancients and the ability of monuments to present, in the shape of images, a historical précis of a great moment in the annals of the world. These images are so very much in tune with the spirit of the events that one has to ask oneself what could be the significance today of the two scourges of *thorny rods* in the coats-of-arms of Ethiopia if they are not a reminder that this province had at the beginning of its history been the granddaughter of *Echidna-the-Bristly-One*? "Sacrilege!" someone will cry. The very Christian crown of thorns on the escutcheon shows that the rods in question are those with which **Christ** was flogged! Surely?

No. We are convinced that we have here a transposition (as so often happens) of a pagan symbol into a Christian symbol, and that the thorny rods have not been put in here purely by chance. We know that the Ancient Abyssinians (particularly the *Gallas*), who drank hydromel from the horns of the bull, worshipped the *ficus*, a tree around which they piled up bundles of *thorny wood* on festival days. This rite was primarily related to the myth of *Echidna the Divine*. The Ethiopian Chimera (*Khimara* in Greek) has the root *khim* in its name, the equivalent of *kham* or *cham* – the name of ancient Egypt; a name which probably included Ethiopia in furthest Antiquity, since these two provinces had been totally inter-dependant from the days of the 11th Egyptian Dynasty.

No doubt it was the root *chim* of the word *chimera* which created a certain amount of confusion about the appearance of the animal thus named, and which encouraged the Greeks (at a time when correct etymologies – on purpose or otherwise – were as much neglected as they are today) to introduce into its figure part of the body of a *goat*. But, we must go back further – to the *Sea People*. The *squale*, which is also called 'chimera', the dogfish (*chien de mer* in French) and also *galleus * canis*, has the peculiarity that its dorsal fins *look somewhat like wings* while, at the front, there is *a part which juts out rather like a horn*.

It is all there. In Danish, the word *kam* means '**crest**' (*crête* in French, *crista* in Latin), '**protrusion**' or '**horn**'; and the word *kim* means '**germ**', '**embryo**' or '**initial cell**' (7). In Gaelic, the word *kam* or *cam* means '**one-eyed**' (8) and refers to the Cyclops. It is easy to see the relationship between all these terms. In Icelandic, *kampr* (cf. Danish *kam*) describes the pointed beard ('**goatee**'), while *kambr* (cf. the French *cambrouse* '**the uncivilised spot where thorns grow**') not only means '**crest**' and '**protrusion**', but also by derivation '**tooth of the comb**', together with the comb itself and, in particular, the weaving comb.

Its pointed beard or its two horns – but (in our opinion) especially its *goatee* – can, no doubt, explain the goat's ancient name *khymia*, which later changed to *kapros*. From *Khymia** we derive the word *chimie* (**chemistry** in English) which is explained by the fact that in this science the composition of initial cells (*kim*) and of their transformations is studied. All these different developments have been derived in the course of centuries, or even millennia, from one original root. We cannot claim to be able to track down all the derivations with rigorous exactitude: we can only take note of the relationship and draw our own conclusions as to their distant origin.

There also seems to be a connection between *shamanism* (based on the *cult of nature and of the spirits that govern it)* and the name of the priest-sorcerer in ancient Mongolia - *chaman*, which is very close to the *calaman** of the druids whose equivalent in *Pali** was the word *samana*, festival of the 1st November, devoted to great transformations, or '*metamorphoses*'.

In the earliest days of Egypt, if we are to believe Herodotus, the crocodile was called *champres*, which reminds us of Icelandic *kampr*. The name was probably given to this animal because of its protective shell covered in scaly bumps.

Like the word *Chamite*, the word *Ethiopian* ended up referring to the *race with the bronzed colour*, which does not mean the *black* race. These were beyond any shadow of doubt survivors of the ancient Atlantan *red race*. All the historians of Antiquity agreed on calling the first Egyptians and Ethiopians *red men*, or else a race with a dark complexion but with a hint of red in it: "A duskier complexion … , brown with a tinge of red", writes Smith (9).

It was only very much later, after they had interbred on the one hand with Semites and on the other with Sudanese Negroes, that the Ethiopians became a mixed race – albeit remarkably homogeneous, and still proud, it would seem, of its principal descent.

All the above can be verified by the fact that, in the time of the Pharaohs, Egypt was divided into two regions: that of the North, or of the Delta, symbolised by the *lotus* of the fertile silt, whose Goddess *Sabena* wore a *white crown,* and that of the South, symbolised by the papyrus root or *calame*, with *Neith* (or *Nout)*, goddess of the *night, crowned with red*.

If we needed further proof of the connection between Egypt and the Atlantan peoples, we could rely on two terms which have left their mark on its ancient civilisation: those of *Memnon* and of *Pharao*. *Memnon*, King of Ethiopia, was the son of *Tithon*, King of Egypt. Tithon himself was the son of the Trojan *Laomedon* who was the son of *Illus* and father of *Priam*. This line of descendants, shown in Greek Mythology, demonstrates clearly the bonds of relationship existing between the dynasties which reigned over the Trojan complex, Egypt and Ethiopia: and we have already shown above that they could all be traced back to the same Atlantan base. Memnon was sent to help Troy. History describes him to us as being dressed for the occasion in armour *made in the workshop of Hephaistos*. This detail is **explicit**. The brothers wage war on each other, agreed. But when the very life of the *clan* is imperilled, they unite against the external threat.

In honour of the glorious exploits of this hero, Egypt built the famous **Colossus of Memnon** in the neighbourhood of Thebes. In the 7th Century AD, *Arctinus* of Miletus (take note of the first name!)

wrote a long poem in honour of Memnon the Ethiopian. It was a continuation of the *Iliad* and was called the *Ethiopid*. It was never completed and literary History has ignored it.

Memnon is a proper noun which, in Antiquity, also had descriptive value (like *August* and *Caesar*). We find it, for example, reproduced in the name *Agamemnon* and in the surname *Maiamoun*, used by Ramses II.

Where can we find a word still in common parlance which, in its meaning and assonance, reminds us of this famous *Memnon*? Where else, if not with the Celts and Scandinavians? First of all, in the second part of the name *Vainamoinen*, son of the giant *Kaleva* who wandered over the water like the *mainée*, his mother. Then there is *meamna*, in Gallic (10), which means **spirit, desire** or **will**. This word is cognate with Irish *menme*, which has exactly the same meaning, and with Welsh *menmawl* (11), meaning **sovereign** or **what tends towards sovereign beatitude**.

In other words, Memnon in Antiquity meant 'sovereign man' or 'man-god'. Since the latter had originally been a giant in Atlantan legend, one can understand the colossal dimensions of the Memnon statue near Thebes.

Littré tells us that *memnonite* was (according to Lamark) the common name for *cone virgo* (a mullusc with a cone-shaped shell). There, again, one can be certain that the similarity of names is not fortuitous and that this *cone virgo* called *memnonite* must correspond, in the order of sculpture and colossal size, with the Egyptian obelisk and the sacred *cone* of the Nordics, whose name also described or designated the quality of sovereignty in this part of the world.

This cone, of which we have already spoken at length, and which associates itself symbolically with all horns and with anything that is like a spike; which, beginning with its Trojan name *hile* or *ille*, will also give its name *Illus* to the great-grandfather of Memnon, brings us by natural association of ideas to the Pharaohs.

Pharaoh, the dictionaries tell us, meant for the Egyptians the 'great dwelling' or 'lofty dwelling' of the sun god; hence the French word *phare* (meaning **lighthouse**, **beacon** or **headlight** of a car). In the Welsh language, *ffair* means 'high place' or 'eminence'; *ffain* is what 'rises up like a cone'; *ffaraon* is 'great power'. In Gaelic, *farleus* is the word for 'light from the sky', *fraoch* is 'radiating heat' and *fraon* is a 'lofty house' (12). *Far ainm* is a common surname. *Far* means 'air'; that which floats over everything. The same word *far* meant both for the Celts and in Old French 'flour' (*farine* in modern French). It is curious to note that the cult of the sun god included in Egypt an offering of cakes made from barley – no doubt because the sun god was also the god who *nourishes*. The *far* is still the traditional patisserie in Brittany.

In Greek mythology, *Phoroneus* is said to be of the Pelasgian race. He is said to have brought the people of Argos both knowledge and well-being; in other words, civilisation. In the Peloponnese, near *Hermione*, Phoroneus had founded the temple of *Demeter*, divinity of the *Night* and symbol of the *West*.

One just has to open one's eyes and one can see that the most obscure facts link up together with complete clarity.

* * *

Translator's Notes, p.139:

* To find the word *galleus* has eluded this translator's most diligent efforts. Could it be a misspelling of *galeus*, whose first meaning is 'lizard-like'? A *dogfish* is also some kind of shark. (A dog in Latin is *canis*.)

* Transliterated into Latin, the Greek and Russian letter **X** is pronounced **ch** as in Scottish **loch**.

* Name of the *dove* or the priestess: cf. the plant *columbine* in English, meaning *dove*-like from the resemblance of the inverted flower to a cluster of five doves. The Latin *columba* (dove) gives the adjective *columbinus* (dove-like).

* **Pali,** an ancient *Indic* language, still used in the scriptures of *Theravada* Buddhism.

15

DRAGONS AND TALES
OF DRAGONS

What was represented by the *Dragon*, another son of Echidna and brother of the Chimera?

History tells us that Perseus, having killed the latter, then married Andromeda by whom he had six children – six sons. The eldest, called *Perses*, was born in Ethiopia and, according to Mythology, it is he who should be considered the father of the Persian nation.

By reason of his triumph, *Perseus* became a hero-god. But, did we ever see a hero – and especially a god – born from the husband of his mother? He has to construct a legend for himself, and the first requirement of a legend is that a god may **not** have a mortal father and also that he should be born of **divine** intervention – that of Zeus, in this particular case. Nevertheless, his mother is *Danae* (often confused with *Dione*) and she was fertilised, so the tale goes, by *golden rain*. Now that is the right way to make oneself unique in Mythology and it bears a clear Nordic imprint.

We know what is meant by *rain* in such cases. In those days, there was great similarity of functions between Man and Nature. Hence the French expression : "*Il n'est pas de la dernière pluie*". The *literal* translation is: "He is not of the last *rain*". However, the idiomatic English equivalent would be something like: "He wasn't born yesterday". This rain could be golden, or otherwise infinitely precious, for the very good reason that it came from Zeus. But, Heaven be praised, in the ancient legend each word means exactly what it says and each metaphor likewise. If the West hadn't been blessed with luscious pastures and rich horned animals, and if Zeus had not known that the cow was the most important goddess, he would not have created the bull in order better to seduce Europa. And when he pours gold into Danae's lap, he knows very well what he is doing. Does the *Kalevala* not tell us of *the gold which is the bed of the dragons* (1)? In the funeral song of *Ring* we read: "The king was not miserly, he spread around himself the dazzling dew of the dwarfs – the dragon's bed, the gold. The gift cascaded from his liberal hand". There can be no doubt that Perseus, begotten by a shower of gold, came *from the bed of the dragons*, in other words, that he was the son of a Chrysaor, or of that race which alone at the time was powerful enough to exploit the mines.

Danae was, of course, the daughter of *Akrisios*, the son of *Abas*, whose mother was the daughter of *Danaos*. If we recall that *Dan* was the name of the legendary kings of Denmark (*Dane*-mark in French) (2) then there can be no doubt that we are dealing with a family of Nordic *dragons*. History relates that the famous *Danaids* were the mothers of the *Danaeans* who supplanted the Pelasgians. Why not believe it?

When he had killed his stepfather (by a clumsy accident when he was throwing the discus), Perseus refused to take his throne, the throne of Argos. Instead, he exchanged this kingdom for those of *Mycenae* and *Tiryns*, which he took over from Crete – about which we know that its ancient fortresses were built by the giants.

At this time, Athena *with the blue eyes* (3) had not yet gained the upper hand. Did she really help Perseus in his struggle with the Pelasgians or did she merely boast that she had, once his victory was assured? If that is so, she must have kicked herself more than once. Until she finally managed to bring them into her fold, the Persians (heirs of the Dragon's possessions) would give her some hard knocks. We see, therefore, that the dragon was the real *bête noire* of the Athenians, a perfect symbol for them of the old hereditary enemy.

It is known that this famous dragon held watch over both the *Hesperides* and the *Golden Fleece*. It is also mentioned in connection with the *Castalian spring*, sanctuary of the virgin *Artemis*. The legend is precise on this score and in accordance with History.

The dragon resembled the Chimera and the Gorgon of Perseus. There was a pronounced family likeness between these three creatures, which is easily explained since they were brother and sisters. According to Hesiod, the front part of the Chimera was like the body of a lion and the rear was like that of a dragon. Homer adds something in between, the shape of a goat's body. We have seen why. As for the Gorgon of Perseus, *it vomited torrents of flames, its feet were of brass and its wings of gold. It had three rows of teeth plus two boar's tusks* (4). This time it is not simply a question of resemblance but almost of a copy. Except for the dragon's wings which were black.

The starting point for this fantastic animal seems to have been the lizard, called "*dragon*", which climbs trees and has two membranes which it releases like a parachute when it jumps from one branch to another or down to the ground. It was certainly to this creature – of which there were doubtless great numbers at a certain epoch, and which were perhaps much larger at the time – that Herodotus refers when he speaks of the *winged serpent which guarded the incense trees.*

But, as a matter of fact, is this *winged serpent*, about which the historian of Classical Greece only speaks for the record, not the *flying fox*; or *goblin*; or *flying dog* – a gigantic *bat*, essentially fruit-eating, which is today only found in New Caledonia? The *Larousse* Dictionary informs us that some of them have a wingspan of a metre. "Their heads are like a dog's, the thumb and first finger alone have nails". Buffon, in his description of them, adds that they "drink palm sap which makes them drunk".

Homer speaks of them in the Odyssey, but Greece of the 5th Century only seems to know of them in myth. On the other hand, they are depicted on the walls of Egyptian tombs erected two millennia before our era. The Hindus, for their part, held the flying fox in high regard and seem to have looked on them as sacred animals.

They must most certainly have represented descendants of the Western conquerors (from the Empire of the Night) since *Moses* would later classify them in his laws as *impure* creatures. Blanville, who quotes this fact, adds that the flying fox had once been found in great numbers in Mesopotamia. In Leviticus they are called **Kallou**!

With the coming of the Christian era, these gentle and inoffensive animals would be called vampires and would become an object of terror and of superstition – which is interesting from a historical point of view.

Men must quite naturally have had the idea of "borrowing" the appearance of these little monsters to frighten everyone, which is the best and **cheapest** way of destroying an enemy. What Herodotus relates, inclines one to think that the men of the North exploited the incense tree – which is quite correct with regard to Armenia. Nevertheless, nowhere in Greek mythology is there any mention of a dragon guarding incense. On the other hand, it is well known that a real song and dance was made about the one which kept guard over the Garden of the Hesperides. Since the Hesperides were the islands situated at the *limits* of the Atlantic (the special preserve of our Nordic people), it is not surprising to see a dragon in these parts. But there is more. There are the famous *golden apples* about which there have been so many theories and about which the dragon can be so illuminating. And, if not the dragon, then the dragon's blood.

Pliny spoke about it in his day. He refers to a tree called *calamus*, 'containing the gum called *sanguis draconis*' (dragon's blood). It grows on the Canary Islands, very properly called the *Lucky Islands*. The tree is called the *dragon tree* in our French dictionaries and it is said that *the trunk splits up into many stems*. Larousse specifies that "the bark of certain species secretes a gum called dragon's blood which, when it dries, becomes friable and red-the-colour-of-blood". Likewise, in Swedish, the expression *sang-dragon* (*drakblod*) is used to describe drops of gum or resin (*gummiharts*). By corruption, the *sang-dragon* becomes *mandragore* (mandrake) – which gives rise to many fables and superstitions.

By extension, the resin which resembles honey (because it not only looks like honey but has the same consistency) becomes *pomme d'or* (golden apple) because, in the **Greek** language as in our **Old** French, the word *mele* meant both **honey** and the **apple** of the apple tree – probably because a drop of honey is just as round and glossy. And, when we flick through *Littré*, we see that in Breton *miel* (honey) is *mele* (just as in Greek). We see too that he quotes the *frène mielleux* (**honeyed** ash tree) and the *mele* or *pomme d'appie* (a sacred apple because it is marked with the red spot of the dragon's blood). It was this kind of honey, or rather resin, which was used in Antiquity to make *hydromel*, a very old drink of the gods which is still drunk in Nordic countries, calling out **skaal**! (a subconscious hommage to the *Echidna* and to the dragon, her son). *Hydromel* was the ancestor of Greek *retsina*, resinated wine.

The exploitation of this resin, particularly abundant and of good quality in the Canary Islands, must have been a source of immense wealth, and it is understandable that the Western Paladins should have defended it fiercely.

We now understand what is at stake with the *Golden Apples of the Hesperides*, and how it was thought that they were defended by a dragon – since the boats of the Nordics which mounted guard over them must already at that time have been displaying the terrifying mask of the animal which had become their emblem. In Celtic languages *droukh*, *droch* and *drought* are still synonymous with 'redoubtable', and the sailors of the North certainly were that! It was also the same basic idea which conferred the title *Dracon* on the Athenian legislator of the 7th Century BC, the man whose laws were so severe (so the historians tell us) that they were said to have been *written in blood*.

This last statement leads us on to a further consideration.

In the Armenian language (and for good reason, as we shall see further on), the root *drg* means *to fall in drops* or *to drip*. This root reappears in an inverted form in Swedish *graad*, which also means *drop*, and for this reason is cognate with *graal* (grail).

The myth of the *dragon blood* and of the dripping resin of the *dragon tree* (and today of the *pines*) was certainly associated in the minds of the Ancients with the myth according to which the Titans had been born from drops of blood from the mutilated *Uranus*. Must we not also **wound** the tree in order to collect the precious substance? Furthermore, the drops of the *calamus which turned from the colour of gold to blood-red* were a perfect symbol. And if that were not sufficient, they are found in a *red soil*, like the *soil* of the earliest days with which men painted their skins in memory of their ancestors! Surely it must have been a *dragon-blood* cult that had inspired this rite?

Must we add that no legend in any other country would ever make so much use of the term *golden apple* to express the most exquisite refinement, or the epitome of tenderness, as the lands and legends of the Celts and Scandinavians – and this seems to fit in very well with the concept of an Atlantan West.

The Canaries, together with the *Pillars of Hercules* (Straits of Gibraltar), had been an integral part of this enormous power for several millennia. It would, therefore, be correct to attribute the conquest of the famous golden apples to *Hercules of Tiryns* and not to his ancestor. And in any case, does Mythology not tell us that when the hero handed over the apples to Athena, she had to return them to the Garden of the Hesperides because *it was not permissible for them to be anywhere else*? This pretext inclines one to suspect that, at the time, it was not known how to acclimatise the dragon tree in Greece.

The myth of the *golden apple* and of the *drop of dragon's blood* has been transformed over the ages, but it is still powerful. The fact that in Celtic legends the Holy Grail is supposed to be kept in a place called *Avallon* [which could be a *Pommeraie* (orchard), since *aval* means *pomme* in Breton (*apple* in English, *Apfel* in German and *appel* in Dutch, etc.], leads one to think that, with the passage of time, Christian myth and Ancient myth have moved closer to one another: or rather, have become confused.

Just like the **egg**, the **spiral** and the **triangle**, the **drop** would also in time take its place among the classical types of architectural ornaments, imagined by Man, which all originally had a sacred symbolic significance. In the pre-Christian times of Athenian Greece and in our Christian era, the drop of **blood**, or the essential liquid, would change into *drop of dew, a celestial power that had come down from the light and the regions of the spirit into the lower regions.* In the Old Testament, for example, we find the following passage: "My doctrine shall drop as the *dew* on the earth, as the soft rain upon the gentle herb".

But, for all that, it was still the blood of the Nordic *dragon* which had opened the way (via the blood of *Uranus*) and it was still the drops of *his* blood that would be depicted on shields carried by the descendants of the *hyperborean giants*. For want of a better explanation, the heraldry experts have up to now interpreted these as an indication of illegitimacy. Such an interpretation can be correct when there are two drops instead of three: but originally, three drops, shown as follows

are a sure sign of one of the oldest and most distinguished lineages transmitted by the *Franks* and *Goths* to various families in Europe. Already in Antiquity, the kings and princes of the Hellenic Peninsula all claimed descent in vertical or oblique line from *Eleinos*, son of *Deucalion*, whom we have seen as the heir of the *Atlantans*. Apollodorus of Athens listed the names from Eleinos himself down to *Orestes*, ancestor of *Aeneas*, including *Amphytrion*, husband of *Alcmene*, the mother of Hercules of Tiryns. Now Athena, as we may remember, had endowed Eleinos with two drops of the Medusa's blood (Medusa being a sister of the dragon): so the Hellenes, whether they wanted it or not, had a dragon in their one eye – only one at this time, because of their falling birth rate.

The power of this fantastic creature was so great – or rather, so great was the power of the race which it symbolised – that the root of its name has left an unvarying mark on all languages and on all dialects, from Sanskrit *drgvischa* and Greek *drakkon* to Bohemian *drak* (via Latin *draco*), ancient Scandinavian *dreki*, Irish *draic*, Russian *drakon*, Finnish *traki*, German *Drache* and Dutch *Draak*.

It still remains to be seen by what path this imaginary figure could invade three continents and is held equally sacred by the Mayas, the Japanese, the Tibetans, the Chinese and the Hindus.

Once again, the path seems to us to lie in the *North* where three continents are joined: *America*, *Europe* and *Asia*.

In France, when the fabulous animal conquered Normandy, *its head rose up proudly* from the prow of the boats of the terrible Vikings. *Its mouth was flaming red, its flanks were flecked with yellow and blue, its tail was coiled in spirals, powerful and bristling with silver scales, and its black wings, edged with red, were spread out proudly* (6).

Could the dragon's *tail* not be at the core of names like *Sinus codanus* and *Codanum mare* which Tacitus gives to the Baltic (*Sinus* in Latin means 'bay' or 'gulf'; *codanus* means 'tail-like') (7)? Several Latin authors called Copenhagen *Codania* and gave Scandinavia the name *Codanonia*. Since *coda* was the oldest version of the classical *cauda*, we could be speaking (figuratively) about the *tail* of the horrible monster whose head protruded beyond the Pillars of Hercules, on the one hand, and, on the other, as far as one part of *Arabia felix*, provinces in which certain tribes bore the name *Codani* (8). Unless, of course, all these names such as *Codania, Codanonia*, etc. were connected with the name of the French *morue* (which is *cod-fish* in English) and, of course, at once reminds us of the American Cape *Cod*. In that case it would be worth remembering that the word *morue* arose from the Celtic *mor* and *hu* – the one meaning 'sea' and the other 'goddess'. And we should also remember that this fish was certainly one of the totems of the Atlantic tribes, since the female is the most magnificent layer of eggs in the whole maritime world – which is why the Latins regarded it as one of the symbols of *lust*. Nor should we forget that Irish legend speaks of *Cod* (or *God*), a hero-god who became king of the world after having had, together with his brothers, *a thousand adventures in Italy, Greece and Asia Maior* (9).

One way or another, the Atlantic always seems to be behind all the conquests and great migrations of proto-historic ages.

So what happened to the dragon in Greece?

We know that the war between Athena and the Second Dynasty, that of the *Sea People*, ended in a compromise. Athena agreed with *Ares*, God of War, *to give Cadmos one half of the dragon's teeth* and the other half to *Aetes*. Basically, this left the wealth of the dragon to its natural heirs. Athena needed peace to be able to establish her power.

Let us identify the cast.

Ares was a giant, a son of *Hera*. He had been born, as befits a hero of this importance, without his birth having been preceded by any sort of carnal commerce: *There was only contact with one of the marvellous flowers from the plain of Oleinos*. Although certain authors have preferred an intervention by the worthy Zeus.

Ares was always hostile to Athena. It was in his blood to be so, as it was in the blood of all the *Argolids*. So he sent his daughters, the *Amazons*, to invade and devastate Attica. He only agreed finally to negotiate because of the fear he shared with Athena for their common enemy, the high and mighty *Cadmos* – a cousin but, nonetheless, an enemy.

Cadmos had lived in Egypt where he had slain a dragon (others say the killing took place in *Boetia*). This dragon was the son of Ares who was, therefore, himself a dragon. And Cadmos had to pay dearly for having dared to kill the son. Nevertheless, he was very strong, so diplomacy was called for. In agreement with Athena, Ares made him *sow the teeth* of the horrible creature which he had received as his share: which means more or less that he was given the right to allow the men of Thrace, who were of Nordic origin, to live and multiply. This was an arrangement of pure genius: these peerless warriors only needed a little encouragement and they would end up killing each other. And this is indeed what happened. So, when there were only *five giants* left on the board (or field of battle), a little bargaining took place. Cadmos married Ares' daughter *Harmonia*, and with his *five Spartans* he founded the city of Thebes.

We should here bear in mind that there could have been confusion in the transmission or translation of the legends between the words *dents* and *Dans*. The latter term, as we have seen, has always, from the most ancient times, been used to identify the *Danish* heroes. It is closely related to *dant* which, in modern Danish, means 'tooth' (*dent* in French). Of course, one could have become an image of the other?

Who was *Cadmos*? He was the brother of *Europa*, *Phoenix* and *Cilix* and like them, he was a descendant of *Io*. When Europa was abducted by Zeus, her brothers ran after her. But, after a certain lapse of time (with Phoenix having succeeded his father on the throne of Phoenicia, and Cilix, for his part, being kept very busy in his kingdom), only Cadmos *and his mother* remained to carry on the struggle, which came to a climax in Thrace.

Essentially, this must mean that our *ex-Westerners*, having been attacked in Phoenicia (a country they had colonised), pursued the enemies who had tried to snatch Crete and Thrace from them over a long period. They did not however catch up with *Europe* who, nevertheless, created a new world in the West.

The name *Cadmos* must have been symbolic and cognate with *Calamos* or *Calaminos*, since the dictionaries tell us that *cadmine* was formerly called *calamine* (having to do with *carbon*). But since Cadmos is in History thought to be the father of the Phoenician alphabet (whose origin we now know), his name must rather have referred to the *calame*; that is, the name of the reed used for writing. And, at this point, we should remind ourselves that the reed in question was the symbol of Upper Egypt where Cadmos lived. This *reed* from the *sacred garden* (represented by a hieroglyph which would become our letter **Y**) was the Egyptian representation of the *alga*, or *grass*, of the *first Atlantic island*.

Now, once again, it is curious that King *Cod* of Irish legend should have been the son of the sovereign of the *mythical kingdom of Ioruath*, **Io** being the Greek name for the mythical *island-mother*, where everything began. It is also curious that, in this same legend, Cod and his two brothers should have *chased after a bewitched woman*, a witch who tried to lead them to the *land of her birth*.

Surely, that is the story of Europe?

* * *

16

THE GREAT "BOSS"

Western Asia was not only conquered by the Paladins of the West via the Mediterranean but also via the Black Sea.

According to *Quintus Curtius* and *Strabo*, "the vast plains which stretch from the Danube to the shores of the Black Sea, from the Caucasus to the Caspian and up to the banks of the rivers Oxus and Iaxarthes, seem to have been occupied by one and the same nation, divided into an immense number of small peoples or tribes" (1).

By *nation* we mean a *race* more powerful than the others and simple logic tells us that, in this case, this could only refer to descendants of the Pelasgians. Since they were in possession of Egypt, Phrygia, Troy, Crete, Scythia and Thrace, they were naturally tempted to close the circle of their empire by swallowing up the lands in question. A computer provided with this data would reach the same conclusion.

The peoples who lived around the Black Sea can be placed in two main categories; the Scythians in the North and the Thracians in the West. According to the historians, these peoples had the same 'blue eyes' and the same 'red hair' and they are said to have been living in these places *since time immemorial*.

There they kept the gates which would one day change into **gateway** (*porte* in French and then into the Turkish *Sublime Porte*) through which one passed from the West to the East. Remember that later, in the Greek mind, the idea of a 'gate' in this part of the world would coincide with that of the entrance to *Tartarus* which would be transferred to this region.

But, where does the Black Sea get its name?

The Black Sea (*Pont-Euxin* in French) is generally believed to be an *inhospitable* sea. But why inhospitable? Because, it would appear, of its reefs and storms. The idea of inhospitable conditions could also be derived from the fact that the word *euxinus* was sometimes written *axenus* (derived in turn from 'axe' or 'hatchet') and that this weapon was used by the giants* during the terrible fighting that took place in these parts. But, in our opinion, the Pont-Euxin was the *Pont-aux-boeufs*, or *Pont-au-boeuf* (Cattle Bridge), since the letters *o* and *eu* are interchangeable (as are **p**, **b**, **v** and **f**). In English *boeuf* is 'ox'. The term is still widely used in Germanic languages (*Ochs* in German, *okse* in Danish and *os* in Dutch).*

Also, in Pelasgian Greece, in Latin countries and in certain parts of Gaul, *boeuf* was written as *bos* (in the nominative case) and it is this root that we find in the place-name *Bosphorus*, an arm of the Black Sea, which connects *Marmara* (*mer Maia* or *mère Maia* in French) with the Black Sea (*mer Noire*), *black* because the empire of *Maia* is *Tartarus*.

Bosphorus originally meant the **lamp** or **tower** of the **ox**. *Pharae* was the name given to cities in Achaia, Egypt and *Messenia*. But there may have been confusion between Greek *phorus* (lamp or tower) and Latin *foris* (*porte* in French and *door* or *gate* in English). So, Bosphorus could have meant, or could have come to mean, *Porte-aux-boeufs* (gate for oxen) or, perhaps, *Passage-du-boeuf* (passage or route for the ox).

Be that as it may, *cattle* are part of the equation, somewhere! Their presence is reinforced by the legend concerning *Io*, who swam across the Bosphorus in the shape of a cow: *Io* being in this case the sister of *Phoroneus*, father of the Pelasgians. It is also reinforced by the legend concerning the oxen of Geryon which Hercules brought to Thrace, crossing Europe in the process.

The ox, by virtue of cult practice and of the way in which it is bred, is an animal of the West. The Celts believed that before anything really existed, there was the *cow*. We also read in the Icelandic Edda that *Ymir*, father of the giants, and the cow *Audhumbla* emerged simultaneously out of Chaos. It was in the Atlas region, one of the most important Atlantan kingdoms, that the *Centaurs* lived. The Orient has never reared cattle for domestic use. If these animals, cows and bulls, have survived, *sacred* and emaciated, since time immemorial, it is in *memory of* and out of *respect for* the great and fabulous Paladins who came from the *West* through Thrace, Egypt, Troy and Crete to impose their Law on the *East*, bringing with them vast herds of cattle.

Naturalists consider the origin of the ox to be obscure. Some of them seek it in Central Asia, where it is fashionable to maintain that everything started, before spreading westwards. But others, including Cuvier, see the womb of "the domestic ox in the *bos primogenitus* (first born), or *fossil ox*, whose enormous skulls are found in the peat bogs of Germany, England and France" (2). Brehm, from whose work these lines are extracted, considers it inadmissible to claim that it was this animal which filled Europe, Africa and Asia with its progeny. In the light of Ancient History, such as it has been written up to now, it is easy to understand the author's surprise. But his surprise is no longer justified – far from it! – in the light of what we know now. The long history of Geryon's oxen, led by Hercules from the Country of the Dead into Thrace, can only give substance to our claim.

We should first add that Brehm also claims that the *bos primogenitus* only died out recently in the West. "In the 16th Century," he writes, "several heads were kept as precious trophies in Warwick Castle, in England. It was said that these animals had been killed by the last lords of the domain."

And what else is there to learn? That the species known as *Bos urus* (ancient Aurochs) is commonly called *boeuf de la Manche* (ox from *la Manche*, on the northwest coast of France) and that the *Cimbrians* used to swear their oaths on a brass bull. [NB: In the Psalms we hear that "fat bulls of Bashan close me in on every side". In Chamber's Encyclopedia (1950) Bashan is described as a country in South-West Syria; "… [i]n the time of Abraham Bashan was occupied by the *Rephaim* (giants) … The men of Bashan were remarkable for their *stature*, the soil and pastures for the richness, the sheep and oxen for their size and fatness …" The last of its Amorite rulers was Og who, with all his sons, was killed by the Israelites under Moses, at the battle of Edrei.]

The tales that are told in country districts are also very revealing because they come from very old traditions. "In every pastoral region", Brehm writes, "there is a *bewitched cow*, placed under an evil spell: it is almost always *red*, and is suspected of being in touch with the *Prince of Darkness*". When we know how to read between the lines, we can see all that that means, and how, once again, we must return to the story of Io and to the story of Europe – which we lost track of in Thrace. And any way, was the paradise of the cows ever situated in some place other than in *Fionnie enchantée*? So, what then are we to say about the fat bull of *Karelia*, which the *Kalevala* describes as being so enormous that a swallow would need a whole day to fly from one horn to the other, while a squirrel could run along its tail for more than a month without getting to the end of it?

In Greek mythology, the bulls of the Empire of the Dead are described as being *milk white*. The naturalists, on the other hand, maintain that only the *Scottish bull is entirely milk white* (Brehm). And yet on Geryon's shield there is a splendid *white bull's* head! How long must we still doubt evidence that smacks us between the eyes?

Our etymology with regard to the Black Sea seems to us to be better founded because, in our everyday speech bordering on **slang** (*argot* in French is a word which reminds us once again of the Pelasgian Greek language), *boeuf* (bull) is synonymous with *enormous* in expressions such as *effet boeuf* (enormous effect), or a man who is *fort comme un boeuf* (strong as an ox), etc. So, once again, we meet up with this animal belonging to a conqueror who is *powerful and huge*.

Loysel, quoted by Littré, has made a truly inspired comment: "One binds cattle by the horns and men by words". Does this not make us think of *Ogmios*, the Gallic god who was transformed into the Greek Hermes, *the cowherd god, protector of itinerants and famed for his eloquence* whom we find represented, without any explanation, pulling towards him a group of men bound together by chains which the hero holds between his teeth? The chains in this image represent the magic of words which *fascinates** men and *binds them* to their leaders. In the same way, the rope tied around the horns of the animals *attaches* them to each other and the animals to their cowherd. This symbol is magnificent and truly Celtic. In the form of the *yoke* of the ox, it constitutes one of the aspects of the *sacred knot* which occupies such an important place in Western prehistoric art – especially since this knot is in the shape of a *figure eight* (8). It is the knot we find in the Roman *fascis* (rod). It is the knot we find in the *ritual knot* which *fascinates* the branches or twigs of the birch which the Finns cut on certain summer nights to use in the sauna. Finally, the yoke of the cowherd would – through the ages and through many myths culminating in the Christian myth – be inseparable from the *Word*, as Ogmios expresses it so well.*

In confirmation of all the above and with reference to the *Pont-Euxin* (Black Sea), Littré tells us that this sea is also called the *Pont des Ioniens* (Bridge of the Ionians) and the *Pont des Illiens* (Bridge of the Illians).

'*Bridge of the Illians*'? Illian was another name for Trojan (Troy being originally called *Illios*, hence the poem entitled *Iliad*), and now we know who the forebears of the Thracians and Trojans were.

Bridge of the Ionians? Once again we must refer to *Io,* the cow. Io was the mother of *Epaphos*. We read in Herodotus: "Oxen are considered to be the property of Epaphos. They are subjected to the following examination: if only a single black hair is found on them, the animal is regarded as impure" (3). Can there be any doubt that we are dealing here with a rite in honour of the *milk-white ox* from the Empire of the Dead whose head is depicted on Geryon's shield?

And there is something else: *Creusa* has been called the mother of *Ion*, eponymous ancestor of the Ionian people. But *Creusa* is no more than a transposition (for the benefit of Athenian history) of *Artemis Crisa or Creusa* of the Black Sea, whose breast is shown us on archaic statuettes covered with the udders of a cow. If *Io* is thought to have given her name to the *Ionian* Sea, why would she not also have given her name to *Ion* and the *Ionians*?

Ion is also written *Eion*, which brings us to something really interesting.

The ancients attributed to the Black Sea the shape of a Scythian bow which looked like the capital letter **sigma** *of the Greeks* (4). This has been confirmed by Smith who wrote, "The Ancients compared this sea to a Scythian bow" (5). In fact, the Ancients did **not** *compare* this sea to the Scythian bow whose shape was totally different; they merely used the Scythian bow as a *sacred idiogramme* to make a *symbolic representation* of it. This brings us back to Geryon's oxen.

The *sigma* of the Ionians, ⋀⋀ , which became the *san* of the Dorians, ⟨ , then the Gothic **S**, ⟨ , was the Phoenician *shin*, ⋁⋁ and it corresponds with our modern **S**.

The root *sig* in the word *sigma* means 'eminent' or 'lordly' and is related perhaps to *som* or *cim*, or else is their equivalent. The horizontal beam, *sommier* (lintel) was called *summer* in Old French and *sagmaricus* in Latin. In French slang *un bon zig* is 'a decent chap'. From this root the Germans have formed the names *Zigmar, Siegfried, Sigurd* and *Sigmaringen*. We speak, too, of the Babylonian *ziggurat*. And, we find the same root via Latin in 'sign' (*signum*). The Dorian *san* is the Modern Greek letter Σ, corresponding to the diphthong *Ei*, engraved on the *pronaos* of the temple of Apollo at Delphi.

We read in the French *Grande Encyclopédie* that the letter **S** was passed on to the Latins from the double **O** via the Phoenician sign W̲, which was itself taken from an Egyptian hieroglyph.

Herodotus also has something interesting to say: "There is something I have noticed in Persia to which no one here pays any attention. The names of people who belong to High Society or who possess this or that attribute or physical quality *always end in the same letter*: the *san* of the Dorians or the *sigma* of the Ionians. You will seek in vain for a single exception to this rule" (6).

It is amusing to read these lines when we remember that the Franks have kept the same usage alive in France. In France we refer to the final **S**, *never pronounced*, in words such as *Louis* and *Reims*, or the **S** at the end of the second-person singular of the verb. And, up to the end of the 16th Century, many Norman and Burgundian lords still indicated their quality by signing their acts with an **S** or an **8**.

But, getting back to the Black Sea: taking into account the double **O** (or **8**) as the shape of the knot in the bovid's yoke, why should it be surprising to see this yoke as a symbol for the *Bride of the Oxen*? Because the shape of the Scythian bow is as follows: the normal curve of the bow, not bent at the middle, so as to reproduce the image of *two ox horns*, joined together by a strip of birchwood on which the bowstring is strung. Such was the shape of the bow which, according to Herodotus, was bequeathed by Hercules to the Scythians.

In time, the *sigma* would evoke the twin-toothed saw, and it was perhaps from this root *scie* (saw) that the word *Scythe* would evolve. *Sci* is related to the Greek root *oxi* or *exi*, a root containing the idea of 'shadow' (as in *sciamachie* meaning 'fighting shadows'), since the ox was the symbol of the kingdom of *shadows* and of *death*; in other words, of *Tartarus*.

According to Herodotus, quoted by Littré, the Scythians, when speaking among themselves, did not use the name *Scythian* but *Scolote*. Since *skal* (or *skol*) meant 'scale' or 'tooth' in the Nordic languages, we see that we keep circling around the same idea.

However, two other possibilities come to mind. Perhaps the sign or letter **X** was born from the crossing of the two arms of the figure **8**. But it is also possible that, in the minds of men, the association of the **X** and of Greek *andros* (i.e., of the **X** and of ***Man par excellence*** – an idea which would survive into the Christian Era thanks to the legend of the crucifixion of *Andrew* on a cross shaped like an **X**) dates from that far distant epoch of the Black Sea's supremacy in this part of the world. The fact that Scythia was evangelised by St. Andrew, and that he gave his name to an order of Russian chivalry, seems to support this supposition.

Before leaving the Black Sea, let us mention the *Golden Horn*. It is generally agreed that this horn owed its name to the heavy traffic at the port of *Constantinople*. But, it is logical to think that the name initially constituted a homage to the *golden horns* of the sacred ox – golden horns whose tradition has been maintained in France up to this day and relives at every festival of the *fatted ox*.

The *fatted ox*! This must be the domestic ox, the ox of heavy labour, the beast of *burden* (*somme* or *summérien* in French), the indefatigable ox, the Western ox, the *Great Bovid*, the *Grand Bos* – symbol of the sons of the Atlantic who took up the torch again after the Deluge. Active men, inventive, pugnacious men who never stop pushing the world forward and waking up those who are slumbering.

In a recent work, Max Weber asks the question, put by so many before him: "To what concatenation of events must we attribute the appearance in Western civilisation – and only in this civilisation – of cultural phenomena which (or so we like to think) have had *universal* meaning and value?" (7) Part of these "cultural phenomena" includes, of course, *science* which leads in turn to industry and to capitalism. The author then states that intensive activity, and the equally intense pursuit of profit, are achievements of Protestant peoples, and that they are to be attributed to the spirit of the *Reformation*. In no Catholic country (he writes), in no country called *Latin,* are work and money so closely associated with a religious attitude.

To explain this Alliance, Weber then speaks at length about the spirit of the Scriptures.

And yet, the fundamental and historical reason for this apparently strange phenomenon is simple. What has been called the *Huguenot International* in matters of finance and industry was preceded by that of the *Templars*, whose families later would people the ranks of the *Rosicrucians* and the *Protestants*. And, going back through the centuries, these were all of *Frankish* stock, or *Ligurian*. In other words, they were offshoots of the Western Paladins, who many millennia before our era were the first blacksmiths, mentioned in Mythology, the first creators of the spinning wheel; in short, they were everywhere the first to exploit all the riches of the globe and to dominate it, thanks to the fortunes created by their industry.

Right from the start, and in their very essence, these industries were for them *bound* up with the religious concept of the *nobility* of man, descended from *Man* or *Mani, the ancestor with the long hand* (or with the **powerful** hand), the first who knew how to use the joints of this hand to manufacture *tools* and emerge from the state of savagery. A concept, a myth that, without question, was born in the Atlantan universe.

Once again we find our proof in the *names* of things. Weber relates the German word *Beruf* (**vocation**) to the English word **calling** and to the corresponding Scandinavian words *kald* and *kallelse*. The latter terms are cognate with the family of words such as *calculation*, *calends* and *Kalendertag*: and we know that these words have, throughout Antiquity, referred in the Western World to the religious festival at each new moon – and, on this occasion, to the festival of *work* (8).*

Maia, the sea-spider which gave her name to the month in which these festivals reached their climax, had yet another claim to the veneration of Mankind, above and beyond all others: she had the symbolic faculty of opposing an independent *nipper* to her four joints (or legs), and this ability to oppose her *thumb* to four other *fingers* would permit man to become *industrious* and to be able to *create in his turn*, so that he could for this very reason *lift himself up* towards the *omnipotent* Creator. Is this not so?

It is possible that one day this race of masters, this race of lords, could have a *black* skin or a *yellow* one, just as the first ones almost certainly had a *red* one. But the *inheritance* on which its power will be built, and which will help it in its turn to shine over the globe, will come to it – whether it is admitted or not – from the ancient *Atlantan* race with which everything began and which for this reason is entitled to call itself *immortal*: throughout the whole of Humanity.

* * *

Translator's notes

P.153 **Giants.* Could these have been the *Streitaxtleute* – "People of the battle axe"?

P.156 ***Fascinate** means 'to bewitch' or 'to hold spellbound'. It comes from Latin *fascinare*, meaning '**to bind together**' as with a *fascis* (rod). Note the old fable of the dying man who teaches his brood of quarrelling sons that only by standing together in a *tight bundle* can they withstand the depredations of their greedy neighbour. Each stick can easily be broken *separately*, but the *bundle* cannot.

P.160 * Even the alternative English expression *vocation*, although borrowed from Latin, fits in here, since *vocare*, (the root of *vocation*) means 'to call'. Different *sound* and appearance, but the same *concept*.

17

SEARCHING FOR TRACES
OF THE
THRACIANS

So, if we are to believe Quintus Curtius and Strabo, Thrace formed together with Scythia "the great nation" of the Black Sea. But again, if we are to believe the Hercules legend, Thrace had preceded Scythia in the order of civilisations. The two claims do not, however, contradict each other; on the contrary, they are complementary to one another and it seems natural that it should have been so. Thrace, which lay to the west of the Black Sea, included the lands stretching from the mouth of the Danube (the river of the *Dans*) and extending a considerable distance along its course. It is obvious that this river (like the *Tanais* which became the *Don*) was the best route that our Paladins could follow to get to the East.

The best route – the best passage – hence our acceptance of the *name* for the empire they created there: *Thrace*, a word which means 'conduit' or 'duct'. But it is possible that the two terms became confused in the minds of men so that their order of precedence was reversed: i.e., they derived the word 'duct' from Thrace. However, speaking etymologically, it is not impossible that Thrace is derived from *Trika*. We have seen that the *trika*, *treka* or *treskeles* was one of the emblems of the North Atlantic and that it symbolised the empire of Geryon. Well now, in Thessaly, bordering on Thrace (a region which the Pelasgians of the Black Sea crossed in order to enter Greece, properly speaking; and which was reconquered in the 3rd Century BC by our Gallic ancestors, the capital city was called *Trika* or *Trikala*, or even *Trachinia* (1). It is also known that the *Thracids* were a priestly family in Delphi, highly reputed for their deep wisdom as were all Western magi throughout the whole of Antiquity. Moreover, this same Antiquity described letters with a magic property as *Thracian* letters which, of course, reminds us of the *Scarlet Letter* as well as of *runic* writing, since *rune* meant mysterious and secret. Did the philosopher Lucius Apuleus not visit Thessaly in order to study the art of *magic*?

It was by starting off from the Atlantic Trika and by passing through the country which was founded beneath its emblem at the frontiers of the Oriental world that the French verb *tracer* was arrived at (*tracier* or *trachier* in Old French). Besides *dessiner* (to draw) it also meant *guider*, *voyager* or *traverser* (to guide; to travel; to cross over). In Latin we find *tracones*, a term which meant 'passage' or 'tunnel' and gave us the French word *trançon* (section or stump), the historical importance of which we shall see later.

Herodotus says of the Thracians that, after the Indians, they were the most important people on earth (2). By *important*, a Greek such as he could only mean the most *numerous* or the most *widespread*. To this historian, the grand epoch of the Thracians was already something of the very dim-distant past and, as far as Athens was concerned, they were no more than a collection of "barbarous" tribes, in the commonly accepted sense of the word. Just as one could ask, by way of comparison, what similarity could there be between Rome in the Middle Ages and the capital of the Roman Empire?

Karl Blind wrote to Schliemann in 1881: "I believe that it is possible to establish with the greatest certitude that the Trojans or Teucrians belonged to the great family of the Thracians" (3). That is certainly our point of view.

Amongst the numerous tribes grouped under the generic names of the Thracians and the Scythians, we should mention the *Getes*, the *Maeotae*, the *Geloni* and the *Dacians*. The *Getes*, who became the *Goths*, were most certainly descendants of the first race of giants. The root *get* is synonymous with the root *germ* which we also find in the French word *germain* – *germe* being, of course, a 'shoot' or 'young shoot' of the main plant. [*]. In botany, the scientific name of *germanders* is *teucrium*. The *Maeotae*, who were mostly settled along the shores of Lake *Maeotis* north of the Black Sea, were certainly a product of the tribe of the *Maetae* who, together with the *Caledoni*, peopled the ancient islands of Ireland and Scotland.

We read in *don Cassius*, translated by Smith: "Among the Britons are two tribes, the Caledoni and Maetae. The Maetae dwell close to the wall, the Caledonians beyond them have neither walls nor cities, but live by pasturage ..." (4). The author informs us further that the latter tribe lived in tents, walked bare foot and held their women in common, *living in a truly democratic state*. He said that they fought in chariots (tanks weren't just yesterday's invention!) and were armed with shields, lances, daggers and swords with pommels of bronze. This is almost word for word what Herodotus writes about the tribe of the *Neures* who also lived by the Black Sea near *Tauric Chersonese*, in other words, not far from Lake *Maeotis*: *their women are common to all*. This means, they say, that *all are brothers*; they all form a *great family* and this avoids all hatred and jealousy. Apart from this detail, the historian adds that their customs are the same as those of the Thracians (5).

As for the *Geloni*, History and Mythology tell us that their most ancient king – *Gelanus,* of course – was the brother of *Danaos,* the most ancient king of Argos. This seems to determine his origin. Moreover, we read in the *Grande Encyclopédie* that the Scandinavian divinities had to struggle for a long time with the giants of *Geleus.* Once again we are compelled to note a connection between the peoples of the North Atlantic and the Thracians – either because ancient *Gelea* could have been some hyperborean but *unmarked* region, or because *gel* was written in place of *gal* and could, therefore, mean 'Celtic'. But we prefer the first alternative which could, *inter alia*, explain the idea of *cold* included in the root of the French word *gel*, meaning *frost*.

When describing the *Geloni*, settled to the north of the Black Sea, and just like Xenophon describing the Thracians, Herodotus emphasises their *blue eyes and their red hair*. He adds that they organized processions in honour of *Dionysos* every two years and he notes that he suspects them of having some Greek blood in their veins mixed with a little Scythian.

Once again, Herodotus had only met up with a residue, now reduced to slavery, of the peoples who many millennia earlier had crossed this piece of territory – Thrace. There they had left their rearguard and gone on their way, taking their old civilization with them into Asia. He refers to them as being "tribes" continually at odds with each other. And yet, before their great defeat, Dacians, Maetae and Geloni had swept down as one man to help Troy, whose ancestors were the same as theirs. They had exploited in those days the rich minerals of Tauric Chersonese, just as men of their blood had exploited the minerals of Cambrian Chersonese (it is not a matter of pure chance that the most common English name is *Smith*). In the Maeotis region they mined the coal which they had long since learned to extract from the peat which was found in such abundance in their old countries of origin: Ireland, Wales and Greenland. And thus, coal would come to be called *geanthrace*, until this was shortened to *anthracite* or *tara* – although the latter name would be specially reserved for *tar*, asphalt or bitumen, in such plentiful supply both on the shores of the Black Sea and of Atlantic Celtic regions.

And so we come to the *Dacians* or *Dais*, which we have kept as a tit-bit. Why? Because, as J. de Saint-Martin has written: "if the Ancients had passed on just a little information about the Dacians and the Dais, this would have revealed that the thrones of Persepolis and of Babylon were occupied at the start of the Christian era by the Goths or Huns. Perhaps it would even have taught us a little more and given us some information about the astonishing relationship that exists today between most of the European languages and the idioms in use in Persia and India. And even without going too deeply into these relationships, they might possibly persuade us to examine the question from an angle completely different from the one currently in vogue"(6).

Nevertheless, be patient! It is evident that we are on the right track. Who were these *Dacians* or *Dais* (or *Daae*) who had been living along the banks of the Danube since time immemorial (7)? They were quite simply the descendants of the *Dans* or *dents du dragon* (dragon's teeth) from the North.

The reason why *Dacia* was the last European province to be conquered by the Romans is quite simply because the Atlantic peoples were the most implacable enemies of Rome which, in order to build **its own** empire, destroyed **theirs** – an empire which had also extended from Europe to Asia. And when *Christian* Rome would in its turn establish its power on the ruins of the *Roman* empire, the Goths and the Getes (like **all** descendants of the Atlantic races in **all** countries where the dragons had sowed their teeth) would remain its enemy on both the spiritual and temporal level and would be the last to remain unconquered.

By what mysterious force does it seem inevitable that today (1966) those (USSR) who (despite their protests) are resuscitating ancient animosities, should be descendants of the ancient Scythians? And by what other mysterious force does it seem inevitable that they too are fighting beneath a *blood-red* banner displaying the *hammer* of *Hephaistos* and a *sickle* exactly like the *scythe with the cutting tooth* (8), (not of gold or silver but of *steel*, in accordance with the old theogonies) which, by mutilating Uranus, gave birth to the *giants*, the *Sirens* and the *Furies*? Even if we think that the hammer and sickle in question have a totally different meaning; even if it is all pure chance, nevertheless, it is no less true that the *gloves fit the hand most strangely.*

164

What an excellent illustration of the ebb and flow of events of which Man is the instrument chosen by fate, as the Ancients believed.

The *Dacians* or *Dais* or *Daae* were also called the *Diens* or *Dyans* (9). The name of *Dione* is related to this appellation, as we have already seen; to *Diana*, a goddess of Latium, a province of Pelasgian origin; and finally to *Dionysos*, where we must pause a moment. This hero was gathered up while still a baby by the nymphs, daughters of Atlas, called *Hyades*, name of the sea spider with the red protective shell. He was in fact anything but a master of bacchanalia and he is of great interest for us Westerners.

A short parenthesis. Since the words *Diens* or *Dyans* meant 'gods' in Asia, we are entitled to ask ourselves whether it was not originally from them rather than from the much later Latin *deus* that we derive our French word *dieu* (god).* There can be no doubt that the *Diens* or *Dyans* or *Dais*, initially men of the *oak* and then men of the *scale* and of the *tooth* were the most ancient heroes known to Antiquity. Because the men of Antiquity worshiped them with a cult which was the due of their ancestors, we have confused this term with our Christian notion of divinity, a notion that did not exist in the minds of the first men who made a distinction between the *dians* (or *secondary* divinities) and the Great Custodian or *Ordainer* of the world. We have thus acquired a completely false idea of their religious spirit.

The Ancient historians tell us that the *Thracians* were the first to practise the cult of *Dionysos*. Although born from the thigh of Jupiter (or, rather, **because** he was born from the thigh of Jupiter), this hero-god was a scion of the race of the *Oeil* (eye), later to be closely involved with that of the *Arc* ('bow' and also 'arch'). One only needs to look at the Bacchic amphoras on which he is depicted, surrounded by enormous *eyes*. We have already mentioned the symbolic sense of the eye, so we should not be surprised to see images of great Zeus displaying the *genital eye* on his thighs. *Cadmos* was an ancestor of Dionysos on the maternal side. Other legends suggest that he was the son of *Persephone*, which certainly makes his claim to Western descent credible. Moreover, both ancient historians and modern mythologists maintain that he *gives the impression of being a foreign god in the Greek Pantheon*. Cicero, for example, states that there were five gods known by this name and that they lived in Crete, Egypt, Phrygia, Thebes and on Mount Cithaeron.

Another tell-tale fact as to his distant origin is that *Demeter*, goddess of Agriculture and mother by Zeus of Persephone (whom

Hades carried off to be Queen of the Underworld for three months in the year), was present at his birth. Dionysos would, therefore, have had a connection with *Hades* by the maternal line, which also places him in the *Western camp.*

Dionysos is said to have been born in *Nysa,* a city which some say was situated in Thrace (the country of Dione and of Artemis); while others say he was born in *Thessaly,* in *Carnia, Lydia,* or even in *Ethiopia, Libya* and in *India.* The reason why each of these provinces lays claim to having been the birthplace of the god is because in each of them he was worshiped with greater devotion. It is, of course, also possible that, as in the case of Hercules, the name Dionysos referred to a *caste* or *dynasty* in which several individuals distinguished themselves in the same cause.

As a matter of fact, there is no proof that the adjective *nysos* coupled with *Dion* or *Dian* refers to a place of birth. There was in Greek Mythology a certain *Nysos,* King of Megara, who – when he lost his kingdom – was changed into a sparrow-hawk. This story is certainly related to the legend of *Horus,* the Egyptian *god-sparrow-hawk,* son of Isis, whose myth is far too complex to be looked at here. We merely note that the Egyptian sparrow-hawk, apart from being the god of *light* and of *eternal renewal,* was also the symbol of *virile friendship.* The myth of the *Companions of Horus* is exactly parallel with the one which represents *Nisus* (Trojan friend of *Euryal* about whom Virgil speaks in the *Aeneid*) as the very incarnation of the spirit of camaraderie. The Latin word *nisus* has always meant both a 'sparrow-hawk' and a 'companion', therefore, the correct meaning of the name Dionysos is actually 'god of the companions'.

The ivy which invariably crowns the head of the hero-god, or decorates his image, or twists round his sceptre, is definitely a symbol of undying friendship and of the union between the strong and the weak – first in friendship and then in love. The ivy complements the **other** attribute of Dionysos, his *first* attribute, namely, the *cup,* which gave him his Latin name of *Bacchus. Bac* (*bak* in Breton and in Dutch) is an old Celtic root which, in a general way, describes any cavity filled with liquid and, more particularly, *the wooden bowl in which the brewer prepares the hops.* By extension, and in the form of a *bacin* or *bassin* (basin in English), the same term meant 'goblet', the cup from which we drink. Littré, in the dictionary where we can glean this information, notes the following about *bac*: "Compare with *bassin,* with whose root those dialects which use *bac* in the sense of French *auge* ('trough' or 'manger') become merged".

The word *liber*, which sometimes replaced *Bacchus* for the Romans or merged with this name, must date from *decadent* times when the sacred rite, which consisted of drinking together in heroic circumstances, became nothing better than a chance to indulge in orgies which involved all kinds of *liberties* or *licence* – since drunkenness *liber*-ates men from all convention (NB: *Liber* in Latin means free].

Having said this, the *Dionysias* of the Ancient Times were not just vulgar debauches. The memory of them has been deformed when it was passed down to us via Attica. Initially, they were above all an exaltation of the community spirit, an exaltation of the living forces of men through a constantly renewed youth, raised up to a paroxysm of emotion by *inebriation* resulting from libations and dancing. It was the rite of forgetting oneself by *communion with the masses* which we find in all traditional dances: it is a spirit which our modern youth obviously yearns for in its *excesses*. It is a very *Western* rite. It was in the North Atlantic (and we understand why) that heroes sought in the cup of hydromel the *exaltation* of their courage simultaneously with its *recompense*. It is an old rite which has survived in the form of the soldier's *cheap plonk* (booze), Anglo-Saxon and Scandinavian *eroticism* and student *drinking* parties.

This is all just a wretched parody. But it is worth remembering that the gesture of *clinking glasses* (*trinquer* in French), a sign of fraternity and good faith, goes back to the time when our Paladins had occupied and created *Thrace*. We cannot see any other etymology for the verb than the one which it may have inherited from the *name* of this country since, on the one hand, *trin* has become **trinquet** (foremast) in shipbuilding terminology – or, alternatively, **traquette**; and since, on the other, we find the same root in the German verb **trinken** ('to drink'). Nor should we forget the *godet à boire* (drinking bowl) which is mentioned in Hercules' adventure in Thrace, a cup which he bequeaths to his children as a distinctive sign of his race.

According to the Greeks, Dionysos invented the vine. This is very possible, but History is rather nebulous on this point. It **does** tell of a descendant of Deucalion and of *Pyrrha* who had a *bitch* which *tore loose a length of a tree branch*: having been inserted into the ground, this produced a vine. On the basis of this explanation we should just bear in mind that *Pyramus* is to this day the name of a dog with a *black* *and rust-coloured coat* and that the word *tronçon* (stump of wood: see above) reminds us of Thrace. Moreover, it is a fact that images of Dionysos (and of Diana) almost always show them together with a dog: could it be the dog of the Empire of the *Night*, possibly given to him by *Demeter* who had been present at his birth; or perhaps, the *Gallic* dog famed in days long past for its speed and courage? Or, more probably, could it have been the dog to which the Finns have devoted a veritable cult since it exemplified for them the *auxiliary genius of the hunter* (10) – which, of course, more or less mirrors the previous eulogy?

Dionysos was on occasions greeted with the epithet *Zagreus*. And, with reference to the dog, the Ancient Persians used the words *zag* or *sace*, which reminds us forcibly of the *zig*, already mentioned, and which we also find in the sense of *beam* or *stump* of wood or log in the Latin *sagmaricus*. At the same time, the Persians were wont to call the Messagetae, a Scythian people from the Caspian Sea area (11), *dogs* or *wolves*. Herodotus in turn refers to *man-dogs*, which were supposed to be widespread in India.

The dog and the wolf have both been symbols of the Kingdom of the Night and of Death. One cannot, therefore, help thinking in this connection of the *rust-coloured dogs* of Constantinople (situated in ancient Thrace) for which the inhabitants of this city still had such a high regard at the beginning of the 20th Century that they would not destroy them – although they were *cursed as harbingers of calamity*. This was a tradition which was just as deeply embedded in custom, and probably just as old, as the Hindu veneration for cows which prevents their killing these animals.

We can now see how important it is to follow the tracks of the dog and the god in the direction of the Orient. We read in the *Nouvelle Mythologie Illustrée*: "As the geographical horizon of the Greeks widened, the cycle of legends, relative to Dionysos and to his expeditions, grows too. It is found in Asia and in Africa, in Egypt and in Libya, in Ethiopia, in Arab lands as well as in Lydia, Phrygia, Bactria, and as far as India ... It is Dionysos, says Pausanias, who was the first to lead an expedition against the Indians ... He was the first to throw a bridge across the Euphrates, and today we are shown the cable which served to unite the two rivers. This cable is woven from vine shoots and branches of ivy ... To cross the Tigrus, Dionysos mounted a lion" (12).

And to cross **what** country did he climb onto a camel? It is indeed perched on this animal that he is shown on the frescoes consecrated to his triumph. And, do we not find in Antique India (as in Phrygia, Thrace and Libya) a city called *Dionysopolis*?

This cannot simply be dismissed as a complete fabrication. It represents, on the contrary, an historical reality before which we need to bow.

Dionysos the successor of Hercules, Dionysos the son of Cadmos, Dionysos the civilizing conqueror, the god of companions at arms – could he not be in the *East* the one who in the *West* is called *Odin* (*O Dinn*, the *Dien* or *Dian*), *the only god to drink wine amongst the gods of Walhala who drink beer* (13)? And, are Odin's daughters, the *Walkyries*, not sisters of the *Amazons*, born on the banks of the Black Sea by *Harmonia*, wife of *Cadmos*?

At the opening of the *Dionysias* (festivals which Athena-the-*rational* never understood very well and which she only accepted fairly late) a voice was raised: *I have come to celebrate the race of glorious heroes and the women of Cadmos' family*. Like all celebrations with an Atlantan origin, *these took place at night and on the top of a mountain*. Long files of torches surrounded the procession in which the infant-god (Dionysos) was carried, lying in a *winnowing basket* in the shape of a *shell, his body wrapped in bandages* ("swaddling clothes"), the ritual wraps in which, according to legend, the body of *Ion* and of *John* lay at their birth – **and** the body of the *infant Jesus*. In the case of Dionysos, it is always the expression *winnowing basket* which is used to describe the manger or basket in which he lies. This proves both the great age and the origin of his cult (NB: 'To winnow' means 'to examine closely in order to *separate the good from the bad*, the *grain* from the *chaff*').

According to M. Jules Girard, "It is because he unites in himself the ethereal source of the life that comes to him from Zeus, his father, and the infernal source which comes from his mother, Persephone, that Dionysos was considered to be the Principle of all things" - or, as the Old Testament puts it, referring to *Jhw* (**Jove**, by another name?): "*Thou judge of quick and dead*". Euripides greets Dionysos as follows: "To thee, sovereign Ordainer, I bring this offering and this libation ... *Shed the light of thy soul* on those who wish to learn what trials their mortal destiny will lay upon them, reveal to them whence they have come, and what is the root of their ills ..." * Already there appears behind these words a yearning for revelation, a soul's torment that sublimates the role of the antique hero-god. Aristophanes seems closer to the spirit of these times when he cries: "O Dionysos, O Evios …" after which the chorus repeats, "Evios! Evios! Evios!" By which the poet is probably saying: "O thou, the greatest, because thou art our ancestor".

Evios, like Latin *avus*, was derived from the Celtic *awen* or *ewen*, which meant both 'water' and 'well-born': 'well-born' because it is a scion of the *Ocean* Dynasty.

For us, Dionysos – *raised by the nymphs* – is the one who created a meeting-point for the *Vanir* and the *Aesir* (the forces of darkness and light), which, by the way, confirms the assessment of Jules Girard. It is said in the *Kalevala* that the two peoples in question (Vanir and Aesir) *spat* together into the bowl (*vase*, *van* or *bac* in French) as a sign of reconciliation (14), and that from this spittle emerged the *perfect man:* or, more exactly, the one who by his *arms* would establish order and who in legend was called *Kuaser*. Would it be too daring to relate this name to a word still in use in Byzantium, namely, *kavas*, which means both 'guardian' and 'policeman'?

Kuaser, in modern Icelandic, refers to a mythical being whose blood, when it was touched by a dagger, was transformed into hydromel. This has an amusing twist to it, namely, that the USSR is at the moment trying to de-throne *Coca-Cola* from the world market by launching a national drink of its own, made (so we are told) from the *apple* (just like the hydromel of the gods) and which it intends calling *kuass*! (15)

Let us hope that when they drink it, men will become the *spitting image* of *Kuaser*, the *perfect man* of the old sagas!

Dionysos is not so dead after all.

Translator's notes

*'Germane' in English means **pertaining to**. In Middle English 'German' or 'Germain' means **having the same parents**. In Latin *germanus* means **of the same race** – from *germen* meaning 'offshoot' or 'foetus'(p.162).

*The Germanic word *god* seems to have been derived from Scandinavian-Icelandic *godhi*, meaning 'military leader' and translated as 'Lord God of Hosts' in the *Old Testament* (p.165).

*In *The Book of Common Prayer* we read: "Shed the light of thy countenance upon them, and give them peace …"

* * *

18

ARIADNE'S THREAD

We know how important the colour *blue* was in Ancient Persia. It was cherished or hated, according to what peoples in turn dominated this province, because in the very dim-distant past it was tied to a religious myth and also to the origin of the first glorious race which civilised the region. *Pers,* the word in Old French, still means to this day 'the colour blue in all its nuances'.

This is a long story, poetically told in the legends of *Ariadne* who, having been abandoned on an island and picked up by *Dionysos,* became the faithful companion of the hero-god. This means that *Ariadne* (or *Ariana* or *Ariya,* the latter being the name of the most ancient Persia (1)) passed one day into the hands of the *Danaians* who at this spot supplanted the Pelasgians along the Mediterranean coasts. It also means the *blue eye* was the distinctive mark of the *Arian* peoples who, several millennia before our era, had founded one of the most powerful white empires on Asiatic territory. The *Danaians,* bearing many presents (arms, culture and progress of all kinds) were *Aryans* or *Aesir* (*as* in French, and definitely **aces** as well!) or else people, if you will, belonging to the *Dynasty of the Air,* the one of which humanity is still a part, and will remain so – until the arrival of the *fourth* dynasty which will no doubt be that of the *Cosmos* for those who will be writing History in 10,000 years time.

This does not prevent Persia's present-day name, *Iran,* being cognate with the ancient *Ariana,* or that the title of *shah,* borne by its sovereign, and which is also written *schah* (2), should in turn be cognate with the *chas* of the sacred eye.

It will be said that *Ir* is not *Ar;* but the two roots **are** a couple. In the language of Ancient Egypt (where *Perses,* eponymous father of the Persians was born, according to Greek legend), the eye was called *irt.* The root of this word, *ir,* is the homonym of *ir,* meaning 'to do' or 'to create' (like *ar,* from which *art* is derived). We have already spoken of '*eye*' as symbol of divine births. The meaning, the **original** meaning of the word *Iran* (before it was 'the land of the conquerors', as it is called today – although this is only a derivation) was in our opinion 'land' of the 'race of the eye' – which was actually the same thing, since 'race of the eye' and 'race of the conquerors' are, in fact, basically identical.

Nevertheless, the concept of the eye **is** important because it explains that Iran is the *country of the throne of the peacock*, since a peacock owes its sacred character to the *eye* which 'looks out' of its feathers. This is why, in Greece, it was sacred to Hera, who took the place of the ancient *Iris*.

Having said this, how is it possible to explain the union of *Ariadne* with *Dionysos* at a time when (the Greeks not yet having *anthropomorphised* everything) this name described (no doubt symbolically) a *sacred animal*?

According to legend, Ariadne was abandoned on the sand of a beach. But since *sand* in Latin is translated by *arena* (from which we derive our circus arena, which is *sandy*), is it not possible that a sandy beach could have been a favourite spot for our old friend the *aranie* (*araignée* meaning 'spider') which had risen up from the depths of the waters? And may we not wonder whether *Ariadne-Ariane*, who was born in Crete, is not a female version of *Arion*, a land-based mollusc which could very well have followed in the tracks of the Pelasgian – and purely maritime – *aranie* as totem for a dynasty (the third) which was a Dynasty of the Air?

All the evidence supports this hypothesis. Animals with shells or scales were certainly cult objects in the Near East at this time, in memory of the Great Ocean Dynasty. It was brothers of Arion who provided the mother-of-pearl and the stone for the cameos and, in certain French provinces, especially Normandy and Poitou, the shells of ammonites were for a long time also held in great veneration. In many old dwellings we still find thresholds of doors decorated with these shells, following a very ancient tradition.

The *Arion*'s great advantage was to be *on land*, that is *in the open air*, and if he differed from related families by not having a shell **as such**, he nevertheless did have a lumpy skin covering three quarters of his body which naturalists actually called a *shield*, or sometimes *armour-plate*. Moreover, his colour was *red* or *black*, like the dog of Dionysos and like the Dynasties of the *Night* and of the *Ocean*. He was also *hermaphrodite*, like the *Ordainer of the World*, and had the singular distinction of eyes at the end of his horns. Remember, too, that throughout Antiquity the *antennae* were sacred, as were the *horns*.

And finally, *Arion* explains Ariadne's thread both literally and figuratively by the large quantity of mucus which that creature leaves behind as he moves forward, because the arion is in fact no more than a slug, or *limas* – a name to remember. The trail of mucus looks like a silver ribbon: on the one hand, this can explain the generic term *ar* for almost all the rivers in the Celtic vocabulary and, on the other, it has many shades of colours like the life-giving rainbow – and like the *medusa* (sea-spider) itself. *Ariane*, the *Great Encyclopaedia* tells us, is supposed originally to have personified *fertile soil*, and her name is said to have meant 'very holy', which meant in turn 'very high' or 'very venerable'. There was, however, also a quality of limpness as in that of the grey slug or leech. In the art of Classical Greece, Ariane is always represented in an attitude of listlessness or languor.

None of this is abnormal. Other molluscs have been honoured as totems by previous civilisations; for example, the *nautilus*, the *Argonaut*, etc. (*Nautilus* and *Argonaut* are both types of mollusc). Many of them appear on medals, and it was probably the *Asian snail*, whose shell (with its four or five clusters of whorls) was the inspiration behind the hairstyle of the sun god on the Assyrian stele in the Louvre where he can be seen dictating his laws to Hammurabi. And, please note that these spirals were in the shape of a cone.

The Asian snail *Ariophanta* is, in fact, nothing more than a common snail with a cone shaped shell. But, where does the French word *escargot* (*helix* in Latin) come from? Littré derives it from *escarguète*, which in Old French meant a 'watch tower'. The relationship is fairly obvious because the eyes of the snail are at the end of its horns, which enables it to inspect the horizon freely, *all around*. Actually, it is also quite possible that *escarguète* is derived from *escargot*. But that is not the issue. What is interesting about this story is the connection that our ancestors saw between the creature and the **tower** – especially when we remember that the Aryans were the first to conceive of the art of fortifications and, therefore, of a **watch tower** initially inspired by an architecture of **spirals**.

But that is enough said about *Ariane*. What about *Ariana*?

After a series of fights between *Egyptos* and *Danaos*, it was Danaos who won, as far as the Argolid was concerned. Mythology tells us that from this moment the Danaians supplanted the Pelasgians. By which we should understand that a maritime and pastoral civilisation was succeeded by a more industrialised civilisation.

Perseus was born later as son of a *Danaian*, descended from the kings of the city of Argos. It would, therefore, seem that the clan of the Argolids provided the first dynasty to reign over Persia – that of the Achemaenids. Surely, we know that Achaeans were the same as Aegeans? History confirms the legend since it tells us that the oldest tombs of the kings of this first Persian dynasty reveal very clearly an Egyptian influence in their art. It is also natural to assume that the first annexation of these territories was the fruit of an expedition (or of several expeditions) which had set out from Egypt or Phoenicia.

The second dynasty, that of the Arsacids, began to establish its power in an Eastern province of Persia occupied by the *Parthians*. Historians describe these Parthians as an ancient Scythian people living on the banks of the *Oxus* (a river in Central Asia flowing into the *Aral* Sea); this is a name to remember. On the other hand, *Quintus Curtius* and *Strabo* relate the Parthians to the tribe of the Dacians by the Black Sea. However, J. de Saint-Martin has another story to tell (2). Referring to the Chronicle of Malala, he tells us that Sesostris, on his return march from Syria, chose 16,000 young men, mighty warriors, whom he transported to Persia... and ordered to reside there. These *Scythians* were said to have lived in Persia since that time, and it was supposedly they whom the Persians called Parthians.

There is nothing to be said against this story. Was it not from amongst these Syrian Scythians that at a much later period – just four centuries before our era – the dynasty of the Seleucids would arise and prove to be one of the principal peoples to take over from the Persians? The Seleucids had the *elephant* as their emblem. Where would Canute IV of Denmark, in the 11th Century AD, have hit on the idea of founding the *Order of the Elephant*, showing the enormous animal with a **tower** on his back, if not in tales about distant conquests by his forebears? And, do we not see Seleucus I, on contemporary coins, mounting an elephant with *bull's horns*? Was it not he who founded Antioch which, up to the early days of the Christian Era, would bear the indelible spiritual stamp of the *Occident*?

Be that as it may, it was the Parthians who, under the name of the *Arsacids*, succeeded to the throne of Persia and to the dynasty of the Achaemenids. Where did they get their name from? Very probably from the fact that they were masters of the art of *iron* and *fire*. *Ars* and *art* are, in fact, two equivalent roots, the first of which we find in the word *arsenal* and the second in the word *artillery*. But it should also be noted that *ar*, *ars*, *arsa* and *arsaich* are, in the Celtic languages, words which mean all things *ancient* and belonging to the *primordial* race (3).

J. de Saint-Martin informs us that the *illustrious race* of the Parthians, from whom Basil the Macedonian (later emperor of Byzantium) claimed descent, spent its time on horseback, making war or hunting. They were also called men of *Bahl* or of *bel* – which is very revealing.

The most ancient cities of the Parthians were called *Europa*, *Arsacia*, *Heraclea* and *Artacana*. There is no mistaking it. And it is curious to note in passing that one of the most ancient cities in Wales was called *Arthiaca* (4) and that, in the time of the Byzantine Empire, one of the six dioceses of Thrace was called *Europa*.

The *Medes*, too, were part of Ancient Persia. History tells us that very long ago they lived in *Cimmeria*, one of the Black Sea provinces. As far as we are concerned, and until there is proof to the contrary, we believe that they were descended from the *Maetae* of ancient *Brittia* who had settled in the marsh lands of *Maeotis* by the Black Sea. We believe that from their name was derived the word *metal*, whose etymology is today still uncertain, but about which we do know that the root *met* or *meth* originally had the meaning of 'metamorphosis', a **transformation** which corresponds rather well with the very essence of the metal industry of which the Occidental giants of old had been the first masters. The fact that the Sanskrit root *mithas* is cognate with this group of words does not prove that it is the *mother*, because we have already seen that Dionysos had civilised part of India and, by Dionysos, we mean the people he symbolised.

Med, *meadh* or *meidh* is a root from which a large number of words have been derived in the Celtic languages. *Medd* means 'original movement', 'centre' or 'balance'. It is the root which we also find in *medusa* and in *Mediterranean*. *Med* means 'compact' or 'perfect'. *Meddelig* means 'possessing joy'. *Meddu* means 'possessing power'. *Meadonach* means 'central'. *Meddvl* means 'to think' or 'to reflect' (5). All these terms seem to be derived from *Mait*, one of the Celtic names of *Maia*. *Meddel* in Swedish is 'middle', as is *Mitte* in German. We should also point out that the Egyptian *Isis*, whose original name was *Mait*, has often been shown with a '*set of scales*' in her hands, symbol of '*balance*' and of the '*middle way*' (Also, the Greek Athena?).

The Medes appear in History with the name of *Arii*. Is it pure coincidence that there is an Indian town called *Ariaca*, the equivalent (so we are told by the Abbé Martin) of our French *Arcy*, as in *Arcy-sur-Aube* (6)? As a matter of fact, we think that this name was taken directly from *arc*, but the notion of 'air' or 'arc' was in any case related in the mists of time to the origin of the *Third Age* which marked the triumph of the *divinities of the Air*. There is one fact that should retain our attention: the fact that the Medes and Persians initially worshipped *fire*, and that later the basis for their religion was the principle of dualism, the never-ending struggle between good and evil which is expressed in nature by the opposition between light and darkness, personified by Dionysos, long before Janus and all other gods-with-two-faces.

What is equally worthy of attention is the fact that with the advent of Christianity, the Christians of *Persia*, of *Chaldaea* and of *Syria*, would oppose *Hebrew* Christianity with the full weight of their faith and traditions; and that from the 1st Century AD they would rally round the sect of the *Nestorians*, sworn enemies of Rome and of the Fathers, which would go on to found **its own** churches in *China*, *Tartary* and *India* (7). Their anti-biblical conception of Genesis made them the initiators of what would be called *Gnosis*, and it is generally accepted that Gnosticism took its sources from Egypt, Babylonia, Iran and even India.

Is it not troubling to note that, in continuation of the tradition, it was the **heirs** of these peoples' **ancestors** who, in Europe also, would wage the longest war against Rome in the name of *true* Christianity – until the explosion of Protestantism which would regroup its forces in Geneva beneath the eloquent banner *post tenebras lux* (light after the darkness)?

Ariadne's thread is a long one, and History unwinds it imperturbably.

* * *

19

THE WIND OF HISTORY

As far as Europe and Asia are concerned, the Wind of History – contrary to what is generally believed – started blowing from the West. Or, to be more precise, from the North-West. This first wind (Fr. *vent*), the wind *par excellence*, was the Nordic *van*; the Breton *foen*; the Saxon *fawn*; the Old German *wanna*. Today the French speak of *vent norrois*, since the oldest Scandinavian language (which is closely related to the Celtic languages) is in fact the *langue norroise*: the Norwegian language.

The relationship between the *West* and the *Wind* has always been so self-evident that in Breton *wind* is generally called *aouel*, and the *West* (Occident) is called *heol*, a word related in its turn to the Greek *Eole* (1). Incidentally, Aeolus was god of the winds. The Aeolians were a major Greek tribe of Central Greece. 'Aeolian harp', also called the **wind harp**, was an open box with strings stretched over it that would sound 'when the wind passed over them' (1).

The *Vanir* of Nordic mythology attributed so much importance to the wind – this wind with which they identified themselves – that, when *Thor* was questioning *Allvis* to find out "what the sky which we see over our heads is called in each of the different worlds", the dwarf replied: It is called **sky** by men; **shining vault** by the gods. The **Vanir** call it **generator of the wind**. And when Thor asks him what name is given to the clouds, the dwarf replies that the *Vanir* call them the *toys of the wind*.

Van was the word used primarily to describe the *wind* (*vent* in French was written *vant* in Old French), and by extension, the men who sailed before the wind, following the example of their great ancestor *Vainamoinen*, which means 'Lord of the Wind'. The oldest word in Finnish meaning 'boat' or 'canoe' is *vene*. In English, the other name for a weathercock, turning in the winds, is a weather *vane*. And it is worth recording that, up to the end of the Middle Ages, only *lords* had the right to have a weather *vane* on the roof, which is a clear indication of the importance they attached to this object. In Swedish, *vanster* means 'to the left', since the notions of *west* and *left* had formerly become synonymous. Moreover, because the wind was supposed to be rise up out of the earth's belly (Fr. ventre), or from a great cauldron or hole in the earth, *van* took on the second meaning of 'hollow'; hence our word 'vanity' and 'vain' – something that can be carried off by the wind.

The *van*, as we have seen, has given its name to the peoples of Norwegian origin. The first to have it were the *Vanir* who would in time become Scandinavian divinities before becoming the Finns themselves whose country (the ancient *Fenland*) without any doubt owes its appellation to the fact that the Vanir settled there – unless it was because this country abounds in *pools of water*. From *Van* the French also derive the *Vindes* of Hungary, the *Vanes* or *Vaniques* of Armenia, the *Vénètes* or *Enètes* (or even *Oenètes*, according to Polybius and Procopius) who populated the Baltic, Illyria, the Adriatic and Brittany. *Vannes* which came to be called *Venetia* (2), was the capital of the latter area, and Douarnenez was called *Vindana Portus*. Vannes was the last city in Western Gaul to defy Caesar, who had to attack it by sea with a considerable fleet which found it difficult to overcome the Breton *Vénétie* [*Veneti*]. We know that the latter city had absorbed part of Finistere where there is still a *Van* headland.

In the Valhalla of the Icelandic Edda, the Aesir and the Vanir were two categories of divinities which were allied but distinct (once again the word 'divinities' refers to sacred ancestors). It seems clear that the Vanir, whose wisdom was renowned, had preceded the Aesir in the evolutionary order. This is confirmed by all relevant mythologies. No doubt they represented the inhabitants of some Atlantic "island" stretching (perhaps, very much earlier, in a single block) from *Ireland* to *Greenland*. This would, in fact, have situated them North West of the Scandinavians as we now know them.

The Vanir were conquered by the Aesir, but they rebelled. Relying on their rights of primogeniture, they demanded that the same respect should be shown to them as to the Aesir. Moreover, the legends seem to imply that some talk of gold also entered into the question of priority. Perhaps a ransom was paid. However that may be, even if the Vanir were finally admitted to the company of the "divinities", they were still very much minor divinities compared to the Aesir. In the hierarchy of the gods, they sat lower than the newcomers.

Could the *Vanaheim* logically be placed higher? Everything in the minds of the Ancients was subordinated to concrete observation, even when this led to an abstraction. The *Vanir* were seen as part of the First Dynasty which had emerged from the entrails of the earth, propelled by a life-giving "steam vent", or else by the steam of hot geysers –

according to the Icelandic Edda. Their place was, therefore, definitely *at ground level*. It is possible that the rite of the sauna, practised in the ancient *Fenland* (which certainly seems to have been colonised right from the start of its history by the Vanir from the West) is based on this old cosmogonic myth – no doubt just like the *Scottish douche* (a kind of sauna in which heat alternates with cold).

Iceland has always been the *country of winds*, and to such an extent that its climate is said to regulate that of Europe. Furthermore, its legends make references to a certain *Wind Captain* who exercises total control over the gusts of wind in the atmosphere.

Having fought each other to a standstill (the *Kalevala* is a long recital of struggle between the two clans), the *Vanir* and the *Aesir* finally agreed to join together in the conquest of other peoples. *Freya with the blond locks*, surnamed *Vanadis* because she wandered like the *Vans*, whither the wind and the waves took her (the name *Venus* would later be derived from this epithet), had to suffer reproaches for having *culpable relations* with the Aesir – although this did in fact constitute the best basis for a really rock-solid fraternity (for which indeed she was destined by her name *Freya**, since it enabled her to personify that love that generates life). Thus did the real Scandinavians and the Celts of the North Atlantic mingle together, and thus – by *spitting* together into the *van* (bowl) – did they create the superior man of whom the *Hellad* has preserved a memory in the legend of Dionysos. (*Freya: Ger. *Freien*, Dutch *vrijen*, both meaning to *court* or to *make love*).

Like all powerful primitive words, *Van* had many meanings derived one from the other. From 'hollow' in general, they moved on to the 'sacred basket', to the 'mystic bowl' and from there to the 'mystic sieve', whose sign is found in the Egyptian alphabet. This sieve (*tamis* in French, *tamma* in Celtic and *tammhi* in Walloon) is the father of the tambourin or of the *Basque tambour* used at bacchanalia dedicated to Dionysos – and perhaps (who knows?), also of the African tom-tom.

The *Creux du Van* (hollow bowl) in the Jura is an ancient religious site.

The ancient town of *Van* in Asian Turkey has become *Artemita*, and this is the moment to recall that Artemis, who has in her time been the Great Divinity of the *Pontus*, was often shown with a hollow basket (or bowl) in the middle of her chest. At this time, the idea of fertilising water by fire (from heaven) was a very great myth. We know it originated in the Nordic countries.

"It is with the help of Scandinavian mythology", writes Georges Dumézil, "with India providing only a distant reflection, that similarities will appear in a way that we think are striking, and which are difficult to understand unless we postulate the survival of a *corresponding* patrimony of legends" (4).

We have already exposed some of these similarities. One of the strangest is still an unravelled secret. It is the one which unites in a straight line the Swedish *Lake Van* (*Vanern* in Swedish) with the Asian *Lake Van* and which shows *Armenia* to have been a sister of *Armorica*. '*Armorican peoples*' was, for a long time, the name given to the inhabitants of the '*Atlantic coast*' from the north to the south.

Today, the Armenians are a widely dispersed people but, like the Jews, they have remained astonishingly faithful to their ancestors and to the virtues of their race.

In the days of *Great Armenia*, the country that bore this name stretched to the Southern side of the Caucasus and as far as the Euphrates and the Caspian Sea. The relief on a map shows a series of mountain ridges, dissected by deep gorges. The dominating feature was a high plain called *Harcq* (*Arc*), a word which in this people's legends had the sacred meaning of 'ancestor' – which need not surprise us.

The country was fertile and the rivers abundant. Armenia was famous for the great quantity of its cattle; for its buffalo, its gazelles, its *domestic* and its *wild* asses.

Its inhabitants, about whom the great dictionaries tell us that many of them (like the Thracians) had *red hair and blue eyes* (quite common in this part of the world), were often called *Vanes* or *Vanics* because they had first lived around a lake of this name – *Lake Van*, in the North of the country.

Lying across busy routes, Armenia was naturally no stranger to wars and was continually dominated by one people or another. But as is stated in the *Great Encyclopedia*, although 'Hebrew' origins have been attributed to this people, "it certainly does seem as if Armenia was originally Celtic".

All the evidence points in this direction.

To start with, there is the name. Since *Armenia* is often spelt *Erminia*, it is generally thought that the name of this province is derived from that of the *ermine*. One name is obviously as good as another: for example, *Arminius* was given a Gothic flavour from which was derived the German *Hermann*. On the other hand, it is also obvious that in Armenia the *ermine* has been bred with particular care:

doubtless for commercial purposes after a certain lapse of time, but certainly for *ritual* or *sacred* purposes in earlier days. It was also called the *Pontus rat*, which tells us what route it took. For it is indeed curious that this animal, native to the Nordic countries, should have emigrated to Persia and Armenia, whereas it is found nowhere else on the same latitude. We think that it was *taken* there and acclimatised.

By whom was it taken and bred? Most certainly by the people of Pontus. But isn't it curious that these Oriental *Vanes* and *Vanics* (the *Armenians*) should have shown such veneration for the *ermine* – which can not only frequently be seen on the escutcheons of ancient *Armorica* (*Brittany*), dominated at the time by the Western *Venetes* – but also on those of *Ostrobonia*, in Finland? Let us not forget that before the Roman conquest, Vannes in Morbihan was called *Dariorig* (5), which means the **Kingdom of Darius**; or of **King Darius**; or again, of the **Kingdom of the Sea** – not forgetting that the word *sea* is translated by modern Iranians as *Daria*. But this last example is probably only a derivation, since King Darius was a scion of the *Achaemenids*, that is, of the Dynasty of the *Ocean.* (Incidentally: *rig* could be cognate with German *Reich*, Dutch *rijk*, etc. Translator).

What then could be the symbolic value of this animal, from whose skin the bag was made from which Vainamoinen took the seven essential grains which he sowed in the earth? What else, in the minds of those whom we are talking about, could the striking contrast between *white* and *black* in his coat mean but the principle of *dualism* on which the *harmony* of their world rested? To this can be added that the ermine makes his burrow *in circles*; that he hibernates (as does the sun) behind the White Mountain; that the animal is *nocturnal*, and finally (be it said to his very great shame), that he is rather *bloodthirsty*.

The principle of dualism of which this animal was the incarnation and which was at the basis of **Gnosis**, the inveterate opponent of **Paul's** Christianity (6), was surely the very essence of the religions of Western Asia (Persia, Chaldea or Assyria), colonised and civilised by the people of the North Atlantic, who were the first to base their whole world system on the opposition of forces? In this connection one may well wonder whether *Harmonia*, daughter of the War God *Ares* (whose palaces stood on the Eastern shore of the Black Sea) and who later became the wife of Cadmos, did not have some kind of connection with the *Herminie* in question? We believe this because (with her husband on the one hand and her father on the other) she too was the incarnation of the marriage between *brute* force and *spiritual* force, between *matter* and *spirit*.

There is another characteristic of the Celto-Nordic *Vans* which reminds us of the most ancient Armenia. Although all documents relative to this kingdom have been completely destroyed, the humble *Armenian paper* has survived to this day. It was made from paper, infused with *incense* – the incense that in old legends was guarded by *dragons*. Is this not another hint that in the very earliest days our people from the North Atlantic had colonised the earth? *

We can cheerfully pursue our inquiry further and, since the investigation with which we are here concerned takes us back to the very origins of the Indo-European languages, we can try and grasp what was the first source of the terms *harmony* and *herminie*.

To do this, what better way could there be than to take a look at the name of the first king of Ancient Armenia: was he a legendary king or a historical figure? It doesn't matter. This king was called *Aram. Aram*, in the Celtic language, means *brass* or *bronze*. In a figurative sense the word meant 'hard'. In Latin, *aeramen* was used to describe a *bronze* object.

Legend tells us that a wall of *brass* (or of *aram*) surrounded the Kingdom of Hades at the bottom of the Atlantic Ocean – as in Caucasian Tartary. We also know that the palace of *Ares*, like all the palaces of the time and all the great cities in this part of Western Asia, has left us a memory of its *bronze* gates. Now, it was the people of Pontus – and we know who they were – whose exclusive prerogative it was to exploit the *copper* and *tin* mines. Thus, the name *Armenia*, which is certainly cognate with *ermine**, could nevertheless have started off originally as a derivation of *aram* or a distortion of *aeramen*, meaning *all in bronze* (or something similar) or even *the country of the king of brass*. And why should one of the successors of the famed *divine smiths* not, in turn, have adopted the surname 'man of brass', or *Aram*? Did not, many millennia later, Joseph Djougachvili choose to call himself *Stalin, man of steel*, or *hard man*? This coincidence is even more delicious when we call to mind that the Celtic word for brass which, applied to copper, gives us bronze, was *stan* (very close to *stal* or *steel*) and that by transposition of the two initial letters, *stan* would become *Satan* (7). (What a symbol of the Anti-Christ!) Another coincidence is that *the language of the Ancient Armenians was related to that of the Georgians* (Stalin was a Georgian) (8).

Taking into account the inner meaning of words at the time in question, who else could have had the name of *Aram* if not someone belonging to the race of the *Ases* or *Aesir*, the more so since Ernout and Meillet in their *Etymological Dictionary of the Latin Language* assimilate the roots *aer* and *aes* to each other, from which we get both English *iron* and German *Eisen* (iron). Incidentally, this etymological point confirms that the Nordic *Aesir* definitely did correspond to the *Dynasty of the Air* in Greek mythology while at the same time corresponding with what the archeologists call the *Bronze Age* and the *Iron Age*.

How else can we explain that the *Aramaean* language, which developed out of the Antique *Syriac* and Antique *Chaldean*, should have been the mother tongue of the great gnostic illuminati, even though they usually wrote in Greek? And at the same time, what was *Armenicism* if it was not a new *Pelasgianism*?

Ermine also has a few other things to teach us. It explains why *Breton* nobility (i.e. *Armorican*) has remained synonymous with *most ancient* nobility.

The words *arme* and *armée* ('weapon' and 'army') entered the French language very late. The chroniclers of the Crusades never used any other word but *ost* (host) when speaking of an army. In Gaelic, *arm* not only meant *bras* (in French) but also *weapon* and, furthermore, *exploit* or *achievement* (10). An *armum* was a hero; *ermin* in the same language meant both 'Armenian' and 'man at arms'. *Armant* was an armed man, *armal* was a young ox and *armelin* was *hermine*.

Lacurne, on the subject of the ermine, quotes the following texts: "Dappled *ermines* and black *jennies* (a small saddle horse or donkey) could only be owned by ladies of the blood royal". And also: "Ermine and sable were only for the *knight*". And again: "A horse naturally *ermined* with its *sable*." The same dictionary tells us that in Lombardy "the tails of the ermine were replaced by small pieces of Lombardy lamb which are shiny black in colour".

All this proves, in the first place, that our idea of a *white ermine* as symbol is totally artificial and only dates from the Christian era. Throughout Antiquity – and for a very long time afterwards – ermine got its symbolic value from a distinct *clash* of the two colours which characterised it. Moreover, *ermined* never meant *white* but dappled *black on white*.

Secondly, these texts prove that there was a connection between ermine and the notion of chivalry-by-birth, from which we are entitled to infer that ermine was an original element of what we classify as heraldry. Since *arm*, as we have seen above, meant both *hero* and *circle* (because the man-at-arms uses his *arm* and because it is his *arm* that *embraces* or *encircles*), we need not be surprised that *rings* are amongst the most ancient pieces of armour. And the *arm* itself, for that matter – especially amongst the Bretons. Because another connection now comes to mind: *Breiz*, the Breton word for Brittany, also meant 'arm' and this word stands in the same relationship to *bronze* as *arm* does to *aram*. Incidentally, the ancient region for forges or smithies in Brittany was called *Arée*.

How can the connection between Armenia and heraldic art be explained except in terms of etymology?

We know that one of the prime objectives of the Crusades (the aims which are pursued in a war are seldom those which are admitted) was to annihilate the Christians of Constantinople and of Asia Minor – the opponents, as we have seen, of Paul's church in Rome. Certain knights (and we can guess which ones) were hostile to this enterprise or, at least, to this part of the enterprise. Another group followed the orders of the Pope and, having destroyed Constantinople, took it upon themselves to destroy Armenia. The Armenian victims took refuge in Cilicia, a province allied to Ancient Phrygia and, like Phrygia, also of Pelasgian origin. Here they established *Little Armenia*. There were already many Gauls who, three centuries before our era, had invaded this area and settled in Cilicia. They were now joined by Crusaders from the West, who naturally joined forces with the Armenian colony.

Was it there, in this region and as a result of this event, that the use of coats-of-arms was adopted, whose chief aim was to distinguish from the others those knights *who had inherited* the true, ancestral Christianity and who would be stigmatised by the pope with a pun on the word *heretics*? It cannot be doubted that a few first steps were taken at the time to regularise family coats-of-arms. However, there is every reason to believe that, above and beyond clan totems and rallying signs that had existed since time immemorial, there were also personal badges of honour that had likewise existed since time immemorial, at least in this part of Asia. Herodotus notes during his voyages that *each Babylonian always carries with him a personal seal and an engraved baton*. A rose, lily or apple, etc. is carved on it, for everyone in Babylon owes it to himself to have his own distinguishing badge (11).

This confirms that, since the most ancient days, [there] had been a very definite wish in the minds of the heirs of the Pelasgians not to break the thread of Ariadne which attached them to the Aryan race.

This origin of the coats-of-arms explains why the first examples were made of *fur* before they later came to be made with *enamel*. The "talking" furs were used to decorate one's tent or one's shield. Perhaps the cult of the '*hair*', introduced via Pelasgia, had something to do with this custom. We read in the *Grand Larousse Illustré*: "The people of Babylon seem to have been the first to invent these kinds of diversified, mottled furs. Zonase tells us that Sapor, King of Persia, who was a contemporary of Constantine, had ordered for his son a superb tent from Babylon, made of the skins of animals that come from that country."

The fact that, with regard to the ermine, the idea of birth and of a certain religious attitude dominated the symbolic meaning, is evidenced by the very drawing of the animal's tail; one is reminded more of the *fleur de lys* ('lily' or 'lotus', symbol of birth) than of the tail of the *Pontus rat* or of the *cross*, as some people have claimed.

One more word about heraldry before abandoning the subject. When, after furs, people started using enamels, the favourite colour was *red* – as in the ancient Irish enamels. In heraldry, this colour which is *red-with-the-colour-of-an-ox-blood*, is called *gules* (*gueules* in French). Not, or at least not initially, as a description of the inside of an animal's mouth (*gueule*), but because *gu* referred in Sumerian to the 'male bovid'; because *gyul* had the same meaning in India (where it is also spelt *gyal*); and because it was also the source of the Persian *gul* which determined the colour of the animal's sacred blood and which was very probably similar to the even older Icelandic *gull*. Then, at the same time, it became associated with a flower of the same colour: the rose, corresponding to the *ross* in Old French.

But, initially, we would not have been looking at the rose which we know today. It would have been the *flower of blood* (blood-red) or *flower of love* with five petals, which in Egypt is still called *rose de Noël*, a very significant name. Its Asian equivalent was the *carnation* (*oeillet* in French) of the same colour, at present known as *arménie* or *armoire*, a kind of wild stock flower with five petals which has on occasion been confused with it.

This Asian stock flower was one whose *clou matrice* or *clou de girofle* ("womb") was filled with seeds which, of course, enhanced its symbolic value. With reference to this flower, Littré mentions a quote from Lacurne which should make us think, "You are the flower of the Danes, you were stocks and lilies for all high-born knights." Elsewhere, Lacurne quotes a text from Menage: "If it were true that the flower called *armoirie* had been transported from Great Britain to Britain-called-Armorica, this would not necessarily make it more probable that Armorica had been, as was suggested, the origin of this title."

The clouds are beginning to clear. To understand History, "there is basically only one subject for study, namely the forms and metamorphoses of the spirit" (13).

On Western coats-of-arms, the rose will seldom appear other than with *five* petals, like the ancient rose. The other flowers, which also have only five petals but of a different colour from red, will be identified in general with the name *quinte feuilles* (*cinqfoil*). Need we be surprised to learn that, during the wars of religion, the faithful of Greek-Christian persuasion often replaced the personal details on their escutcheons with the rose or with one or other *cinqfoil* which served as their profession of faith? Need we be surprised to see it on the seal of the *Rosicrucians* where the cross of St. John (the Celtic Cross) appears – two symbols which we also find in the coat-of-arms of Martin Luther?

The second heraldic colour – although some people give it the first place – is 'azure'.

Azur, *Asur* or *Azul* is the equivalent of **Air**. This word – like 'Asia' and like *Azania* (which has sometimes been used for Persia (14)) – is cognate with the Scandinavian *Aesir*, divinities of the regions of the **Air** who one day defeated the "red race" of the giants. We read in the *Kalevala* that *Vainamoinen* says to the giant *Joukahainen*: "Yes, it is I, Third, who have helped fix the gates of the Air, to place the vaults of the sky, to sow the stars in space …"

It is for this reason that the stone called *lapis lazuli* was once – in Chaldea, Persia and Armenia – thought to be the precious stone *par excellence*. It was from this *azure stone* that the eyes for the statues of the gods were carved to remind people of the eye of the Nordics and of the Scythians. Reduced to powder, this stone gave us *ultramarine, a colour which resists the passage of time*. It was the colour of the French flag – before it was recently changed. (NB: We may be mistaken, but we suspect that the authoress – when referring to the "recent" replacement of the beautiful old *fleur de lys,* emblem of the French monarchy, by the *Tricolor* of the *Révolution* – meant exactly what she wrote. When one is dealing, like Mme. Talbot, in *aeons* of time, the passage of a mere two hundred years can hardly even merit the term "recent": perhaps the *blink of an eye* would be more appropriate? *Translator*)

The astonishing thing about the *blue eye* is that we can read from the pen of a contemporary Finn, describing his country: "… when the land hollows had filled up with water, the lakes made their appearance and endowed Finland with myriads of *blue eyes*, famous throughout the world" (15).

This is a banal image, people will say. Banal? Certainly – for men of the 20th Century, but **striking** for anyone who understands the ancient value of words and symbols. Such a person knows, for example, that the *eye* represented for Pagans the genital hollow (*hile, cal* or *van*) where all life was born and where *life itself* was born, according to the Finnish *genesis*. This blue that was the colour of the *Venetes* confirms for us that the name of Finland (*Fenland*) does indeed mean the land of the *Venes* or *Vanes* and also the land of the *vans*, meaning land with 'hollows full of water' – i.e. '*lakes*'. Should we not group the Finns together with the *Vanics* of Armenia, the *Venetes* of the Adriatic and the *Vennes* of the Ancient Atlantic Celts? And, besides the *cinqfoil* which appears in Finnish coats-of-arms, does one province of this nation, *Ostrobonia*, not display six ermines on its escutcheon? These ermines – *raha* in Finnish (a generic term) and *Pontus rats*, according to Herodotus – *make a pair* with the *Scythian bow* (yes, also from Pontus, originally!) which adorns the coats-of-arms in the province of Savo.

* * *

Translator's notes: P.184

*Paper infused with Incence. I am uncertain about this translation. In Chambers Encyclopedia it is stated that *incence* has a "Resinous base, such as gum olibanum, benzoin, storax and powdered cascarilla-bark". So I am merely making a suggestion. P.184

*Incidentally, the *Readers' Digest* Dictionary tells us that the valuable fur of the ermine is used in England for the robes of peers or judges, and that the expression 'to take the ermine' means to assume the office or dignity of a judge or peer.

20

THE STRAW AND THE BEAM

In the year of grace 1045, *mounted on their sea dragons*, the Normans sailed up the Seine until they reached Paris. And what trophies did their leader take back with glory to Denmark? *A beam from the convent of Saint-Germain des Prés and a nail chosen at random among those on the great gates of the city* (1). We shall speak later once more about the *nail*. Just as in the case of the *beam*, the removal of the nail was a deliberate choice. But let us first look at the beam, one of the sacred emblems of the men of the North.

The *beam* (translated in Old French by the words *sommier* or *sumer*, *soumi* in Walloon and *sagmaricus* in Latin) was, of course, a symbol that was dear to the Sumerian peoples. By *Sumerian peoples* we mean, not only those of Mesopotamia (no one knows why this name should have been given exclusively to this area), but also those of the Black Sea (Thracians and Scythians) and above all those who were the fathers of all; the people *en-sus-de-la-mer* (*above* the sea), at the *summit* of the earth – the people of the *North*.

As far as we are concerned, there can be no question that the Sumerians of Mesopotamia were a colony of the Great Power established on the shores of the Black Sea. Indeed, most historians are agreed on this point. If the language of the former is related to *Ancient Turkish*, as has been established, this need not surprise us. The inhabitants of the Black Sea shores are frequently called *Cimerians* or *Cumerians*. Expressions such as *cimerian caverns, cimerian darkness* and *cimerian Bosphorus* took root from the fact that the authentic *Cimeria* was situated partly in Tartarus and also beyond in that area where the *lands of sleep* and of *the night* lay, in other words, in the regions of the North-West Atlantic (NB: *chimaera* in Greek means *deep-sea* fish).

Homer calls the Pelasgians *Cumerians* (2). There can be no mistake here because we read elsewhere in the *Odyssey*, regarding Ulysses' visit to Proserpina: "For a whole day, the ship sails at full speed, the sun disappears, the shadows obscure all routes and we reach the opposite shore of the Ocean of *great depth*. That is where the city of the *Cumerians* stands" (certain authors translate the name as *Cimerians*).

Elsewhere, in the *Primitive Antiquities of Norway*, we read: "There is every reason to believe that the Cumerians were also Celts, because Posidonius, Strabo, Diodorus of Sicily, Plutarch and Etienne of Byzantium all agree that the *Cumerians* were identical with the *Cimbri*. But the *Cimbri* are called *Celts* by Appian, *Celto-Scythians* by Plutarch, *Galates* by Diodorus of Sicily and, finally, *Gauls* by Cicero".

There is nothing here to surprise us. The root *sum* that we find in *sumerian* (as in Latin *summum*) means *superior* or *higher*, both literally and figuratively speaking. Thus, by extension, or rather symbolically, the word *sumer* has come to mean 'foundation stone' or 'main beam', according to the type of materials used.

The root *sum* is directly equivalent to the *sum* in English *summit* and to the *som* in French *sommet*, to the root *cim* in French *cime* or *cimier* (tree-top or crest of helmet) and, finally, to the root *culm* in Latin *culmen*, synonymous with *summum* in the same language (NB: also, *culminer* in French and *culminate* in English).

It is at this point that we see a coming-together of the *beam* and the *straw*. *Culmus*, or *calame*, seems, for the descendants of the *Southern* Pelasgians, to have symbolised the idea of *high birth*. It was they who had, amongst other countries, civilised Egypt, where the *calame* or *reed* certainly did have this symbolic value. The *sommier* or *soumi* (beam) do in their turn seem to have symbolised the same idea for the descendants of the *Pontus* Pelasgians who, of course, needed to distinguish themselves from the others with whom they fought endless wars to achieve supremacy of power in Western Asia. In heraldry this *beam* tops one of the two pillars of the *Hellespont* which is one of the emblems on the Austrian coat-of-arms.

But why the beam in the eye (Fr. *oeil*)? Why the straw (or *calame*) in the *oeil*? That is where the real history of the **O** begins. We now know – at least since the beginning of this book – what the symbol of the eye was in Antiquity (*oeil*, *hile* or **cal**). It was like that of the *van* (the *productive cavity* or, more poetically, the *well of love)* which heraldry experts now call the *disc of life*. It is this interpretation of the word *oeil* which leads us to call a buttonhole *oeil* in French and it is also the reason why the French say *oeillet* (little eye) for the hole through which one inserts a shoelace or the crosspiece of a brooch. The Celts symbolised the eye with the letter **O** for *oeil*, a round **O** which naturally had a sacred character for them since it symbolised *life* or the *miracle of love*. This letter corresponds on the one hand with the Greek *phi* (French **f**), which comes from the Ionian alphabet.

Now it so happens that the root *phi* also has within itself an idea of *love, friendship* or *attraction*. So how is the letter *phi* written? The small letter is an **O** crossed by a straw, while the capital letter is an **O** crossed by a thick beam. As if by chance, the same letter is found in the *Danish* alphabet, where it corresponds with *o* or *oe* in the *Swedish* alphabet.

The *Celtic* **O** seems, however, to correspond with the *omicron*, **O** (no story attached) of the *Greek* alphabet, which – when it is joined with an *adjective* – gives it the value of a *noun*. Did this not probably happen with the Celtic **O** as well, whenever it came before an *adjective* – by which process it turned the adjective into a *noun* and even into a *proper noun*, as in the case of *O'Brien*? Did it not perhaps in this case play the part of a *definite article*, like that of the Greek omicron and like that of the Breton *le* (as in the case of *Le Minou*), after which it gradually took on the quality of a *particle* indicating *provenance by birth*?

Strange to relate, but there may initially have been a similar process involved with the Dutch *van* and, consequently, the German *von*, both meaning 'of' – bearing in mind that *van* (bowl) or *tamis* (sieve) was represented by the Ancient Egyptians with a *circle* or an **O**, and that in Gaelic the word *van* could mean, together with many other things, *origin* or *beginning*.

It is also worth noting that in Latin manuscripts the word *ille* (which has the same history) is often indicated with a simple *oblique line* just like the Breton word *ker*, which has a similar meaning.

So, whereas the *straw* in the *oeil* was an indication of birth throughout the *Mediterranean basin*, the *beam* had the same value in the region of the *Hellespont*. It is very possible that the first-named peoples were more especially Celtic, whereas the second group was more especially Scandinavian, although in the early days there must have been a fairly constant mixture of the two races.

And there is another interesting point. In the Latin word for *beam*, *sagmaricus*, we find the root *sag* or *zag* which we also find in the Nordic word *saga*: the latter word means, as well as 'tradition', anything to do with *race history*. So that *saga* is in effect an epic tale of the (family) *Zag* or *Sag*, just as the *Illiad* is an epic tale of *Illus* and his descendants.

Incidentally, anything to do with, or concerning, *Thrace* was translated in Latin by *travus*. The beam or crosspiece was, therefore, made-to-measure as an emblem of this people: not only because its place on the "portico" of the Hellespont was *higher* in a *geographical* sense, indicating the regions whence this people had *come down*, but also because it *supported the whole edifice* – the civilisation of the Hellespont with its two pillars, one European and one Asian. Finally, we must point out what might seem obvious: that a place of *passage* is **traversed** – which perfectly symbolises the geographic position of the Thracians.

But where do we find, in the very first ages, the idea of a sacred *beam* if not in the Kalevala? We read: "Here, at the far end of this iron bench, this pine plank, this famous beam ..." (4). On all archaic depictions of Northern boats, the bench or crosspiece made of pine *will always be seen*, no matter from what perspective, because it is of the greatest importance. We are also tempted to wonder if the *half-timbering* of houses built by the Old Normans was not primarily an act of hommage to the sacred cross-pieces from the first stirrings of their history? (The word *half*-timbering in French is cognate with *column*, *beam* or *post*: **colombage.**) In Finland, the glory of the house depends on the *age* of the **beam** – just as the glory of Breton churches depends on their **glory beam**.

Are we now permitted to seek a connection between *Suomi* (the ancient name for Finland) and the words *Suômi* and *sumer*? The word *Suômi* is usually derived from *Suo*, meaning 'marsh'. We know that marshes abound in Finland: but without necessarily rejecting this etymology, we feel that it would not be **too** presumptuous to connect *suômi* to *sommet* and to *Sumerian*. We should not forget that men's vocabularies were formerly *very restricted* and that, by the association of different ideas, *various concepts* could have been attached to the *same root*.

Thus, by a meandering path whose various twists and turns it was useful to follow, we arrive at the Sumerians who founded a very great empire in Mesopotamia.

The ancient kings in the valley of the Tigris gave themselves the title of Kings of *Sumer and Akkad*. This gave historians the idea of adopting the two names to describe the pre-Chaldean or Babylonian stage of the civilisation. Let us not quarrel with this initiative.

Everything does seem to confirm that *the Sumerians played the most important role in originating and moulding the Babylonian*

Empire (5). We know that *Akkad* (or *Accad*) corresponds to *Agad*, that is, to *Aegean*. The Aegeans, in the sea that bears their name, took over from the Pelasgians. That they also played a part in Lower Asia is confirmed by the discovery of helmets of a purely Aegean design in the exploratory diggings around ancient *Akkad* or *Agade*.

Our modern historians all agree that these Sumero-Accadians *were a people of pioneers, very advanced in the development of agriculture and in the metallurgical industry which had started in the Caucasus* (6). *These people*, we are told by other historians, *spoke a language which was very closely related to Armenian* (7). These same historians tell us that the ancient region of *Sumer* and *Accad* was originally called *Kalam*. Now, that name really does sound Celtic and reinforces our impression that the southern-most part of the country, which is also the most *swampy*, was colonised by the *Aegeans* of Celtic origin, as is proved, moreover, by the *Promontorium Chaldone* at the mouth of the Euphrates.

Certain scholars assert that the true natives of this region were called the *Azanians*. But, since Persia was called *Azania* (8)* and, since the Azanians have also been called *Hari* while the *Parthians* were called *Arii*, we suggest that we should be talking about neighbouring peoples of the same basic extraction who at a given moment in time flooded into this region and were the first to civilize it. Since we do not claim to be writing the *factual* history of Mesopotamia and are merely trying to indicate, with the aid of *names* and *symbols*, the distant origins of the great civilisations which flourished in this region, we shall now mention not only Sumer and Accad but also Assyria and Chaldea.

It was the *Nordic Aesir* who gave their name to *Asia*. The word *Aesir* did not only refer to the Scandinavian divinities but also to a *collection of ancient peoples who were part of the great Scythian family* (*Grande Encyclopédie*). It was from the word describing a *people* that the first-name *Asen* or *Osen* (given to ancient Bulgarian princes) was derived. "In *Sumer-Akkad*," writes Charles Autran, "the letters *As* refer to the man or male, and therefore, comprise the idea of overwhelming power" (9). It is probably this root that survives in our slang. The oldest Irish legends speak of *aes dana* as ancient *heroes-made-gods*.

Assur, the great Mesopotamian god to whom Assyria no doubt owes its name, is related to Persian *azul* and, in India, where Western Asia extended its civilisation, the *Assouras* are the ancient *Titans* (10). The term *Asur* in Gaelic means 'afresh' or 'anew', which fits in perfectly with the concept of the *Third Dynasty*, that of the *Air* or of the *azure* (blue sky). "It is curious," writes Smith in his Dictionary, "that *Scyllax* and *Caryanda* place Assyria among the nations of *Pontus Euxinus* (Black Sea)" (11). But it is not at all curious, unless it is also curious that *Xenophon* should have spoken of *Chaldea of the Pont* and of the *Chaldeans from the north of Lake Van* (12). C.F. Lehman who reports this fact, also says that, in the time of Constantine Porphyrogenetus, *Chaldea*, with its capital *Trebizonde*, was one of the military provinces of the Byzantine Kingdom. Even if we are speaking here about historical times, this link is not unimportant.

Let us say that wherever Chaldeans settled, there was a Chaldea. So can we not say the same about the Celts of Ireland or Scotland, whom the Greeks called *Khaldos* and whose country of origin was *Callde* or (Gaelic) *Callda* (13), i.e., *Caledonia* – where *Deucalion*, the father of mankind, got his name? Certain tribes of this region must have settled in Scandinavia, since Ptolemy mentions the *Chaldoni* as being one of the nations in this area (*Dauciones*, *Levoni* and others) (14). If we then add that the priests of Babylon, who played a most important part in this city, were called *Chaldeern* and that the monks of Scotland were still in the 9th Century AD known as *Kuldern* (15), then we cannot see what possible doubt there could still be about a family relationship so close and so obvious although – just at the time (six centuries before our era) when Athens had triumphed – a man as eminent as Herodotus could be ignorant of the very existence of the British and Scandinavian islands in the North Atlantic!

Whether the Chaldeans ended up by dominating Babylon from the North or from the South is not very important. What is certain is that Pliny calls this city the capital of the Chaldean people (*Chaldaicorum gentium caput*). When Babylon, near its end, was invaded by the Semites, the Chaldeans still provided the "cadres" for the city, i.e., warriors and sages. We read in Smith: "They [the Chaldeans] appear among the magicians, sorcerers and astrologers and speak in the name of the rest. They are described as the King's wise men … The name [of Chaldea] used to be applied without distinction, or at least with little real difference, to the inhabitants of Babylon and to the subjects of the Babylonian Empire … *Nabuchodonosor* is called King of Babylon but his armies are called *Chaldees* … In *Isaia*, Babylon is termed *the glory of kingdoms*, the *beauty of the Chaldean's excellency* … Darius is king over the realm of the Chaldeans" (16).

To tell the truth, there are so many proofs in favour of our thesis that we are surprised that anything so blindingly obvious should not have been noticed long ago. Since we are dealing with a time when every syllable had a mystic meaning and held sway over a group of words with the same authority with which a chieftain dominated his tribe, these philological relationships cannot simply be dismissed as absurd flights of fancy. On the contrary, they go hand in hand with the purest rationality. How could *Sumer* and *Akkad* have been able to live between Persia and Phoenicia without belonging to the same world and, indeed, to the **only** world which in those far distant times knew how to hammer iron and build towers – not only **knew how**, but **loved** to hammer iron and build towers!

Where else could the idea of a *tree of life* and a cult of the sacred cedar have come to these parts, other than from the Celto-Nordic *oak* which, like the cedar, was the most powerful tree in the country?

And the boats, shaped like a *cal* or a *van*, round and deep like our *cauldrons*, are they not copies of the boats used by the Angles and the Scandinavians? And what about identical rafts made of planks caulked with *tar*?

And the laws of Hammurabi, which Moses would one day borrow, were they not also engraved in brass by Minos, a Cretan and Pelasgian?

And *Nebo*, the ancestor-god, the most ancient King of Nineveh, whose name is cognate with Latin *nepos* ('nephew' or 'kinsman'), is he not *heir* of, and joined by an *umbilical cord* to *Illus*, venerated as inventor of all the arts and all the sciences, and as the man who can write, use the *calame*, read destinies and resuscitate the dead? *God of fire, of water and of the horn*: from whom could he have been descended, if not from the Occidentals or from *Neivez naf Neivion*, the sage of Breton legend who saved the race of men after the Deluge (17)?

Is it not related in an old Sumerian legend that Mesopotamia had been *invaded by a sea people*?

And were there not *ten* great kings famed in fable before the Deluge? – ten, like the Atlantan kings?

Do we not see on a stele of *Naram-Sin*, King of *Agade*, an image of the *White Mountain*, the cone of cones, the sacred cone, the cone whose summit is touched by the sun *up there*, far away in the *Hyperborean North*?

Are the **eight** floors of the *zagurat* towers not a sign of homage to the sacred number of the Atlantic Celts?

And where could the sacrificial *bull* have come from, if not from the West? Mesopotamia only had the buffalo.

The great lord of Mesopotamia, the *limus* who gave his name to the years, was he not the brother of our *limes*? And were they not related to the *élymes* of Sicily and *Suzianna*?

If we try and trace the meaning of the word *élyme* to its earliest source, we find that it shares its root *lim* with the French word *limon*, and not only means silt in **French**, but also in ancient Scandinavian and ancient Catalan. And it is because the two Latin words *limus* and *limes* are so very *old*, that they are venerable and powerful.

Moreover, *limes* and *limus* are also cognate with the word *limbus* (**abode** of the dead) and with *lemures* (**spirits** of the dead). As regards **meaning**, *lemures* can be regarded as synonymous with *lares* (**household** gods: cf. Littré).

Finally, it might also be possible to include the Norwegian *lemming* in the above family of names: does it not belong to the Dynasty of the Air, having quite literally "fallen from the sky"? He too is a very important emigrant, and most curious animal that has often been described as an *ermine*.

It is now high time to look even more carefully at other equally eloquent relationships.

* * *

Tranlator's note:

With reference to note 8 p.195, it is thought that *Azania* is possibly derived from Arabic *Zanj* via Latin *Azania*. *Zanj* means dark-skinned African.

21

IN THE MAGPIE'S NEST

The magpie was a quasi-sacred bird for the Scandinavians. This was also true (and for obvious reasons) for the Aegean people whose name was cognate with the magpie's: *agash*. How so? Because in France the *pie-grièche* or Greek magpie was known (in Old French) as *agase* or *agace*.

For a long time the magpie was a symbol of all that was considered praiseworthy and excellent. For example, *être au nid de la pie* (to be in the nest of the magpie) came to mean 'to have achieved the highest honours'. The literal French meaning had nothing to do with this bird's supposedly making its nest in the highest places (which is certainly not true) but because *being in the magpie's nest* was the equivalent of being *born from Jupiter's thigh*.

Littré tells us that people often speak of the magpie and the eagle in the same breath. This could only be because of their shared symbolic character. By opposing black and white in its plumage (in the same way that the ermine's coat does), the magpie was in fact reminding us of the eternal dualism between light and darkness, the principal belief of the Chaldean religion, and also of the Persian. However, this principle did not – as has been said too often – imply an absolute separation between the two forces and the rejection of one in favour of the other. Very much to the contrary, the Gnostics (carrying on in this particular point the Celtic and Nordic tradition) regarded the fusion of contraries to be the primordial law of the world. This view was so convincing that the *revealed religions* which supplanted the *philosophical myths* of High Antiquity were compelled to oppose their god with a *devil*.

It is interesting to note that the French *pie* is translated in English as *mag-pie*, which is the equivalent of Latin *pia mater**, the term for the membrane that envelops the nerve-centres. *It is called **pie-mère** because it gladly envelops the brain just like the happy mother wraps her arms round her son* (1) (* *Pia mater* means *pious*, or *devoted, mother*).

In Gaelic, *mag* means *born of **good stock***. This terminology is very logical and very revealing. For it is possible that the French term *pie-borgne* (one-eyed magpie) is a result of confusion between '*pie-born*' (as symbol of excellent birth) and the ancient race of the *Cyclops* from whom the Aegeans claimed descent. We see this confirmed by the fact that in Low-Breton *borgne* was written *born* (cf. Littré) and that the idea of the "valorous one-eyed warrior" survived over a long period of time, as is shown in the following text of Amyot: "*Amongst the ancient captains, the most warlike and those who did the greatest deeds by ruse and cunning in war, well planned and executed, have been* **one-eyed**, *such as Philippus, Antigonus, Hannibal and Sertorius*" (2).

With regard to the word *borgne*, this has to be an error in the translation or, at least, in its interpretation, due to transition from one civilisation to another. These great captains of History were probably not *borgnes* (one-eyed) but would doubtless have proclaimed that they had been *bien nés* ('well-born' in English) because they were descended from the *first race* of warrior-civilizers. Since the advent of the Christian era, the goal-posts have, as it were, been changed, and to be *borgne* has become a mark of malediction (like the hare-lip, which for the Celts was a good omen), so that the word now has a pejorative sense. * All this is an introduction to the word *Lagash*, an antique city in Mesopotamia, whose name may possibly contain the French **noun** *pie* (*agash*), either because it was the *holy city* (the French **adjective** *pie* also translates the Latin adjective *pius*, while *aga* reminds us of *august* meaning 'majestic') or because it was built by the *Aegeans* – which comes to the same thing! In modern German everything to do with the Aegean world is translated by the word *ägäisch*.

Which were the other cities of Mesopotamia?

Calach. This word needs no explanation. It is the Gaelic *callaich*, meaning 'clay soil', the fertile 'hollow' or 'crescent'; it is *Calais* in our modern French. In Chaldean, the 'hollow' boat was called *kelek*.

Niniveh was dedicated to the great goddess *Nin* or *Nana*; no doubt the equivalent of Egyptian *Neith*, goddess of the forces of the night or of subterranean forces. But where else do we find a goddess *Nin* or *Nana*? We find her in the *Edda* (the sacred legends of Iceland) where it is said that the *goddess Nin or Nana, who was bored with her life on earth, took on the form of a wolf* (3). The *wolf* and the *dog* symbolised in the Celtic universe the empire of *Manala*, that is, the underground Kingdom of Death. We know that dogs were greatly venerated in Armenia and that, at a certain moment, the Persians referred to the Messagetes or Scythians, peoples of the Caspian, as *wolves* and *dogs* (4). The expression '*Christian dogs*', which is no doubt as old as the first Christians of the Asian Church (Armenian or Chaldean), could have originated there.

Ur was the city of the god *Bull. Urus* and *Uri* were the names given in Gallic lands to the wild bull which in the days of Charlemagne was passionately hunted by this prince and his lords and whose horns were brandished as a trophy after he had been killed. The Latin *urus* was certainly the equivalent of the Mesopotamian *uruk*. In the classification of the animal world, *bos urus*, which Fitzinger regards as the descendant of the *aurochs*, is similar to the *boeuf de la Manche** (a *Manche* ox) and, in particular, the *Frisian* (5). When he speaks of *Ur*, the Mesopotamian city, Strabo always specifies: "Ur of the Chaldees". (**Manche* – Department of North West France).

But here the bull is winged, for he is no longer the bull of the Dynasty of the Night but the bull of the Dynasty of the Air. The French word *aile* (wing) is not derived from Latin *ala* but from Celto-Nordic languages. In Danish and in Swedish, 'wing' is *ael*. In Old French we find exactly the same word *ael* – sometimes written *ele*. All these terms are cognate with Celtic *aouel*, meaning 'wind', just as the English word 'wing' (*aile* in French) is cognate with 'wind' (*vent* in French). The expression *aile du vent* (light winged) must be very old. In the Celtic world the *elles* (who in appearance could be sisters of the *elves*) were spirits of the air (NB: *aile du vent* ['light winged'] means literally: *wing of the wind*).

Erech, today called *Tello*, had one of the oldest Western names and one of the most expressive. *Erech*, or *Eric*, had in fact developed from *Oirc*, the Celtic god of the underworld empire from whence they *shot out like a geyser*. *Tello*, who followed *Erech*, is in fact connected to the same myth, that of *Talos* or of the *Talle*, which tells of the "emergence of the sap".*

With the passage of the ages, the same symbol gave birth to several legends which are inter-connected. We know that in Greek Mythology *Erechte*, or *Erechtonios*, was the son (or descendant) of the giant *Hephaistos*. It was he who, with the name *Eleinos*, became the father of the *Hellenes*, by virtue of a mutation of names similar to that which changed *Iris* to *Illythy*. Mythology tells us, moreover, that Erechtonios was half-man and half-serpent. But, have we not found in Assyria gods with the body of a man and a long serpent-like tail, which were a product of the most ancient art in that region? (6) Well now, what men, or what gods, could have laid claim to the serpent's tail other than the heirs of the Celto-Nordic peoples?

So far so good. If we pass on from cities to the Assyrian-Chaldean civlisation in its essence and details, the bonds with Troy, Crete and the Atlantan West stand out black on white. In the course of the millennia during which this high civilisation lasted, power passed from hand to hand. Each dynasty, each people, imposed its own language or dialect and its own pronunciation on its subjects. We know how greatly these things could vary from one province to the next, even in France. What needs to be considered, through so many fluctuations, is what was of lasting and outstanding value in the religion, art, customs and *roots of the most important verbs*.

We should, for example, note that the most ancient cities of Mesopotamia were built, like Troy and the cities of the Delta, in the shape of a sometimes artificial rock, standing for preference on a piece of land subject to deposits of alluvium.* This corresponded with the cult of the sacred Atlantic *Fertile Isle*. It was this same ancient concept which also gave the name *Palud Royale* to the region stretching from the Rhone to Durance. The Parisian *Marais* may too have originally acquired its name from the fact that it was made up of a circle of dwellings for people who had contact with the *Court* and who, for this reason, were **born** (*nés*) and **crested** (*huppés*) like the birds of the **marshes**, venerated in Antiquity. It should not be forgotten that in Nordic mythology the *Egres*, a word from which we derive *aigrette* and all those terms dealing with cultivation of the soil, were the *spirits of agriculture* (7)

We should also note that the city of Babylon, whose structure we know, was surrounded by canals, like *Troy*, *Troezen* of the fabulous Atlantis, and like so many other European cities built on or near water (including Bruges, Amsterdam and Venice) whose circle of canals is part of a very ancient tradition. Have we not heard that *all the ancient sovereigns of this part of the globe* (that of Western Asia) *were great builders of canals* (8), and not just because they wanted to irrigate the desert! Many Assyrian monuments show the gods sailing on boats through reed-filled marshland. That is an important symbol. We see the same thing with the *Frisian marshlands* from which would emerge the Franks, these heirs of the Phrygians and of Western Asia who returned to their ancestral lands when their Asian empire collapsed. And what would be their specific emblem other than the *lily of the marshes*, the *fleur de lys*, ancient symbol of birth and fertility in the silt-covered lands of the deltas, which in Danish are called *Kalmus* or *Calamus*!

What can we say about the *ziggurat*, or *zagurat*, of Babylon and of so many other Mesopotamian cities? It seems that each city had its own, and although we have already referred frequently to the roots *zig* and *zag*, we must do so again.

André Parot reports that Diodorus of Sicily spoke of an old Syrian who had told him that it had been *built by giants who wanted to climb up to Heaven* (8). We feel compelled to accept this story. The idea of gigantic high buildings was indeed a brainchild of the race of the *eye* (*oeil*), that is, the race that had emerged from the Atlantic *island* (*ile*) where the rain-**bow** had touched the earth to engender life there. This race wanted to repeat the miracle, or to be more exact, to erect a symbol of the miracle that was the marvellous beginning of the world. Let us take note of the term climb (*escalader* in French, meaning 'to scale'), regularly used to characterise the desire of men to unite, in another sense, the earth and the sky, a term which, clearly, is derived from the Nordic root *skal*.

What else do we find in excavations undertaken in Mesopotamia that confirms the bond between this region and the ancient *Atlantic block*? We find a great number of objects made of bronze, and enormous gates of the same metal which mark out the walls of the great citadels. Once again, History has no memory of any race of *smiths* who can be compared with those of the *North Atlantic* and of *Tauric Chersonese*, mothers of the giant Prometheus and of the giant Hephaistos. The Icelandic Edda emphasizes that the *Aesir had smiths and hammered out gold.*

Bronze objects found in Assyria are in their great majority *drinking horns* (shades of the gods of Walhalla and of Dionysos who passed that way!) or little *cones* often held by the gods and by *Illu* in particular. It is to the *cone*, *cal*, *hile* or *ille* in this part of the world that *Illu* owes his name. We are told that his name is synonymous with joy and especially with *sexual* joy. *Pardi! By Jove!* (By God!) *Cal*, in Celtic languages, was a symbol for the penis – just like *cone* and its equivalent *gal*. We have said before that each word in very ancient times meant *one* thing and also its **opposite**. A *galoise*, in Old French, was still a '**lady-love**', and are *marie-galantes* not *filles de joie* (*girls-for-joy*)? The word 'hilarity', in its most original meaning, was directly connected with *Illu*.

In Mesopotamia, as in Persia, the statues of the gods have blue eyes made from lapis-lazuli. We find in this same country little leaves of *willow* and *ash* made of precious metal. The willow is the willow of the marshes, the one shaped by *Esus* in Gaul, and the ash is the ash sacred to Celts and Nordics – the ash, *eternally green*, called *Yggdrasel* in the Edda of Saemund the Wise, under whose crown of foliage the three virgins kept constant watch.

Finally, we often meet (amidst other ornamental motifs) what is in our opinion wrongly interpreted as *crescent moons*. We think that this crescent represents the *van* or 'sacred basket' whose symbolic value we already know. In Western coats-of-arms in which this symbol would be maintained (as in the arms of Calais), and even in Greek painting, we can see quite clearly that this is no star or planet but a *basket*. It is a symbolic receptacle because this crescent lies *horizontal* and is very often marked with two strokes inside, which would be totally out of place if we were dealing here with the *night star* and not with a piece of *basket work*. This basket, in which the gods would be *ritually placed at birth*, could quite naturally be confused in time with the moon in as much as the moon represented the **opposite** of the male principle, which was in turn represented in the sky by the sun. And, of course, the recurring crescent shape of the moon would also play its part in this confusion. The old myths would lose their meaning with the passage of centuries but the moon would prevail – if only because it was still there!

In Assyrian tombs the dead are buried making a drinking gesture – another very Western custom. In the eyes of the Semites, the Aryan Indo-European is always seen as the man who drinks and intoxicates himself with wine. This could be an Assyrian gesture of hommage to Dionysos, greatly revered in this province.

In these tombs, next to the dead, there are also little cups containing a palette of several colours – black, yellow, pink or pale green (9). Can this singular custom be interpreted in any other way than as a reminder of the *robe of all colours* of the Egyptian *Isis*? But this, too, reminds us in turn of the scarf of the *Greek Iris*, messenger of the gods, because she represents the *rainbow* to which the race, the first race of the *Bow* or of the *Eye*, is related. For the Ancients, scions of this race, is the rainbow not the *shining path of many colours,* the *living way leading from earth to heaven* (10), in short, the path which the dead only had to follow in order to attain beatitude? (In the *New Testament*, too, we read: *I am the way, the truth and the light.* Translator)

There are many other similarities which justify the West's claim to being first in the line of civilising influences. What are the Assyrian round tablets (Gk., *culindros* also *calindros*, meaning 'cylinder') if not a symbolic reminder of the Promethean ferule, the fire-producing rod, father of the magic baton? In the Finnish Kalevala, Vainamoinen calls it the *heavenly baton* (because it symbolises the sun's *lance*) and he challenges his enemies to conquer him because they do not possess it. Indeed, at the time, those that possessed fire enjoyed the same advantage as those who today possess atomic power. They **had** to be the stronger.

Finally, Assyria, like Persia, was the country of the *Magi* who were mostly recruited from the Chaldeans. They were called the *wise councillors of the king*. Once again we ask where it is possible to find a body of soothsayers, doctors, sacrificial priests, astronomers and astrologers of such great repute in the world, if not in Assyria? What was in Asia the origin of the word *magi*, whom *Bourdaloue* calls 'Sages of the Gentile Nations' and about whom we can read in Voltaire that they "adored one god and rejected all shams, but revered in fire (which gives life to nature) the symbol of divinity" (11)?

The magi occupied in Persia and in Assyria the place occupied by the *druids* in Gallic society. When our modern historians admit that before our era the druids were in touch with the magi and the *brahmins*, what they are saying is that the brahmins were simply a **caste** *from an Occident* where the conquests had originated, and whence they had set out. In the legend of *Gilgamesh*, is it not said on the twelfth tablet that the first king to reign over *Erech* was a descendant of a great dynasty of which he was the fifth member and that his name was said to mean *The Fire-god is a commander* (12)? But who, other than Prometheus, a Titan, was the god of Fire and, if we are trying to get our bearings in an unknown locality and need to *orientate* ourselves (always the **Orient!**), is this not a reason to believe that the first great migrations took place on a *West-East* axis?

We need to talk about *Gilgamesh*. In his legend, so very similar to that of Hercules, we find another trait which is a very visible reminder of the connection between the antique civilisation in the valley of the Tigris and of the Euphrates, and that of the Western Paladins. Without going into the detail of the origin and exploits of these two heroes, we must draw attention to one characteristic that concerns and classifies them – the cult of *virile friendship*. Whether it be Gilgamesh and Enkidu or Hercules and Hylas, we always see the same sacred fellowship, the same despair of a friend over the death of his companion and the same manner of expressing his anguish: here by the bellowing of the ox and there by the roaring of the lion. Victorian *restraint* did not operate in those times and heroes didn't have to hide their emotions. It was even considered to be in the *best taste* to be able to get angry on occasion and to roar like Jupiter.

In the case of Gilgamesh and of Hercules, we are looking at a sentiment born of combat, the sentiment of fellowship in the face of death. It cannot be denied that such a sentiment *in this form* has remained especially powerful in the Nordic and Germanic peoples and everything points to the likelihood that these specialists in warfare transmitted it to the East.

The Assyrian legend describes Enkidu as a powerful and good creature living in the forest, not far from *Erech*; a friend of the animals and clad simply with a belt of leaves: a true portrait of the giants of the *Great Age*. Although Gilgamesh (King of Erech) had been alerted about the presence of Enkidu in the woods, the latter had been described to him as a *fearsome* creature. However, as soon as the two men meet face to face, they quickly experience a feeling of reciprocal goodwill because (so the legend tells us) they were *informed about each other*. So instead of fighting, they unite and fight together against their common foes. Of course, we know the old song: is this not the theme of the *Twins*, a union of the *astute* and of the *strong*, of *brute force* and *intelligence*, a union of the *Vanir* and of the *Aesir*?

If we transpose the story back to its own time, we reach the conclusion that Enkidu, if there was such a man, was one of the last giants and that Gilgamesh knew that he himself was, in one way or another, of the same blood. It is after all possible that Enkidu is the same as the giant *Oenochoe*, father of the Dynasty of the Anachids. Assyrian legend tells us in effect that Enkidu had many progeny and that the word *enki* in Sumerian meant 'god of the deep' – in other words, the Western 'Empire of Death and of the Ocean'. If we recall that the root *oen* is interchangeable with the roots *uan* and *van*, and that the *Vénètes* (or Vanir) were in Antiquity called the *Oenètes*, the similarity with *Oenochoe* appears that much more plausible, since the Vanir belonged to the gods *in the entrails of the earth*. It was, moreover, in the Kingdom of the Dead, in the country of the *scorpion-men whose appearance is so terrifying that it causes mountains to disintegrate*, that Gilgamesh would go and look for the companion who had disappeared (13). But is it not said of Car-hon, in Western legends, that his red eye *rolls in wrathful pride* (14) – like that of the *Inachi?*

We hear a very *Western* note in the name Gilgamesh if we remember that in Sumerian *gil* had the meaning of 'willow' or 'reed' while the *gui* (mistletoe), used for the same rite of the *talle*, was *gillon* in Old French. *Gal*, in Sumerian, meant 'powerful man' or 'very male', like Celtic *cal*, *gal* and *gille*. On the other hand, the root *gam* is a key root in Norwegian languages. *Gamall* means 'ancient' (and therefore 'venerable') and *gaman* means 'an exploit'. *Gamli* is a poetic name for the *eagle* in Ireland, and *gammur* is the word for *vulture*.

We read in Herodotus that the ancient island of *Aphrodisia*, lying to the north of the African coast, had long before been founded by the *gilgammae* – a name which is clearly related to that of *Gilgamesh*, on the one hand, and to *Gillcoman* or *Gillagamnon*, on the other which, according to MacBain's dictionary, are both Gaelic proper nouns.

Finally, we see in Assyria great respect for anything resembling a *tooth*. This will explain two particular characteristics of Assyrian custom: growing a pointed beard and wearing tunics bordered with fringes or with material cut in such a way as to look like the teeth of a comb. We have said before that the root *kam* or *cam* had two meanings, both in the Scandinavian languages and in the language of Egypt: *tooth in general* and the *tooth of a comb*. Moreover, Herodotus notes in his writings that in Egypt the men were clothed in linen tunics with *fringes* at the bottom. He says that these tunics are called *calasires* (a word which is like French *camisole* (vest) or *chemise* (shirt), *camse* in Celtic Kimri (Welsh, Cornish and Breton) and *camice* in Italian.

The tooth of the weaving comb, related by reason of its *conic* shape to the *hile*, *cal* or *cam*, was a sacred symbol for the *Phrygians* and *Trojans* (and later too for the *Franks*) and there is no reason to doubt that, traditionally, it was also a sacred symbol for the *Chaldeans* and the *Assyrians*. Numerous objects have been found during excavations of Assyrian cities, including statuettes of different animals all made with a *comb* motif. The same can be said of pre-Roman *Gaul*.

It is also possible that the fringe, as an item of decoration for clothing, could have been, in all the abovementioned countries, a distinctive sign for a class of free or freed men. This is postulated on the basis of a distant analogy between the terms *fringe* (*frange* in French) and *Phrygian*. The source of this idea should be sought in the fact that both the concept and the fabrication of the fringe originated without any doubt in Phrygia, which at the time was famous for its weaving. We should also mention that French *frange* is *fransa* in Spanish and *Franse* in German. Moreoever, Littré tells us that, for a long time, Orientals used to call Western Europe *Frangistan*, in their opinion the country of the *Franks*. And in the same period the Russians called this nation the *Friazin*. But, as we have already said, the Franks were direct descendants of the Phrygians, whose name was synonymous with *free*. And need we remind readers that the dukes of Burgundy, heirs of the Kingdom of the Franks, displayed *two combs* in their coat-of-arms?

In Littré we find a sibylline text which is certainly rather vague but seems to confirm what we have said. The text is from the 12th Century AD. We read: "This (the love of Christ) is the ointment which goes down from the head to the beard, which also goes down to the seam of the garment so that not even a small fringe should be without ointment". (*Cist est li oignement ki dessent del chief en la barbe ki dessent assi en l'orrle del vestement ensi que nes une petite frange ne soit senz oignemenz.*)

Whatever may be the precise meaning of these words which, we admit, escapes us, there is nevertheless a coincidence of terms and concepts which is most eloquent. (NB: Surely, this is not **all** that sibylline? It is obviously inspired by some verses from Psalm 133: *Behold, how good and how pleasant it is for brethren to dwell together in unity! It is like the precious ointment upon the beard, even Aaron's beard, that went down to the skirts of his garments.* Translator*).*

But let us return to Gilgamesh. Some historians have identified him with Nimrod, another fabulous Assyrian hero. They may be right. We do not believe it. How does Nimrod appear on Assyrian bas-reliefs – Nimrod, who is said to have founded *Erech, Babylon, Accad* and *Calach*? Strange to relate for a man of this country, we see him brandishing a *trident* in each hand and pushing a *dragon* before him! (15) Could Nimrod not rather be the old Celtic *Neimdeih*, about whom legend says that he had travelled far, this way and that, and which sometimes describes him as an oriental patriarch? And could he not be the same as *Neptune-Poseidon* who is said, in Greek Mythology, to have been the first founder of Troy and the incarnation of the Ocean Dynasty? But, whatever his true identity may have been, a mythical or real hero armed with a *trident* could only have belonged to the *race of the sea peoples*. That he may later have reappeared as *a great hunter before the Lord* does not in any way discredit his distant origin. The peoples of the North Atlantic also produced great hunters!

So, what about the divinities in the Assyrian Pantheon of whom the most important were *Bel, Astarte* and *Ea*?

Bel, the husband of *Astarte*; *Bel* to whom on feast days *bulls* were sacrificed; *Bel* who is the *Baal* of the *Phoenicians*; *Bel*, god *par excellence* of the *Gentiles*; *Bel* who, literally and figuratively, would be the *bête noire* of the Semites and the incarnation for them of the *demons* and *false gods*; and finally, *Bel* who personifies the **forces of nature** – could he be any other than the *Bel* of the **Germani** and the *Bel* of the **Gauls**? In Gaelic this name was given to the god of war: *Bel y duw cadr* is 'Mars the powerful god' (16). In the same language *bel* is also used for *tumult* and the *wolf*. We should point out that in the Scandinavian paradise the *eagle glided over the wolf as a symbol of the battlefields* (17) in the Empire of the Night and of Death. Is not Odin, an *Aesir* and an *Ase*, always shown with two *wolves* at his feet? Often the crest of the Assyrian bull is represented in the shape of a sun, a *red sun*, which reminds us of the god Thor's *beard of fire* (Thor, the ancestor of *Barberossa* – Red Beard!) And do not forget that, according to Herodotus, it was specifically the Chaldeans who were the priests of *Zeus-Belos* in Babylon.

Astarte, star of the sea, is the eternal Virgin of the Waters, conceived in the North Atlantic but also cherished by the Phoenicians. She is almost always shown together with the virgin *Artemis*, and *Aphrodite* shares her name as second name. *Artemis* is shown with the udders of a cow and with the head of a wolf or dog, while *Aphrodite* is a goddess foreign to Attica, since she is the daughter of *Dione*.

As for *Ea*, her role and person are not very clearly defined but, in Assyrian legend, she is the divinity who intervenes with *Nergal* begging him to call up the spirit of *Enkidu* to console the unhappy *Gilgamesh*. Since Nergal reigned in the *Kingdom of Shadows*, that would indicate that *Ea* had some acquaintances in those parts.

In our opinion *Ea* is identical with *Isis* and represents the forces of the earth. It is possible that her name is cognate with *Gea* (the earth) as *eisir* is cognate with *geysir* – quite apart from the fact that, in the order of Latin pronouns, *ea* is the feminine of masculine *is* and that this same pronoun *ea* exists in Irish, sometimes in the form of *eja* which is pronounced *era*.

So there we have it. The Assyrian *Ea*, or *Aea*, becomes *Gaea*, the universal earth-mother who gave birth to the *world* by *Uranus*. Possibly her name became confused in time with that of *Rhea*, her daughter (mother of the Ocean), or with that of her granddaughter *Hera*, mother of *Herakles*. We think it was more probably *Rhea* because, according to Assyrian legend, *Ea* gave birth to *Zeus-Belos*, or because, in Mythology, *Rhea* is mother of Solar *Zeus*, younger brother of the divinities of the underworld.

*   *   *

Here then we end our very rapid sketch of the ancient adventure of the Western World. We know that the Aryans pursued their conquests as far as India and invaded the plains of the Indus and the Ganges. The similarity between Sanskrit and the North Atlantic languages, and especially North Atlantic spirituality, need not therefore surprise us.

All the lands that our Paladins fertilised with their industry and with their intelligence were also fertilised equally with their *seed*. Everywhere they went, everywhere they established themselves, they procreated abundantly. This was the custom in the old days, and it was an excellent custom. In Medieval France this way of managing affairs was common to all princes and all great lords, and was called *more danico* (the *Danish way*, the way of the *dians*). The ancient Nordic Sagas tell of the exploits of the hero *Heimdall* who adopted the surname of *Rig* (King) and who set off on his travels. Everywhere he went, the legend says, he entered the marital beds and fathered offspring. In other words, this warrior nomad and all those who accompanied him mingled their blood with the blood of the natives in the lands they approached thereby creating, in every place they passed through and in every place where they settled, powerful and *regenerated* races where the natural virtues of these natives, adapted to locality and time, could flower thanks to the creative, dynamic and inventive impulse of the *Aesir*.

And so there was a great mixing of races, a mixing of myths, arts and industries – and surely this ought to make us, quite literally, bury the *hatchet* of national hatreds and blind fanaticism?

The first step to be taken is to give all due respect and honour to historical *truth*. It was indeed those that Athena – their *daughter* – dismissed as barbarians (a term which at the time meant the *foreigner* and psychologically the *enemy*) who civilised the Eastern Mediterranean. So it need not surprise us that historians should have noticed the many affinities between these great Asian empires and those of the Celts and Nordics.

Having returned to the West after the fall of Troy, they created Europe. Up to the French Revolution and up to the First World War, they were its great *princes*. They have remained its great *bosses*, those who always defy heaven with the innovations of their science – worthy sons of Prometheus.

The movement started with them at the very dawn of the civilised world. Referring to the lands of the North, *Léouzon le Duc* wrote: "One loves to contemplate such regions. Somehow one feels there as if one were at the centre of divine eternity, and one is no longer surprised that men who had drawn their blood and received their life from it should have had an arm strong enough to grasp the sceptre of the world."

When these men went into decline, the old and imperturbable Vainamoinen *sat down at the rudder, set off for the open sea and while his boat ploughed through the waves, raised his voice and said:* "Other times will come; other days will dawn and pass; then I shall once again be needed. They will wait for me; they will ask me to bring another *sampo*, to build another *kantele*, to find once more the moon and the sun which have disappeared. They will ask me to restore the joy that has been exiled on earth."

Having spoken, the imperturbable one set forth in his copper boat through the stormy seas and reached the distant horizons, the spaces beneath the sky.

And the bard who was scanning these songs had to stop, too, *because no one was listening.* And yet the bard did still say: "I have marked the way for a new host of readers of the runes … As of now, the path has been pointed out, the quarry has been opened up. Other readers of the runes who are better that I, readers of runes whose songs are richer in content, will enter the quarry and sing their songs for a younger race, for the young sons of our people …" (18).

Our people cover the whole earth, as we are now rediscovering.

* * *

Translator's notes:

*This confusion of French *borgne*, *born* and *né* with the English word '**born**' can possibly be clarified by referring to the German noun *Born*, and the German past participle *geboren*. Thus, the adjective *borgne* in French means 'one-eyed'; the past-participle *né* means English '**born**'; the German noun *Born* means 'source' or 'well' [*Lebensborn* means 'source' or 'well of life']. The German past participle *geboren* means English '**born**'. P.200

Manche: a Department in NW France. P.201

*Sap, p.201: see *Talle* under Information for General Interest at the end of the book.

Alluvion or *Alluvium* – inundation by flooding. This leads to the formation of new land, especially along a riverbed, p.202

END NOTES OF THE AUTHORESS

I. THE HAIR AND THE FEATHER

1. Renville (DE), *Coûtumes Gauloises.*
2. Th. De La Villemarqué, *Contes Populaires des Anciens Bretons*, Paris, 1842.
3. Quoted in the *Dictionnaire de l'Ancienne langue française* of Lacurne de Saint-Palaye.
4. Rosenthal (Julius de), *Ostriches and Ostrich Farming.*
5. Léouzon le Duc, *La Finlande,suivi d'une traduction complète du Kalevala,* Paris 1845.
6. *Icelandic EDDA*, songs collected by Saemund the Wise.

II. TORCHES AND LILIES OF THE VALLEY

1. Léouzon le Duc, *La Finlande, suivi d'une traduction complète du Kalevala*, Paris, 1845.
2. Marie-Hélène Pauly, *Fleurs de lys, castors et calumets,* Montréal, 1958.
3. Whiley Stokes, *Togail Troi* (The Fall of Troy), from the Leinster Manuscript, Calcutta, 1882.
4. Smith, *Dictionary of Greek and Roman Geography*, London.
5. Mulk Raj Anand, *Kama Kala,* Geneva, 1958.

III. RED AND GREEN

1. *Several ancient authors, including Diodorus of Sicily, have reported that the Ancient Gauls applied a mixture of grease and ash-tree cinders to their hair in order to give it a reddish colour.*
2. Maurice Pézet, *Durance et Lubéron*, Paris 1958.

IV.   PHRYGIA AND PHOENICIA : TWO COLONIES OF THE
      ATLANTAN WORLD

1. *Découverte du Monde Antique, Voyages et Relations
    d'Hérodote d'Halicarnasse.* Club des Libraires de France,
    Paris 1957.
2. See Quicherat.
3. *Nouvelle Mithologie Illustrée,* published under the direction
    of Jean Richepin, Paris 1920-1921. And : Whitley Stokes,
    Togail Troi (The Fall of Troy), based on the Leinster
    Manuscript, Calcutta, 1882.
4. Léouzon le Duc, *La Finlande avec la traduction complète du
    Kalevala,* Paris 1845
5. Neil Mc Alpine, *Gaelic Dictionary,* London 1877.
6. *Histoire des Gaules, Extraits des Auteurs Grecs,* translated by
    Cougny, Paris 1878.
7. Dr. Gauillaume Freund, *Grand Dictionnaire Etymologique de
    la Langue Latine.*
8. See GRANDE ENCYCLOPEDIE.
9. *Icelandic EDDA,* songs collected by Saemund the Wise.
10. Ernest Renan, *Mission en Phénicie.*

V.   THE KING'S HORN

1. A.E. Brehm, *Les Merveilles de la Nature,* Paris s.d.
2. Ditto.
3. Smith, *Dictionary of Greek and Roman Geography,* London.
    See entry on *Scandia.*
4. Voltaire, *Prince de Babylone,* quoted by Littré.
5. A.E. Brehm, *Les Merveilles de la Nature,* Paris. s.d.
6. *Le monde Antique, Voyages et Relations d'Hérodote
    d'Halicarnasse,* Club des Libraires de France, Paris 1957.
7. A.E. Brehm, *Les Merveilles de la Nature, Paris, s.d.*
8. Ch. Autran, *Histoire Ancienne et Perspectives Modernes, à
    propos du livre "Kingship of the Gods",* by H Frankfort.
9. Regine Pernoud, *Les Gaulois,* Paris 1957

VI.   GONDOLAS AND CANTILENAS

1. Léouzon le Duc, *La Finlande, avec une Traduction Complète du Kalevala*, Paris 1845
2. *Découverte du Monde Antique, Voyages et Relations d'Hérodote d'Halicarnasse*, Club des Libraires de France, Paris 1957
3. Owen Pughe, *Dictionary of the Welsh Language,* Denbigh, 1832.
4. We read in Strabo, 1, IV, p.195: *Hos ego Venetos existimo Venetiarum in Adriatico sinu esse autores* (I consider these Veneti to be the forebears of those in the Gulf of the Adriatic). Referring to this statement in *Les Martyrs* (Vol.II, p.145), Chateaubriand writes: "According to this author, the Venetians are said to be a colony of Bretons from Vannes".
5. *Découverte du Monde Antique. Voyages et relations d'Hérodote d'Halicarnasse,* Club des Libraires de France, Paris 1957

VII.   ONCE UPON A TIME THERE WAS A KING IN THULE

1. Dr. F. Kahn, *Le Livre de la Nature*, Paris 1958.
2. Smith, *Dictionary of Greek and Roman Geography*, London.
3. "... Thule is extremely large, being ten times larger than Britain, from which it is very distant, (lying) towards the North".
4. Smith's translation: "Thule, as far as it is known to men, lies at the farthest extremity of the Ocean, towards the North."
5. Throughout Greek Mythology, the Race of the Arc is seen as being identical with that of the Giants, sons of the Heavens and of the Earth. See the legend of the birth of Hercules.
6. Littré, see *coupe* (bowl, cup).
7. Gleasby, *Icelandic-English Dictionary.*
8. Jean-Pierre Vernet, *Islande terre de glace et de feu,* Paris, 1962
9. See *Torches and Lilies of the Valley*, above.
10. Gerard de Nerval, *Les filles du feu – Isis.*

11. Aurélien Sauvageot, *Les anciens Finnois,* Paris.
12. Quoted by Littré under the letter G.
13. Lewis Spence, *The problem of Atlantis*, London, 1925.
14. Owen Pugh, *Dictionary of the Welsh language.*
15. *Dictionnaire des Antiquités grecques et romaines, vol.II.*
16. Pasteur, *Discours à l'Académie de Médicine:* "The essence of true theories is the ability to give expression to the facts; to be at their command and to be controlled by them; to be able to foresee new facts with assurance, because these are, in the nature of things, linked with the old ones. In a word, the best theories are productive (of new ones)."

VIII.   TONTAINE AND TONTON

1. *Le Phèdre.*
2. Thomas Davis, *Seven centuries of Irish learning, 1000 to 1700,* published for *Radio Eurean* by Brian O'Cuiv.
3. *Le Phèdre.*
4. Among the most important there were: *Canute Dana-ast* (10th c.); *Canute the Great-of-the-Sea* (*Knut den Store ved Havet*) who reigned over Denmark, Norway and Ireland in the 11th c.; *Hardy Canute* and *Canute the Holy,* who lived more or less at the same period.
5. A. Blinkenberg og M.Thille, *Dansk-Fransk Ordbog.*
6. Léouzon le Duc, *La Finlande, suivi d'une traduction complète du Kalevala.*
7. *EDDA* Icelandic songs collected by Saemund the Wise.
8. Léouzon le Duc, *La Finlande, suivi d'une traduction complète du Kalevala.*
9. H. Martin*, Histoire de France*

IX.   FROM HERCULES TO QUEEN PEDAUQUE

1. F.Wagner, *Les poèmes Mythologiques de l'Edda,* Paris 1936.
2. *Découverte du monde antique, Voyages et Relations d'Hérodote d'Halicarnasse,* Club des Libraires, Paris 1957.
3. La Villemarqué, *Dictionnaire français-breton.*

4. See: the dictionaries of *Godefroy* and of *Lacurne Saint-Palaye*.
5. Smith, *Dictionary of Greek and Roman Geography*, London.
6. MacBain, *Etymological Dictionary of the Gaelic language*.
7. La Varende, *Guillaume le Bâtard Conquérant*.
8. Découverte du Monde Antique, Voyages et Relations d'Hérodote d'Halicarnasse, Club des Libraires, Paris 1957.
9. *Nouvelle Mythologie Illustrée, sous la direction de Jean Richepin*, Paris 1920.
10. *Découverte du Monde antique, Voyages et Relations d'Hérodote d'Halicarnasse*, Club des Libraires, Paris 1957.
11. Ditto.

X. THE GREAT FAMILY OF THE THREE-LEGGED

1. *Nouvelle Mythologie Illustrée, sous la direction de Jean Richepin*, Paris 1920.
2. *Anthologie de la Poésie Grecque, traduction et notices de Robert Brasillach*, Paris 1955.
3. Smith, *Dictionary of Greek and Roman Geography*, London.
4. These days, the *Saint John's wort* is known by this name.
5. A.E. Brehm, *Les Merveilles de la Nature*, sd.
6. See *Phrygie et Phénicie, deux colonies du Monde atlantéen*.
7. J.H. Gurney, *The Gannet, bird with a history*, Witherley, 1913.
8. Mme de Réneville, *Coûtumes gauloises*.
9. *Rabelais, 1V, 41*, cité par Littré.
10. Cité par Chateaubriand, dans *Les Martyrs*, Paris 1810, vol. I, p.287.

XI. COME BACK, BOOMERANG!

1. Françoise Henry, *Art Irlandais*, Dublin, 1954
2. MacLachan & Stewart, *Gaelic & English Dictionary*, Edinburgh. We read: *Lochlin or Locharn, admitted to be the ancient Caledonian name for Scandinavia*.
3. See Régine Pernoud, *Les Gaulois*, Paris 1957.

4. Céram, *Des dieux des tombeaux des savants,* Paris 1953.
5. Joachim Barckhausen, *L'empire jaune de Gengis Khan.* We read about one of G.K.'s ancestors that, *after an absence of two years, he returned from the wars to find his wife pregnant. Asked to explain this clear case of infidelity, she offered the following defence: One night I was lying awake in bed. A beam shone through the opening above, sent by a star. It took the appearance of a blond and blue-eyed young man. He touched my breast several times, and from that moment I was pregnant.*
6. Mc Alpine, *Gaelic Dictionary.*

XII.   HOLY MAKREL!

1. A.E. Brehm, *Les Merveilles de la Nature, Paris.*
2. Id.
3. Id.
4. *Icelandic Edda,* songs collected by Saemund the Wise.
5. Eugène Beauvois, *Les Antiquités Primitives de la Norvège,* Paris 1889.
6. A.E. Brehm, *Les Merveilles de la Nature, Paris.*
7. Id.
8. Smith, *Dictionary of Greek and Roman Geography,* London, 1856.
9. A.E. Brehm, *Les Merveilles de la Nature, Paris.*
10. Id.
11. Léouzon le Duc, *La Finlande, suivi d'une traduction complète du Kalevala,*Paris 1845.

XIII.   TOM THUMB

1. In the old Berry dialect *agneau* (lamb) was *igneau*, in Irish and Gaelic *ian* or *uan*. The Walloon word was *ognai.* I*gneau* is cognate with Latin *ignis* (fire) and by derivation with French words like *ignifuge* (fire-resistant). In the sailor's vocabulary *agnan* is sheet-iron with a hole pierced through it,

while *agnat* means "of the same blood". These relationships are significant.

2. Gerard Murphy, *Saga and Myth in Ancient Ireland,* Dublin.
3. Id.
4. *Nouvelle Mythologie illustrée,* Jean Richepin, Paris 1920
5. Id.
6. *Dictionnaire Larousse.*
7. Marguerite Yourcemar, *Les Mémoires d'Hadrien,* Paris 1951
8. Strange to relate, the national costume of Icelandic women includes a kind of neck-piece or ruff, very much like the *gorgonoion.*

XIV.   THE BLUE COUNTRY OF THE CHIMERA

1. Jordanès (or Jornandès), *Origine et Histoire des Gètes.*
2. *Nouvelle Mythologie Illustrée, sous la Direction de Jean Richepin,* Paris, 1920.
3. *Découverte du Monde Antique, Voyages et Relations d'Hérodote d'Halicarnasse,* Club des Libraires, Paris, 1957.
4. Smith, *Dictionary of Greek and Roman Geography,* London.
5. *See Lengyel.*
6. *Nouvelle Mythologie Illustrée, sous la Direction de Jean Richepin,* Paris, 1920.
7. A Blinkenberg, *Dansk-Fransk Ordbog.*
8. Alex MacBain, *Etymological Dictionary of the Gaelic Language.* 1911
9. Smith, *Dictionary of Greek and Roman Geography,* London.
10. Alex MacBain, *Etymological Dictionary of the Gaelic Language.*
11. Owen Pughe, *Dictionary of the Welsh Language.*

XV.   DRAGONS AND TALES OF DRAGONS

1. Léouzon le Duc, *La Finlande, suivi de la traduction du Kalevala,* Paris 1867.
2. A. Blinkenberg ogg M.Thille *Dansk Fransk Ordbog.*

3. *Nouvelle Mythologie Illustrée sous la direction de Jean Richepin,* Paris 1920

4. Id.

5. La Villemarqué *Dictionaire français – Breton.*

6. Léozon le Duc, *La Finlande, suivi d'une traduction complète du Kalevala,* Paris, 1867.

7. Guillaume Freund, *Grand Dictionnaire de la Langue Latine.*

8. Id.

9. Thomas Davis, *Seven Centuries of Irish Learning, 1000-1700,* lecture series published by Brian O'Cuiv, 1961.

XVI.   THE GREAT "BOSS"

1. J. De Saint Martin, *Fragment d'une Histoire des Arsacides,* Paris 1850.

2. A.E Brehm, *Les Merveilles de la Nature,* Paris.

3. *Découverte du Monde antique, Voyages et Relations d'Hérodote d'Halicarnasse,* Paris 1957.

4. *Grand Dictionnaire Larousse Universel.*

5. Smith, *Dictionary of Greek and Roman Geography,* London.

6. *Découverte du Monde Antique, Voyages et Relations d'Hérodote d'Halicarnasse,* Paris 1957.

7. Max Weber, *L'Ethique protestante et l'Esprit du Capitalisme,* Plon, 1964.

8. See *Torches and Lilies of the Valley*, last three pages of our translation.

XVII.   SEARCHING FOR TRACES OF THE THRACIANS

1. Freund, *Grand Dictionnaire de la Langue Latine.*

2. *Découverte du Monde antique, Voyages et Relations d'Hérodote d'Halicarnasse,* Paris, 1957.

3. Letter quoted by H. Schliemann in *Ilios, ville et pays des Troyens,* Paris 1850.

4. Smith, *Dictionary of Greek and Roman Geography,* London.

5. *Découverte du Monde Antique, Voyages et Relations d'Hérodote d'Halicarnasse,* Paris, 1957.

6. J. de Saint-Martin, *Fragments d'une Histoire des Arsacides*, Paris 1850.
7. J.de Saint-Martin, *Mémoires Historiques et Géographiques sur l'Arménie.*
8. *Nouvelle Mythologie Illustrée,* sous la direction de Jean Richepin, Paris 1920.
9. Alex. Pillon, *Vocabulaire grec-français,* Paris 1858.
10. Léouzon le Duc, *La Finlande, suivi d'une traduction complète de la Grande épopée, le Kalevala,* Paris 1845.
11. J. de Saint-Martin, *Fragments d'une Histoire des Arsacides,* Paris 1850.
12. *Nouvelle Mythologie Illustrée,* sous la direction de Jean Richepin, Paris 1920
13. Em. Aegeter, *Les Grandes Religions,* Paris, 1950.
14. Léouzon le Duc, *La Finlande, suivi d'une traduction complète de la Grande épopée, le Kalevala,* Paris 1845.
15. The New-Yorker, 6 June 1964, *"The talk of the Town".*

XVIII.   ARIADNE'S THREAD

1. Smith, *Dictionary of Greek and Roman Geography,* London.
2. J. de Saint-Martin, *Fragments d'une Histoire des Arsacides,* Paris 1850.
3. Macbain, *Etymological Dictionary of the Gaelic Language.*
4. Smith, *Dictionary of Greek and Roman Geography,* London.
5. Neil MacAlpine, *Gaelic Dictionary,* A. MacBain, *Etymological Dictionary of the Gaelic Language.* Owen Pughe, *Dictionary of the Welsh Language.*
6. Abbé P. Martin, *La Chaldée, esquisse historique,* Rom, 1867.
7. Id.

XIX.   THE WIND OF HISTORY

1. La Villemarqué *Dictionnaire français-breton.*
2. Eug. Beavois, *Les Antiquités Primitives de la Norvège,* Paris 1869.
3. De Laborde, *Emaux,* p.533

4. Georges Dumézil, *Les Mythes Romains,* Paris, 1947.
5. Alfred Lallemand, *Origines historiques de la ville de Vannes,* Dr. Guil. Freund, *Grand Dictionnaire de la Langue Latine.*
6. Jean Doresse, *Les Livres secrets des Gnostiques d'Egypte,* Paris, 1958. We read: "In the 18th Century, when people started to question the historical accuracy of the Bible, some were concerned about the discordant notes that could be heard in different parts of the Old Testament, and also about the moral significance of Original Sin ... With Paul, there is an irreconcilable clash of opinion with the Gnostics ... Expounding on the name, *Son of Man,* our sectarians (the Gnostics) made this the **Son** of the **Primordial** *anthropos* in the **Higher** world. For them, his incarnation is fictitious; his crucifixion, too". The author concludes that the Gnostics associate themselves with the Pagan Mysteries.
7. On the subject of Satan, we find in Littré a quotation of Voltaire: "This term, which is in Job, was unknown to the Jews. They heard of it from the Chaldeans".
8. J.de Saint-Martin, *Mémoires Historiques et Géographiques sur l'Arménie,* Paris 1818.
9. A. Ernout and A. Meillet, *Dictionnaire étymologique de la langue latine,* Paris 1959.
10. *Etymological Dictionary of the Gaelic Language,* MacBain.
11. *Découverte du Monde antique, Voyages et Relations d'Hérodote d'Halicarnasse,* Paris, 1957.
12. It should however be noted that in heraldry *vair* is a little like the form described as "bell shaped", when speaking of flowers called *snap-dragon* which are of a violet, tinted with red.

XX.   THE STRAW AND THE BEAM

1. Réne Héron de Villefosse, *Histoire de Paris,* Paris, 1955.
2. J. de Villeman, *Pluton, père des Gaulois ,* Clamart, s.d.
3. Eug. Beauvois, *Les Antiquités primitives de la Norvège,* Paris 1869.

4. Léouzon le Duc, *La Finlande, avec la traduction complète du Kalevala,* Paris 1845.
5. Leonard King, *A history of Sumer and Akkad,* London, 1916.
6. M.David, *Les dieux et le destin de Babylone,* Paris, 1949.
7. Dr.G. Conteneau, *La Civilisation d'Assur et du Babylone,* Paris, 1949.
8. Alex. Pillon, *Vocabulaire grec-français,* Paris, 1858.
9. Ch. Autran, *Histoire ancienne et Perspectives modernes à propos du livre "Kingship of the Gods",* de H. Francfort.
10. Jean Doresse, *Les livres secrets des Gnostiques d'Egypte,* Paris, 1948.
11. Smith, *Dictionary of Greek and Roman Geography,* London.
12. C.F.Lehman, *Der Name "Chalder",* 1895.
13. *Lexique de Togail Troi* (The Destruction of Troy), by W.Stokes, Calcutta, 1882.
14. Smith, *Dictionary of Greek and Roman Geography,* London.
15. See Littré. The roots *kul* and *kal* have become interchangeable. *Oengus the Caledonian,* who lived in the 9th century, wrote his name *Oengus the Culdee.* See Stokes, *On the Calendar of Oengus,* Dublin, 1880.
16. Smith, *Dictionary of Greek and Roman Geography,* London.
17. La Villemarqué, *Contes populaires des anciens Bretons,* Paris, 1842.

XXI.   IN THE MAGPIE'S NEST

1. H. De Mondeville.
2. Quoted by Littré.
3. *EDDA,* Icelandic songs collected by Saemund the Wise.
4. J. de Saint-Martin, *Fragments d'une histoire des Arsacides,* Paris, 1850.
5. A.E Brehm, *Les Merveilles de la Nature,* Paris.
6. Dr. G. Conteneau, *La Civilisation d'Assur et de Babylone,* Paris, 1937.
7. Léouzon le Duc, *La Finlande, suivi d'une traduction complète du Kalevala,* Paris.

8. Dr. G. Conteneau, *La Civilisation d'Assur et de Babylone,* Paris, 1937.
9. André Parrot, *La Tour de Babel,* Neuchâtel, 1953.
10. F. Wagner, *Poèmes mythologiques de l'Edda*, Paris, 1936.
11. Voltaire, *Moeurs,6.*
12. *The Babylonian story of the Deluge, as told by the Assyrian tablets,* British Museum, London, 1920.
13. Id.
14. MacPherson, *Les Poèmes d'Ossian.*
15. Chaldean bas-relief, British Museum, London.
16. Owen Pugh, *Dictionary of the Welsh Language.*
17. F. Wagner, *Poèmes mythologiques de l'Edda,* Paris, 1936.
18. Léouzon le Duc, *La Finlande, suivi de la traduction complète du Kalevala,* Paris.

***

Translator's Afterword

It had been my intention to let Mme. Talbot's book speak for itself. But a recent cartoon in the *Daily Mail* reminded me of a report I had read some eight years ago: also in the *Daily Mail*. Both the report and the cartoon (one of many in similar vein) are typical of an attitude which, more than 40 years after publication of Mme. Talbot's book – and, indeed, of any book on a similar subject – is still promoted with almost religious fervour by representatives of the Press and Media who are nevertheless always keen to assume in public an air of balanced and open-minded propriety about contentious issues. But let the reader judge for himself.

In her introduction, Mme. Talbot refers to the hostility and derision she and her school of thought must expect from opponents. What better illustration of this could there be than a cartoon in the well rehearsed tradition of Hagar the Horrible.

And what could be more depressing than a worldly-wise sophisticate's tired comment on a potentially exciting archaeological discovery, reported some years ago in the national press:

> *Daily Mail*, 14.4.2000: Vikings wore spectacles. Clear discs uncovered in Viking settlements in Gotland, Sweden, which were first thought to be jewellery, are in fact sophisticated lenses. Technicians at the Aalen Polytechnic in Germany who examined the finds were astounded by the

high level of sophistication, attained by men working between 700 and 1000 A.D. "to advanced specifications".

Olaf Schmidt, a spokesman for the group of researchers, says that the principles they used to make the lenses were not generally understood until many centuries later and yet they were being applied at this early period to create lenses that were suitable for a wide variety of uses. Their cut is practically perfect and the surface almost perfectly elliptic. The optical quality can be compared with that of modern spectacles.

We can only assume, he added, that the craftsmen who made them had a basic knowledge of the workings of the physical universe that was far in advance of the scientists of the day.

The size of the lenses also indicates that some were used to make the first crude telescopes, 500 years before Dutch opticians who, it is thought, invented them for seafarers.

Needless to say, these findings were dismissed out of hand by the Swedish archaeologists who had found the lenses in Gotland and could not believe that their forefathers had been capable of anything other than "raiding and pillaging". Magnus Sundstrom, a member of one of the teams at the dig, said: " They probably stole the lenses from merchant caravans that travelled across from Eastern Europe, or from the Byzantine Empire".

Mme. Talbot doesn't really need my intervention. Nevertheless, readers who have found the idea of a North-West Atlantic *Genesis* more stimulating than that of a *Fertile Crescent* in the Near East, may care to look at reviews of three other books which appeared within ten years of her publication and which illustrate certain aspects of her theory rather aptly.

Finally, I am including in an appendix a list of classical and non-classical gods and heroes, myths and legends, place names, names of towns and other geographical data which will, I hope, be of general background interest and may serve as a kind of pre-History Tourist's Guide Book.

THREE BOOK REVIEWS, RELEVANT TO MME. TALBOT'S LINE OF ARGUMENT.

I **Ex Nocte Lux**: (dust jacket)

In its decisive periods the development of Man has been closely associated with the effects of glaciation. But up to now Science has been unable to explain either the very early glaciations of the southern hemisphere or the more well-known glaciations in the north – the so called Great Ice Age – as regards cause, inception, development and end. All attempts to find an acceptable explanation have failed because research workers could not as yet agree to some form of comparative analysis, which is of course a *sine qua non*: "The divide between them was simply too deep".

The result has been an incomplete picture of all those thousands and hundreds of thousands of years of Ice Age development: incomplete, hazy and even totally distorted in decisive stages. And yet, into this unreliable picture the progress of Man to religion and art, culture and civilisation, language and writing, cities and states has been projected willy-nilly, by force. Inevitably, what we call the History of Man (which – as Jaspers states – "we not only know **about**, but from which we also **draw our very existence**"; and which alone is able to "provide us with those standards which are necessary for our life today") remains incomplete or even erroneous since it turns decisive events in our development upside-down. This distorted picture is then passed from hand to hand, and prevents us from directing an unblinkered gaze at past reality and, consequently, at our life today.

Horken shows us the world from a great height, and on a splendid canvas: factually, without prejudice, and systematically he then corrects our view of geological and human pre-History, point by point. In the process he makes a rigorous analysis of the most recent research by archaeologists, experts in pre-history, geophysics and meteorology, chemical analysis, language, religion and animal behaviour, ethnology and sociology. The result is amazing, revolutionary, persuasive. We learn how an ice age begins and ends, and we discover that we are already in the first stages of a new period of glaciation. We discover how large areas of land emerge from the sea, and then disappear again; how a rain-paradise turns to desert, and then becomes a paradise once more, thousands of years later. We see early man behind the ice barrier, living in six months of darkness in a fertile land beside the Polar Sea, from which he has to flee when the water level rises: and in so doing he exports in a worldwide, southerly sweep his sun monotheism, his symbols, his culture, his knowledge of navigation and ship building, smelting processes, agriculture and cattle breeding, horse breeding and wagon building, writing and calendars. Ex nocte lux! Light FROM the darkness! And at the same time light shining ONTO the darkness of our knowledge about pre-history. Incomprehensible circumstances become clarified; our forefathers – albeit in a different way and in a different world – appear as people such as you and I, struggling with the same problems that assail us today: over-population; lack of space; hunger!

Verlag Ernst Wasmuth,
Tübingen (1972)
[Translation from the German]

II Quetzlcoatl – a foreign god?

Quetzlcoatl is the name of the fifth sovereign who reigned over Mexican Anahuac in the second half of the 10th century. The Toltecs regarded him as a god, son of the Sun, which had given them their calendar, and also the arts of agriculture and metallurgy.

There is every reason to believe that Quetzlcoatl was a historic figure who had arrived by sea with a group of companions and womenfolk. He is probably also the same figure that we meet with in Mayan traditions, but known as Kukulkan. Both words, incidentally, have the same meaning: *feathered serpent*.

Descriptions, garnered by Spanish chroniclers from the natives, vary except on one point: in all of them, Quetzlcoatl appears as a white man, very tall and with a long beard. He must therefore have been a foreigner. In certain texts he is described as a priest with austere habits, without wife or children, spending his time in the mountains, engaging in ascetic exercises. Other texts make him out to be a redoubtable warrior. We are left with the impression of two persons who are totally different, but gradually melt into one another and become one, with a generic name that suggests a common origin.

The Mayan traditions seem to confirm this impression, referring to two distinct white gods: Itzamna, who has all the characteristics of an ascetic Quetzlcoatl; and Kukulkan, the warrior.

In his book *Le grand voyage du dieu soleil**, Prof. Jacques de Mahieu offers us the hypothesis of a Scandinavian origin for Quetzlcoatl. No one doubts today that the Vikings discovered America five centuries before Christopher Columbus. But was it possible for these Vikings to have conquered the high Mexican plateaus, crossed Venezuela, and then founded (only a few decades later) the pre-Inca Civilisation of Tiahuanaco, before expanding their influence to Paraguay and to Brazil?

Jacques de Mahieu has collected a mass of archaeological and ethnological clues which have already shaken the foundations of our knowledge about the Aztec, Mayan and Peruvian civilisations. No one had previously been able to explain the origins of these two white civilisers of pre-Columbian America. Jacques de Mahieu's hypothesis is not yet generally accepted but is still the first rational and coherent explanation. (Translation from the French)

*Jacques de Mahieu, *Le grand voyage du dieu soleil,* Edition Spéciale, Paris, 1971. See also, by the same author*: L'agonie du dieu soleil,* Robert-Laffont, Paris, 1974. A third book, not yet published in French, is available in German: *Des Sonnengottes heilige Steine,* Grabert Verlag, Tuebingen, 1975.

(Review from the French Magazine *Eléments*, one of the publications of the French cultural movement *GRECE*. 1957)

III From the Far North to the Indus

Bâl Gangâdhar Tilak (1856-1920), exegete of Vedic literature and pioneer of Indo-European studies. He was also one of the finest figures of the Indian National movement. His work is presented to us herewith by Jean Rémy, translator of his most important works.

Bâl Gangâdhar Tilak is almost unknown in France, and yet he is the father of Indian Independence. Western history books hardly mention him, preferring Gandhi. It nevertheless deserves to be known that Tilak was the inspiration behind the movement for Indian national liberation from 1895 to 1920. He was the first to awaken aspirations for freedom and independence which were becoming manifest in local ways, and to unite them within a pan-Indian popular movement.

What is however a matter for even greater concern is that nothing is known about his work as a scholar, as historian of religions and of philosophy – work which is nevertheless of a not inconsiderable importance, and can be divided into two parts: on the one hand, research into the origins and dating of the Vedic Tradition; and on the other, an enormous volume of synthesis of Indian philosophy, studied chiefly from the point of view of ethics.

Tilak was born on 23 July 1856 into a family of Brahmins. After a brilliant student career, he joined four friends to found a school for advanced studies in Poona. The five men, Nationalists from the very start, also launched two newspapers: the *Kesari* and the *Mahratta*. After several years in journalism, Tilak found himself increasingly drawn to Politics and became leader of the Mahratta nationalists.

India was experiencing various social and cultural disturbances between 1870 and 1900: the rise of local Bourgeoisie, the ruin of the peasant class, the disintegration of traditional structures, the birth of an Intelligentsia, trained in the West. Tilak sought inspiration for, and love of, *Swaraj* (self-government) from his profound knowledge of Indian tradition, and he acquired from his studies an extraordinary rigour of doctrine and great pugnacity.

To mobilise the masses, Tilak relied on *Popular Religion* and various *Cultural* movements. During the great famine of 1896/1897 Tilak launched a full-scale war against the Colonial Power, and created slogans calling the population to refuse payment of taxes and to boycott all British manufactured goods. Within ten years the movement had touched all levels of society and become irreversible. However, in 1907/1908 rebellions, general strikes and acts of terrorism frightened and alarmed the Indian bourgeoisie and prompted the English to intervene. Then Tilak was banished from the country for eight years. This period of imprisonment more or less put an end to Tilak's leadership role in Indian politics, but it enabled him to write a remarkable book on ethics in Indian culture: *Esotericism in the Gita.*

This monumental work also includes a translation and commentary of the *Bhagavad Gita.* It was composed in particularly harsh conditions, in Burma. *Subhash Chandra Bose*, the "Lion of Bengal", who was also detained in this prison, had the following to say of it: "I often wondered how he could, for more than five years, occupy himself with prolonged intellectual activity in such conditions. Only someone who could exercise the greatest self-control, and who was indifferent both to pleasure and to pain, could have endured such wretched conditions".

The book entitled *Polar Origin of the Vedic Tradition* was in fact conceived in 1898 and published in 1903. Its basic argument is that the *common cradle* of the Indo-Europeans is situated *within* the Arctic Circle, and dates from a period *before* the end of the last major Ice Age (Wuerm IV: 12.000 to 9,000 before our era).

The arguments which the author puts forward to substantiate this hypothesis rely on various disciplines of Western Science at the time (geology, anthropology, palaeontology, archaeology), complemented by a Vedic exegesis, which is the author's speciality. He shews that most of the passages, left unexplained by other specialists, can be clarified in a satisfactory and coherent manner when we place ourselves at the vantage point of an observer *inside the Arctic Circle,* taking due note of all characteristics in this zone:

- **No rising or setting stars.**
- **Long night followed by a long dawn.**
- **Normal days and nights.**
- **Long dusk and once again long night.**
- **Complete rotation of the stars from left to right.**
- **Importance of *Ursus Maior* (the Great Bear) which is always directly above the head of the observer.**
- **Sunrise in the South after the long night, etc.**

From Stonehenge above (reconstruction of the megalithic edifice erected 1400 BC) to the *Jantar Mantar* Observatory, built in 17th century India, there exists a direct link between the *various waves* of Indo-European conquerors who undertook that great trek, starting from their *common place of origin* in the *Polar Regions*, and *confirmed* in the oldest *Vedic* sources.

A study of the most ancient sacrificial system shews that men believed in years of *variable length* (eight, ten or twelve months, *according to Latitude)*. This reminds us of the Roman tradition which envisaged a year *suitable for human activity* (the "living year"), complemented by a *dark, evil* period (called *Kshapah* in the Vedic texts).

Avestic (Persian) writings provide many supplementary details, especially a list of *sixteen* countries traversed by *Mazdaean* ancestors, following a *cataclysm* of *snow* and *ice* in their country of origin: *Airyana Vaejo.*

European mythological literature is also analysed from various points of view:

> The Greek legend of *Helios* who owns 350 head of cattle and as many sheep, representing a year of 350 days and nights, leaving an intermediary period at the junction of the two years.

> The tradition of *Ivan*, in Slav literature, who takes it upon himself to kill a snake because of the never-ending darkness.

A similar legend attaches to *Indra*, champion of the Vedic gods, who fights against the *Powers of Darkness, frees the waters* and *enables the Sun to re-appear.*

A propos of this legend, Tilak makes a monumental contribution to the exegesis of Indo-European concepts of the earth and the cosmos: it appears that they (the Indo-Europeans) believed there to be rivers in the sky that carried the stars around the heavens; that were the source of the rain; and that transported the seeds of all the plants growing on the Earth's surface.

Tilak's work is very reminiscent of studies undertaken by a French scholar in the 18th century: *Jean Sylvain Bailly* (1726-1793). This astronomer had examined astronomic tables brought back from India by missionaries and had come to the conclusion that they *made no sense* in **India'**s latitudes – but *made very good sense on a latitude 49 degrees* **North.** His work was based on an important historical study of astronomy and science in Antiquity. Bailly believed that astronomy was born when the *Peoples of the North* (whom he called *Atlantans,* since the term *Indo-European* did not yet exist in his day), while coming down to the South, noted that "the earth was round, the globe tilted": they would also have observed the "obliquity of the Zodiac at the Equator and the revolutions of the planets, about which they could previously have known nothing ..."

"During this purely hypothetical march (Bailly continues), astronomy would not have been initiated or could not have been *developed,* until men, moving southwards between the 60th and 50th degree of latitude and discovering in the process a *new sky,* would have been able to see the sun *every* day, got to know an *entire* Zodiac, and divided this zone into four *Quarters.* It would indeed seem that an ancient and knowledgeable people settled in this climatic zone and that it became the theatre of a very advanced astronomy of which only a few traces remain. This hypothesis could perhaps explain why the Chaldeans, the Indians and Chinese, who were the *first to get possession of these precious remnants, were unable to take matters any further...*"

Modern research on Europe's megalithic astronomical observatories (for example, *Stonehenge*) fully confirm Bailly's hypotheses about the *northern origins* of astronomy. Just recently Prof. Gerald S. Hawkins, author of *Sun Over Stonehenge (Copernic,* 1977), assured us in a letter that the theories of Tilak, set out in this article, were "entirely valid".

Jean Rémy

Lokamanya Bâl Gangâdhar Tilak: *Polar Origin of the Vedic Tradition,* Editions Archè, 384 pages.

Source: The *Gréce* publication *Elèments,* late 1970s. (Translation from the French)

***

Information for General Interest

LES PALADINS DU MONDE OCCIDENTAL
(Knights-Errant of the Western World)

For Reference. Items of general interest which readers may consider
relevant to Mme. Talbot's theme: a list of classical and non-classical gods and
heroes; some myths and legends, place names, towns and geographical
data.

***

A.

Abas: 12th king of Argos.

Achaemenides: Achaens.

Aeacus: son of Zeus/Jupiter by Aegina. Because of his just government,
made Judge of the Lower Regions with Minos and Rhadamanthus. His
male descendants, the Aecides, include his son Phocus, and thereafter
Peleus, Achilles, Pyrrhus son of Achilles, and Pyrrhus king of Epirus.
Also Perseus, king of Macedon, conquered by Aemilius Paulus.

Aegean: the Aegean Sea, part of the Mediterranean lying between Greece
and Turkey.

Aegina: Mother of Aeacus. Also island near Attica. Hence *Aegineta*: native
of Aegina.

Aesir: (see: Vanir).

Aeetes: father of Medea, who deceitfully promised Jason the Golden Fleece.

Afer/Afra/Afrum (Masc., Fem. and neuter forms of Lat. adjective):
African/of Africa, especially in the narrow sense of the district around
Carthage.

Africa (Lat. noun): In the narrower sense, *Africa propria* or *Africa provincia*:
the country around, and formerly belonging to, Carthage. After 146
BC: Roman province of Africa.

Africus: the South-West Wind, the *Sirocco*.

Agnatic: hereditary.

Alcidae: family/genus of birds.

Alcides (also: Alcaeus) of Tiryns: Heracles/Hercules.

Alcmaeon/Alcmaeo: son of Amphiarus and Eriphyle. Ordered by his father
to kill his mother, and was pursued by the *Furies*.

Alcmaeon: son of Nestor, son of Neleus, king of Pylos. An Achaean hero.

Alcis: Deity of the Germanic Nahanarvali (or: Narharvali). Macedonian name for Pallas Athene/Minerva.

Alcmene: mother of Heracles/Hercules.

Alfes (Fr.): *Alfar* (dwarfs in Nordic Myth). In old English (O.E): *aelf.*

Alkis/Alcis: awk (see: Alcidae).

Amasis: Pharaoh, c. 570 BC.

Antaeus: a giant, son of Poseidon and Gaia. He lived in Libya and made all travellers fight with him. Having defeated and killed them, he decorated his father's temple with their corpses. Antaeus was invulnerable as long as he kept in touch with his mother (that is, Gaia, the Earth), but when Heracles fought with him, he choked him to death by hoisting him onto his shoulders, with his feet OFF the ground.

Apulia: in S.E. Italy, today Puglia. Apulus: an Apulian

Aranie (Fr.): *araignée de mer* (sea-spider).

Ares: Gk god of war (Lat., Mars). ALSO: Ares the Argolid (see below).

Argo: boat. Argonaut: sailor. Argos: most ancient city in Greece, sacred to Hera (Lat., Juno). Capital of Argolis.

Argolid: from Argos, capital of Argolis in the Peloponnese. Hence: Argivus, an Argive (Gk.).

Arine – Erine – Errinies – Erinyes: the *Furies*.

Arsacidae: followers/descendants of Arsaces, first king of the Parthians.

Artemis: daughter of Zeus and Leto. Elder twin of Apollo. Very important deity: virgin and huntress; presided over women's **transitions**, e.g., from *parthenos* (virgin) to *gyne* (adult woman), and over child birth and child rearing. She was also important for men. (Lat., Diana).

Asia: daughter of Okeanos and Tethys, wife of Iapetus, and mother of Atlas, Prometheus and Epimetheus. According to some traditions, the continent of Asia derived its name from her.

Astarte (see **Ishtar**).

Attenborough, David. "In a BBC Radio 4 talk (**Scars of Evolution**) in April 2005, Attenborough asked whether humans evolved close to the sea, foraging along the shore for nutrient-rich shellfish, taking to the water when predators approached. In this new two-part series he recalls that this theory, known as the aquatic ape hypothesis, was first put forward in academic circles by Sir Alister Hardy 45 years ago and later promoted by writer Elaine Morgan. There is plenty of evidence to support the idea – most humanoid fossils have been found close to water; we have the ability to swim and dive; and we have an insulating layer of fat that apes lack. However, the theory caused much controversy and Morgan was singled out for ridicule. But now, finally, opinion is coming round to this revolutionary idea". (Ex *Radio Times*)

Aulis: seaport in Boeotia, where the Greek fleet set sail for Troy.

Auk/Awk: genus of the Alcidae (see Queen Pedauque).

Axil: upper angle, between a leaf and the stem it springs from, or between a branch and the tree trunk. Here: *filament axile du spermatozoon* is the axial thread of the spermatozoon.

Azane – Azania: Azianic – Azanian: (to do with Persia).

B.

Balenas: penis of whale.

Bacchus (Lat.): Dionysos. (Gk.)

Basan/Bashan: see Og, King of -.

Boeotia: in Northern Greece, between Attica and Phocis, with Thebes as capital.

Brittia: southern tip of Italian toe.

Briges: see Friges (Grimm's Law: letters **p,b,v** and **f** are interchangeable).

C.

Calamus: see *culmus*.

Caledonia: Highlands of Scotland

Callirhoe: daughter of Achelous, second wife of Alcmaeon. also: name of a fountain in Athens.

Calumet: North American peace pipe.

Calypso: daughter of Tethys and Helios (see Circe).

Cantel – kantele – cantilena: lyre.

Caria: province in South-West of Asia Minor.

Casseterides: Tin Islands (Scilly).

Castalia: from Delphi. Pursued by Apollo, she jumped into the spring, sacred to him. The spring was given her name. In another version she was the daughter of Achelous and wife of king Delphus by whom she bore a son, Castalius, later king, in turn, of Delphi. For Achelous, see Callirhoe, above.

Castor: (Fr.) Beaver, or beaver hat.

Cecrops: first king of Attica. His top half was human and the bottom half, snake. He is said to have come from Egyptian Sais and to have founded Athens.

Chalciope: daughter of Aeetes, sister of Medea. (See: Phrixus).

Chalcis: chief city of Euboea, opposite Aulis (now Egripo).

Chaldaeus: Chaldaean. The Chaldaeans of Assyria were renowned for their knowledge of astrology and astronomy.

Chamite: Hamite.

Chaos and Creation Myths. As point of reference we can begin with *Genesis* in the *Old Testament*: "In the beginning God created the Heaven and the earth. And the earth was waste and void; and darkness was upon the face of the deep. And the spirit of God moved upon the face of the waters."

Compare this with the **Hindu** myth: "A vast expanse of sea, the limits of which went far beyond the expanse of space and eternity. In the middle of this vast ocean was a giant snake, and in its coils rested the God Vishnu ..." (*Before Creation*, as described by Dr. Lipner of the Department of Comparative Religious Studies in Cambridge, during a discussion on the BBC World Service, 2.8.1997, 1 a.m.)

The Latin poet **Ovid** wrote in his *Metamorphoses:* "Ere land and sea and the all-covering sky were made, in the whole world the countenance of Nature was the same, all one, well-named Chaos, a raw and undivided mass, naught but a lifeless bulk with warring seeds of ill-joined elements, compressed together ..." (*Metamorphoses*)

Stephen Hawking, while discussing in a radio programme various theories about the creation of the universe, said that, according to the *Principle of Imaginary Time*, the universe had "no beginning and no end. It just curls up on itself like the surface of the earth. And it avoids the *concept of singularity* (another theory the professor had been discussing). It is of course unproven but it has interesting implications. Without boundaries, the universe has no beginning and no end. We don't have to explain creation: the universe simply **exists** ..." (BBC Radio 4, Sept. 1997)

Finally, The histories of **Central** and **South American** Indians have in recent years received a great deal of attention in books, television documentaries and newspaper articles, but those of the **North American** Indians are no less interesting for the purposes of this book. Here are two creation legends from the northern continent, and one from **Egypt**, for good measure.

Gros Ventre Indian: According to a myth of this tribe of *Algonquian* Indians their god *Nichant* destroyed the world by fire and subsequently by water. The **Iroquois** tribes believed that *Athensic*, ancestress of Mankind, fell from heaven into the waters of the Deluge as it was receding. She found herself on dry land which soon became a continent. Life was reorganised by the twin brothers *Enigorio* and *Enigohatgea*. The Iroquois later migrated to the land of the **Stone Giants** whom they overcame with the help of the thunder god Hinun, and his brother, the *West Wind*. Here too we see the concept of opposites in operation. Enigorio was the benign creator of rivers, fertile plains and fruitful trees, while Enigohatgea neutralised these activities by making deserts and harmful plants, and by causing catastrophes. This dualism is echoed in the **Huron** legends which tell of two brothers (*Ioskeba* and *Tawiskara*) who were of virgin birth and became the two leaders of the tribe after the deluge. Having opposing philosophies, like Enigorio and Enigohatgea, they were bound to quarrel and fight.

The **Nurunau** tribe of the Polynesian **Gilbert Islands** also tell of a period of universal darkness, followed by a deluge.

In Egypt, the **Shilluk** tribe tell that, in the beginning, the Great Creator Juok made the sacred **White Cow** which came up out of the Nile and later gave birth to a manchild called *Kola*. Kola's grandson, Ukwa, had a child, Nyikang, went to the swamps near the source of the Nile and founded the Shilluk nation. (*Everyman*)

Chersonesus Taurica: The Tauri were a barbarian tribe of the Crimea who
    sacrificed foreigners to Diana.
Chersonesus (Lat. Noun): peninsular.
Chersonensis (Lat. adj.): inhabitant of the peninsular.
Chersonese (Eng.). Tauric - : (Crimea, famed for its mines)
                    Thracian - : (European side of the Hellespont)
Chinese, "white". "Are China's mummies our lost cousins? Bodies unearthed
    in remotest Asia may belong to a lost European tribe". (Heading of
    article in *The Times* of 23.3.1998.) **Also:** Toby More writes from New
    York about the discovery of the remains of "white" Chinese, 2000
    years old. With accompanying pictures. (*Daily Mail*: 20.1.1999)

Incidentally, the *Illustrated London News* of 11.7.1925 published pictures of Chinese, living at that time, whose immediate forebears had not intermarried with Europeans but whose features showed unmistakable traces of a Northern European origin.

Chrysaor: rider of Pegasus.

Cimbri: NW European mainland tribe.

Cimmerians: North of Black Sea. (Having emigrated from NW Europe?) They were said '**never to have seen the sun**'.

Circe: daughter of Tethys (goddess of sea and river waters) and Helios to whom Tethys was married, although she was mother of Perse by Okeanos. Circe was the sister of Calypso.

Cithaeron (Kithaeron): mountain named after Cithaeron, king of Platea, in Greece.

Colchis: country in Asia, E of the Black Sea (see: Phrixus)

Creusa: name borne by several mythological figures, including:
1. A daughter of Creon, king of Corinth, and married to Jason. A daughter of Priam, and wife of Aeneas.
2. Creusa is also a town in Boeotia.
3. There is a Naiad with this name, loved by the River Peneius. She had two children: Hypseus, king of the Lapiths; and Stilbe. Andreus too is sometimes cited as her child. (The Lapiths were a Thessalian people, or originally from Pindus, Pellion and Ossa. They drove out the Pelasgians.)
4. Erechteus and Praxithea had a daughter called Creusa. She was raped by Apollo on the Acropolis at Athens: this produced a son, Ion. She then married Xuthus, son of Hellen and Othreis. She bore him Diomede and Achaeus.
5. Creusa, daughter of Creon, is sometimes called Glauce. The mother of Creusa, daughter of Priam, was Hecuba.

French *creux – nef – cal - van*: all mean, or suggest: hollow, hollowed out.

Culmen: like *culmus*, a stalk, upright thing. Also: summit. Also: summit/height (of ambition, good fortune, etc.).

Culmus /calamus: reed, stem, stalk (esp. of grain). ALSO: a thatched roof.

Curtius (Quintus): Lat. Author, historian of Alexander the Great.

D.

Daae/Dahae: Scythian tribe beyond the Caspian.

Daci: Dacians from Dacia in Thrace, on both sides of the Lower Danube.

Dacia: Thrace (today: NW Romania.)

Danaus: son of Belus and brother of Aegyptus. He came from Egypt to Greece and became king of Argos. His tribe adopted the name Danai (Greeks). They were also called Danaids. All the daughters of Danaus except one murdered their husbands and were punished by Tartaros, who made them bale out water endlessly with vessels having no bottom.

Dauphin (dolphin): Dolphin is also a constellation. (Perhaps the origin of the title borne by the pre-Revolutionary French *Heir Apparent*? Translator).

Decalidones: Scots? (from Calidones).

Dien – Dian – Dyan. Secondary God: the *Great Custodian/ Ordainer/Regulator of the world*.

Diodorus: peripatetic philosopher, famous dialectician (see: *Siculi*).

Dione Naia: mother of Venus (called *Aphrodite* by the Greeks). Shared an oracle with Zeus Naios, which dealt primarily with private problems.

Dionysos (Gk.): called *Bacchus* by the Romans.

Djoub: Is this Juba, South-East of Ethiopia? There is also a Juba at the source of the Nile. (Translator)

Dodona: Sanctuary of Zeus Naios in Epirus, NW Greece. Reputedly the oldest Greek oracle. Probably of pre-historic origin. Odysseus (Lat. Ulysses) claimed to have visited Dodona to 'hear Zeus' in the rustling leaves of the **sacred oak**. Achilles too prayed to the Pelasgian Zeus at Dodona. The sanctuary never really recovered from the ravaging of Epirus by the Romans in 167 BC.

Douche écossaise: Shower of alternately hot and cold water. (Scottish version of the Sauna? Translator).

Draco, also **Dracon**: severe Athenian lawyer.

E.

Egre (Nordic): ogre.

Eight (figure 8). On 01.11.2005, not long after he had begun working on Mme. Talbot's book, the translator happened to see an advert on TV which informed the public that 'because the Chinese believe the eight (8) to be a lucky number, HSBC Hong Kong is now offering an 8% investment…' The school of **Ex Oriente Lux** will say: Eastern influence on the West. Mme. Talbot (were she still with us) would answer: Not at all – the other way round! A view which was, incidentally, argued most persuasively by H.K.Horken in his book **Ex Nocte Lux** (Light from the North), first published in 1970.

The Hindus too were interested in the figure *eight* – witness their concept of the **Regents of the Eight Quarters of the World**. These were:

1. Indra 2. Agni 3. Yama 4. Surya 5. Varuna 6. Vayu 7. Auvera
8. Soma (or Siva)

Ellis – Elea – Hyela (adj., eleatic. Lat. **Velia**): an ancient city SE of Paestum.
(See: Grimm's Law – p, b, v and f as interchangeable letters.)

Elyme (Fr.): Elymais, district of Susiana, in Persia. The adjectival form is
Elymaeus, an inhabitant of the region.

Enceladus: one of the **Giants** buried by Zeus/Jupiter under Mount Etna.

Ennuque (Fr.): I cannot find a translation of this word, but according to
Procopius the 'Galles ennuques' could enter the Gates of Hell without
being overcome by the fumes. However, masculine Lat. *gallus* is a
priest of Cybele, and feminine *galla* is a priestess. In French, the noun
would be *galle* (plural *galles*). This could be relevant. Cybele, a
Phrygian goddess, was often called the "Mother of the Gods", or the
"Great Mother": she governed the whole of Nature. In time her cult
spread all over the Greek, and later the Roman world. Her major
importance lay in the fertility/orgiastic cult which grew up around her
and survived to a fairly late period of the Roman Empire. Perhaps the
anti-life attitudes of the Early Church Fathers prompted them to equate
this fertility cult with the Gates of Hell? The **Gallas** were however also
an ancient Ethiopian people. (Translator)

Erine – Arine – Erin – Aranie: (see: Aranie)

Erytheia: Island in the Bay of Cadiz where Geryon lived. The '**red or
blushing one**' (sunset coloured). One of the Hesperides. Daughter of
Geryon.

Erythrae: one of the twelve main cities of Ionia.

Eumenides: the Gracious Ones (euphemism for the Furies).

Euboea: largest island in the Aegean, now Negroponte, separated from
Greece by the Euripus.

Euryalus: four different histories.
1.Son of Mecisteus: took part in the expeditions of the Argonauts and
of the Epigoni. Fought at Troy. 2. Son of Odysseus. 3. Companion
of Aeneas. 4. Friend of Nisus, killed, fighting the Rutuli, a Central
Italian tribe that opposed Aeneas. (So all four histories have some kind
of connection with Troy.)

Explicate rubro: clearly in red. (Adj. *explicatus*: clear/ unambiguous/
explicit. *Explicate* from verb *explicare* [to explain], 2nd person sing,
imperative. *Rubro*: masc. abl. sing. of adj. *Ruber, red.*)

F.

Fils de mer (Fr.): literally "sea threads". Thus: seaweed, or algae? (The adj. of algae is algal.)

Iles Fortunées (Fr.): The Lucky Islands.

Friges (Lat.): the Briges of Macedonia. (see: Grimm's Law on letters p, b, v and f.)

G.

Gaia (or Gea): Earth Mother.

Galates: Various descriptions. 1. Son of Heracles/Hercules by the daughter of a local prince near the town of Alesia, founded by the hero. (See Celtus below). 2. Galeotes: Hyperborean ancestor of a race of soothsayers who went to Sicily and Caria after consulting the oracle at Dodona, which had instructed them to proceed further: some to the East and some to the West. 3. Celtus: When Heracles was passing through Britain with Geryon's cattle, Celtine (a king's daughter) hid the herds and refused to return them unless Heracles married her. He agreed, and Celtus was born. 4. According to another tradition, Celtus was the son of Heracles and Sterope, one of the Pleiades (but a lady of many other affiliations as well.)

Garon – garus – garum: a spicy fish sauce.

Gelon: king of Syracuse.

Geloni: Scythian tribe.

Germandes: misprint for **germander**, a term in botany? It would fit into the general context, e.g. **germander speedwell**, a creeping plant. From med. Lat. *Germandra* ex Gk. *Khaimaidrus* ex *khamai* (on the ground) + *drus* (oak).

Getes – Geti – Getae: from Thrace, on the Lower Danube.

Gul Persan: a colour in heraldry?

H.

Hache (Fr.): here, cutting edge (of hatchet?)

Halicarnassos: town of great antiquity in Caria. Birthplace of the historians

Herodotus and Dionysius.

Halys, or **Kizil**: river in N. Central Turkey.

Heir Apparent, definition: *indefeasible by Law*, and *cannot be annulled.*

Hellen: son of Deucalion, king of Thessaly. The Greeks are said to take their name from him. (Hellenes)

Heracles (Lat. **Hercules**): Chambers Encyclopaedia gives a very detailed biography of this 'greatest and most popular of the Greek heroes', but for the purpose of this translation we shall confine ourselves to listing the famous twelve labours. These labours (or tasks, in the Greek) were undertaken at the behest of Heracles' kinsman **Eurystheus**, king of Mycenae, whose thrall the hero had become for reasons that vary in different accounts. They are as follows: 1. To kill the **lion of Nemea**. Heracles strangled it, and afterwards wore its hide. 2. To kill the hydra (water-snake) of **Lerna**, a many-headed monster whose heads grew again as fast as they were cut off. Iolaus, son of Iphicles and Heracles' faithful helper, cauterized each neck as its head was cut off, and so the creature was killed. 3. To catch the **boar of Erymanthus**. 4. To take alive the **hind of Cerynea**, whose stag-like antlers were said to be of gold. Heracles caught it, showed it to Eurystheus, then let it go. 5. To kill the **birds of Stymphalus**. 6. To clean the **stables of Augeas** (or Augeias), king of Elis, in a day. Heracles diverted a river through them and washed away the huge accumulation of cow-dung. These first six labours were all accomplished in the Peleponnesus, the rest outside it. They were: 7. To catch the **Cretan bull**. He did so, let it go, and it went to Marathon. 8. To take the **horses of Diomedes** of Thrace, which fed on human flesh. (In some accounts Heracles fed Diomedes to them and they became tame.) 9. To fetch the **girdle of Hippolyta**, queen of the Amazons. He fought and defeated the tribe and took the girdle. 10. To capture the **cattle of Geryon**, a triple-bodied monster living in the extreme west. After much fighting Heracles killed Geryon and drove the cattle to Greece. 11. To fetch **Cerberus**, the three headed dog, guarding the entrance to the underworld. This meant fighting Hades himself. Heracles succeeded. 12. To fetch the **golden apples of the Hesperides**: 'daughters of the evening' (or of 'the evening star'). There are **two versions** of the story. In one, Heracles had to **overcome a dragon**, guarding the apples. In the other, **the giant Atlas** (whose task it was to support the sky on his shoulders) **was involved.**

There were also numerous subsidiary exploits, but only the wrestling match with the African giant, Antaeus, need be mentioned here, as

Mme Talbot deals with it in her text. (*Chambers Encyclopedia*)

Heraclia/Heracleia: 1. Parthian town 2. Seaport of Lucania on the River Siris, in the Gulf of Tarentum, Calabria (SE Italy).

Hilum: scar-like mark on a seed, formed at the point where it joins the stalk, connecting it with the placenta. (Bot.)

Hybodont: hump-backed.

Hybodontidae: 'with compressed, cone-shaped teeth'.

Hyades: group of seven stars in the head of the constellation **Taurus**.

I.

Iber: Speaking of physical traits, common to the old Iberians (Spanish) and the Hibernians (Irish), but still noticeable in modern times, we could suggest that Mme. Talbot might also have mentioned the 'typical Irish beauty': black hair and blue eyes. (Translator)

Ilian: Minerva (Lat.), Athena (Gk.)

Ilithya: Gk goddess. Associations with midwifery like the Roman Juno Lucina.

Illus: son of Tros/Trios, father of Laomedon, founder of Ilium (Troy).

Inachus: 1. River deity of the Argolids, son of Okeanos and Tethys. 2. First king of Argos. Also: father of Io and Phoroneus. Followers and descendants of Inachus are the Inachides (Eng. Inachians).

Indra: god of battle and of rain. Described as a "jolly, fair-haired fighting-man of the Nordic type ..." (*Everyman Dictionary*. See too *Regents of the Eight Quarters* under *Hindus*.)

Ino: daughter of Cadmus and Hermione, second wife of Athmas, king of Thebes (see Athmas and Phrixos).

Io (gen. Ius), or Ion (gen. Ionis): daughter of Inachus, king of Argos. Beloved of Zeus, she was changed into a cow for fear of Hera, wife of Zeus. She fled to Egypt where she recovered her former shape, married king Osiris and was later worshipped as the Egyptian deity Isis.

Ion: son of Xuthus (not to be confused with Ion, daughter of Inachus). He created a colony in Asia: Ionia in Asia Minor, on the Aegean Sea between Caria and Aeolis, on the west coast of Anatolia.
NB:
In spite of (or possibly thanks to) a lifetime living abroad, the English amateur ethnologist, Roger **Aston**, developed some interesting theories about population movements. One of them fits in well with the previous paragraph. Aston suggested that an over-spill of Ionians could

eventually have moved as far East as the area that has become known as **Java/Yavan/Yuan** – a transformation of Ion. Meanwhile – and at different periods - other colonists could have moved South, and eventually reached the land which came to be called Aethiopia: Aethio-(p)ia. An interesting suggestion and one which seems to be at least partially confirmed by an entry in Smith's *Smaller Classical Dictionary* of 1888. Here we read that although the 'origin of the name is not certain', it was 'perhaps really a foreign (word) that had been corrupted…'

Ishtar: Babylonian goddess of fertility. Her cult was first recorded in **Erech**, but probably started much earlier and spread to the whole of the Middle East, even to Greece. On the Mediterranean coast she appears as Ashtart, but without alteration of her essential characteristics. She was adopted into the Pantheon of many races, and appears as the consort of **Marduk, Asshur, Tammuz** – and even as **Ninlil**, consort of **Enlil**, the storm god. She has also been identified with **Damkina**, wife of **Ea**, in which capacity she is the mother of **Tammuz**. She was sometimes considered to be the daughter of **Anu** or of **Sin**, while Frazer equated her with **Esther** of the *Old Testament*. There is a very interesting article on **ESTHER** in Chambers' Encyclopedia, but the story is not strictly relevant to the main thrust of THE PALADINS (Chambers).

J.

Jordanès: Gothic historian, 5th century AD.

L.

Laemedon: founder of Troy.
Leda: mother of Pollux, Helen, Castor and Clytemnestra. She was a daughter of Thestius and wife of Tyndareus. She had many other children, some of them said to have been sired by Zeus, disguised on one occasion as a swan.
Lerna/Erne/Arine/Erine/Erin/Erinyes (Eumenides): the *Furies*.
Liguria: in NW Italy.
Limes: a boundary (normal or fortified).
Limus: (Primordial) mud/slime.
Luce Appulée (Fr.): Lucian Appuleius, a turbulent Roman tribune.
Loki: one of the Aesir, possibly related to the dwarfs. There is confusion

about his background: he is often seen as a kind of malicious magus.

Lydia: in Asia Minor. The capital was Sardis. It is said to have been the original home of the Etruscans. Hence: Lydius can be translated as 'Lydian' or 'Etruscan'. Virgil called the Tiber 'Lydius fluvius'.

M.

Maieutique (Fr.): midwifery.

Maia/Maja/Mara (Ger. *Meer*): symbols of the eight-legged crab and of the jellyfish. (Eight legged creatures were very venerable for the Nordics, as was the number 8, in general: e.g., the 8-legged horses of the **Valkyries**. See also 'eight' under the letter E.)

Maeones: ancient name of the Lydians. Hence: Maeonia/Lydia. (Lydia is also called Etruria because the Etruscans were said to be descended from the Lydians (see Lydia).

Maionides: native of Maeonia. Also: a poetic name for Homer, said to have been born in Lydia.

Maeotae: a Scythian people living on Lake Maeotis. Hence: Maeotis, a Scythian (Pl. Maiotides). The sea of Azov was called *Maeotis palus* (or *lacus*).

Maia: a nymph of Mount Cyllene in the Peloponnesus, on the frontiers of Arcadia and Achaia. The mountain was sacred to Hermes/Mercury who had a temple on the summit. Maia bore him by Zeus/Jupiter. She was the daughter of Atlas and Pleione and was therefore one of the Pleiades. The month of May (*Maius*) is named after her. Cyllene is also a seaport town of Elis.

Maia (69): isles of the old Empire of the Night. For **69** see *sens gaulois* under letter **S**.

Melos: 1. Islands at the base of the Greek mainland. 2. Tune/air/song.

Messina: 1. Capital of *Provincia Messina* in Sicily. 2. Ex Siculan colony. *Siculi*: ancient Italian people, some of whom emigrated to Sicily and gave the island its name. 3. Ex Chalkis/Chalcis, called *zankle* (a sickle) by settlers. 4. Later called Messene, in honour of Messenia in the Peloponnese, by Anaxilas, tyrant of Rhegium. (See Siculi and Chalkis)

Millet (Fr.): Miletus (important town in Asia Minor).

Mont de Piété: pawn shop/pawn broker's

Morbihan: modern department of Brittany.

Mou-moute (de la nourrice): literally "rich syrup of the wetnurse", but here "rich milk"?

N.

Neleus: king of Pylos, son of Poseidon/Neptune, father of Nestor.
Neuri: tribe living North of the Scythians.
Nisos: king of Megara, father of Scylla. Not to be confused with **Scylla** and **Charybdis**, two very dangerous rocks between Italy and Sicily.
Nordic Nine Worlds:
> **Ljosalfaheim** – heaven of the righteous
> **Muspellheim** – home of the flame spirits, led by Sutur.
> **Godheim** – dwelling of Aesir.
> **Vanaheim** – dwelling of the Vanir.
> **Mannheim** – abode of Mankind.
> **Svartalfheim** – cavern world, dwelling of the elves.
> **Jötunnheim** – land of the giants.
> **Helheim** – region of death.
> **Niflheim** – lowest region.

Nose size. In his book **Ex Nocte Lux** H.K.Horken discusses the anatomical features of the **creatures-become-modern-men**, after having been isolated for a million years or more beyond the ice barrier within the Arctic Circle. One of the features he mentions is the **Size and Shape** of the nose – the importance of which he emphasizes and explains. Like Mme. Talbot, he argues that "after the Deluge" (end of the Ice Age?) the dramatically rising sea levels (more than 100 metres over the past 10,000 years) forced the inhabitants of those regions to flee in all directions (West, East and South) to seek safety on higher ground. One of the areas where they eventually found new homes was what today could loosely be termed "Arabia". We know that the Hindu **Vedas** tell of their distant ancestors' having been driven out of the Arctic Circle (See **Vedas**). It is therefore very interesting to learn from a modern source that the Arabs too might have similar memories. In a BBC Radio 4 Programme (*Front Row*, 11 March 2005, at 7.15pm) an artist was being interviewed about his work. He mentioned in passing that, when painting the portraits of Arabs, he took care to show off the noses of his subjects to proper advantage: the size and the prominence of the nose was, he said, a "mark of distinction".

Nysa: 1. A city in Caria, now Nasli. 2. City in India where Bacchus was brought up.

O.

Odin and the *Odinic Trinity*: the Trinity of the Nordic Myth, consisting of the *High*, the *Equally High*, and the *Third*, referred to in the second chapter of the prose Edda. (One of the sources for God the Father, God the Son, God the Holy Ghost, in Christian Dogma? Translator)

Oeil génital (lit. "genital eye"): female vagina.

Og, King of Basan/Bashan. The *Everyman Dictionary of Non-Classical Mythology* has an interesting entry under the heading: "**Og, the Giant King of Bashan**", from whose name we may have acquired the word OGRE, coined by Charles Perrault to describe man-eating giants. The name is frequently paired as **Gog Magog**, when Magog was the Moon Goddess and Gog or Og her spouse or son. The ogre killed by **Jack of the Beanstalk** originally had three heads, in a similar manner to **Svantovit**, the Slavonic god. Dr. Margaret **Murray** has noted that ogres were **not only** very tall but **big boned**, having a broad face with coarse features, high cheek bones, lumpy nose, wide mouth with large teeth, and coarse, straight and straggly beard. All these are characteristic of the **Ugrians** of South Russia, who penetrated to Europe and the Near East from the Black Sea. In addition they were cannibals till Roman times, as were their kindred, the Scyths. Og, King of Bashan, may well have been a Scythian intruder from the North who assumed the leadership of the tribe. **Ogier** the Dane, who is mentioned in the Charlemagne epics, may have been a man of exceptional strength who assumed this title. There is a distinct link-up with **Ogra**, the Celtic God, whose winter festival is celebrated at **Hog**-manay (p. 259.).

Ogdoad: the region about Og. OR: the realm of Og.

Ogre: from Latin *orcus* (the **Underworld**, the **Abode of the Dead**. Then, by extension, god of the **Infernal Regions**: Orcus/Hades/Pluto. See also **Og** in the *Everyman* quote.)

Orthrus: monstrous dog of Geryon, offspring of **Typhon** and **Echidna** and therefore a brother of **Cerberus**.

Oscan: see Samnites.

Ostrobonia. In Finland

P.

Palud Royal: in the Rhone valley. (*Palud*: dialect for "palais"?)

Paradise, Terrestrial: The possibility of rediscovering the lost paradise of mankind inspired explorers for centuries. Perhaps the earliest reference to it occurs in the **Peregeisis** of **Prescian**, itself a rendering of an earlier work by Dionysius – that is, apart from the Biblical version. The earthly paradise was always placed just outside the region known to Man at the time, but the very nature of the descriptions tends to show that at one time the ancestors of the Aryan and Semitic races lived under climatic conditions which can only be described as more favourable than any they have enjoyed since then. Their enforced exile from there dates back to the beginning of the last Ice Age when tropical areas became icy wastes, when meadows became arid deserts, when the bitter struggle for existence turned friends into enemies and whole nations into dispossessed refugees, wearily making their way towards a climate in which they could survive. The fact of sudden climatic changes is shown by the mammoths in Siberia, who were suddenly wiped out, with undigested meals in their stomachs. (Everyman's Dictionary)

Herewith the poet Ovid's description of life in the Terrestial Paradise before "enforced exile":

Of their own free will they kept good faith without the compulsion of law. There was neither punishment nor intimidation, nor did a suppliant throng have anything to fear from the words of a judge, for the people, safe from threat, needed no champion. The pine tree, not yet uprooted from it's hillside slope, had not plunged down into river torrents that would carry it away to spy out foreign lands. Men knew no other shore but their own: towns were not yet encircled by deep ditches. There were no helmets, no swords: people secure and with no need of armed soldiers, lived their lives in gentle ease. The earth, too, unharmed and untouched by hoe or ploughshare, gave freely of itself to all. Men gathered wild strawberries and mountain berries, cherries and blackberries, clinging to hardy brambles, chestnuts, hanging in abundance from Jupiter's richly laden trees. Spring was eternal, and a mild West Wind gently stroked with it's warm breath flowers that grew without seed. The unploughed land brought forth it's fruits in season, and fields, left fallow, shone like gold with heavy ears of corn. Rivers flowed now with milk, now with nectar, and golden honey dripped slowly off the green holly ... (Translation from the Latin)

Parnassus: high mountain in Phocis with two peaks, sacred to Apollo and the *Muses*. On their slopes were the city of Delphi and the Castalian Spring. (See: Castalia.)
Parthians: a Scythian people. (See: Arsacidae.)

Pel/Pen/Pal/Pieu: stake, pole.

Pelagian: connected with the sea. From Fr. *pelagie*. ALSO: *pelagie la méduse*: "jellyfish". Originally, Gk. Pelagos.

Pelasgians: the most ancient race of the Greeks (Lat. *Pelasgi*).

Pelias: 1. Adj of Pella/Pelle, city of remote antiquity in Macedonia. 2. Peliades, inhabitants of Pella/Pelle. 3. Peliades: daughters of Pelias, king of Iolcus/Iolcos, in Thessaly. The uncle of Jason, he was murdered by his daughters at the instigation of Medea.

Penis bifide (Fr., biology): split penis.

Perse: daughter of Okeanos, and wife of Helios (sun), by whom she became the mother of Aeetes, Circe, Pasiphae and Perse.

Perses/Perseus: king of Macedonia. NOT Perseus, son of Zeus and Danae.

Persians, and the African-American Prof. Henry **Gates** of Harvard University USA. During July and August of 1999, Prof. Gates presents four programmes on British TV about the forgotten past of black Africa. He is surprised when two young men from **Zanzibar** tell him they are **Persians**. He protests that they look just like himself: they are surely cousins? No, they reply, they are Persians: their fathers told them so. And their fathers were told this by their fathers before them.

Pessinonte: town in Galatia, where Cybele was worshipped.

Phrixus/Phrixos: Complicated story of which there are several versions. 1. Son of Athmas and Nephele, and brother of Helle. On the advice of his second wife, Ino, Athmas decided to sacrifice Phrixus and daughter Helle to Zeus, but Zeus (or Nephele) sent a ram with a golden fleece that saved them. They flew off to the East on the ram, but Helle fell off into the sea, drowning in the straits, thereafter known as the Hellespont. (In another version, Poseidon saved her and fell in love with her.) Phrixus arrived safely at the court of Aeetes, king of Colchis, who gave him his daughter Chalciope in marriage. 2.. Phrixus now sacrificed the ram to Zeus and gave the fleece to Aeetes, whose daughter Medea later became involved with Jason and the Golden Fleece. 3. In yet another version, mentioned by Syginus, Aeetes killed Phrixus because an oracle had predicted that he himself would be killed by a descendant of Aeolus. In this text Phrixus and Helle, saved from sacrifice, were driven mad by Dionysos for trying to avenge themselves on Ino. (Shortened, from *Penguin Dictionary of Classical Mythology*.)

Plutonium: region or realm of Pluto (Gk. Hades), in the Netherworld.

Procopius: Byzantine historian.

Pronaos/Pronax: son of **Talaos/Talaus**, king of Argos.

Pronoia: "forethought" (**Stoic** term), allied to *providentia* (learned term for *prudentia*, meaning "capacity to distinguish **good** from **bad**").

Pyramos/Pyramus. Lover of Babylonian Thisbe. The story of the two lovers could possibly be described as a Babylonian version of Romeo and Juliette. In a second version, Pyramos and Thisbe committed suicide when Thisbe became pregnant before marriage. The gods metamorphosed Pyramos into the river which bore his name (a Cilician river) and Thisbe became the spring that fed into it.

Pyramus: town in Boeotia.

R.

(*Reine*) *Pédauque*: the "queen with feet turned outwards".

Rune. Rune staff, or magic wand, inscribed with runes.

S.

Samnites and **Oscans**. The Samnites inhabited Samnium, a country in the centre of Italy. The Oscans (Osci), near neighbours of the Samnites, were one of the most ancient tribes of the peninsular. They were subdued by the Sabines and Tyrrhenians, and disappeared from History at a comparatively early period. However, their language (closely connected with the other ancient Italian dialects from which Latin was formed) was still spoken by the inhabitants of Campania long after the Oscans had disappeared as a separate people. In very remote times they were called the Opici, or Opsci.

Sampo: Finnish associations. Perhaps a kind of Finnish "world pillar" (reminiscent of the germanic **Irminsul**, destroyed by order of the Emperor Charlemagne after the final defeat of the Saxons? Translator.)

Sapor: 1. Latin name for Persian *Shapur*; Arabic **Sabur**; and Greek **Sapores**. Kings of the Sassanian dynasty from the family of **Sasan/Sassan**. They ruled Persia from 211 to 651 AD.

Scolotes: name given to themselves by the Scythians.

Seleucid: follower of **Seleucus Nicatur**, a general of Alexander the Great. His similarly named descendants became kings of Syria.

Sens gaulois (69): naughty/smutty (as in a **smutty story**).

Siculi. An ancient Italian people, some of whom migrated to the island to which they gave their name: *Sicilia* (Sicily). Diodorus of Sicily lived in the time of Augustus. (See: Diodorus.)

Sinbad the Sailor: The journeys of Sinbad, as told in the **Arabian Nights**, have some items in common with those of the **Irish Sea Captains**, having been drawn from many travellers' tales, known at the time of writing. They come mainly from cultures where the compass was unknown, but where quite large ships were in use. There are also echoes from Homer in the **Island of the Grotto**; the **Valley of Diamonds and Gold** (in which the use of sheepskins for gold washings recalls the Golden Fleece of Colchis); the **Cannibal King**; the **Land of the Magians** (tale that recalls *Circe*). (*Everyman*)

Som: summit (from Fr. *sommet*)
Sour: Tyre. The modern name is **Sur**.
Sphérique: "bounded by arcs".
Suzianna: Susa, or Shushan. Modern Gk. Susiane. Shush: capital of Elam (Susianna/Susiana), administrative centre of the Achaemenian king, Darius I.

T.

Talle (Fr., bot.): "sucker". The sucker is a shoot that emerges: 1. from the rooted part of a stem; 2. from a root at a distance from the main stem; 3. from an axil, or occasionally; 4. from a branch. (See **axil**.)
Tamis, mystic: perhaps connected with riddles? Or with **Tamesis**, in Celtic Myth one of the **lake/river/spring** goddesses whose name became *Tamise* in French and *Thames* in English?
Tant and **Cadmus/Kadmos**: perhaps a connection with **Tanit(h)**, mother of the Egyptian Harpokrates/Horus?
Tara (**Taras?**): 1. Eponym of Tarentum, in Southern Sicily, son of Poseidon? OR 2. Gaulish Culture Hero.
Tenes: son of Procleia (daughter of Laemedon) and of Cycnus/Cignus (son of Poseidon/Neptune), king of the Ligurians. After the death of Procleia, Cycnus remarried. His wife, Philonome, falsely accused Tenes of trying to rape her: he had in fact repelled her amorous advances. Cycnus had Tenes thrown into the sea in a chest. The chest landed on an island off the Trojan coast which was later named Tenedos, after him. When Cycnus realised his error, he had Philonome buried alive, and he tried to effect a reconciliation with his son, but was rejected. There are many variants of the story (e.g. Joseph and Potiphar's wife? in the Hebrew *Old Testament*), but for our purposes it is only

important to remember that Cycnus was a son of Poseidon, the Ocean god, that he was nevertheless a king in NW Italy; and that the alternative form of his name (Lat. *cygnus*) became *cygne* in French, meaning **swan**, indicating a connection with **Gaul**. Also, it need not surprise us that after his death, Cygnus was transformed into a swan.

Téorbe (Fr.). Theorbo in Eng., a musical instrument.

Thessalia (Eng., Thessaly): most northerly area of the Greek mainland

Thracid (adj.): "of Thrace", "Thracian".

Timeas: One of Plato's dialogues.

Tithonus: son of Laomedon, consort of **Aurora**. Immortalised by being changed into a grasshopper.

Trachyn/Trachin: town in Thessaly on Mount **Oeta**, where Heracles/Hercules burned himself.

Trebizon/Trabzon: ex Trapezus, the most easterly Ancient Greek settlement.

Trescalon: place name in French *Provence*.

Trézène (Fr.): in English, Troezen. Very ancient city of Argolis where Theseus was born

Treskeles: three-legged.

Trika/Tricca/Trikkala: Trikkala is an agricultural area in Thessaly. It is the legendary abode of Asclepius, god of healing.

Trinacria: Sicily. The adj. *trinacrian* (three-pointed) describes Sicily's geographical outline.

Triquetrus (Lat.). French *triquèdre*: triangular.

Troas/Troad/Troias/Troade/Troia. Also: **Ilios/Ilion**. Eng., Plain of **Troas/Troad**: the land of Troy. (*Encyclopedia Britannica*)

Turkmen: "No one knows where they came from. However, they came on horseback. They were magnificent horsemen, the last of the Central Asian tribes to be subdued by the Czars, in 1860. They themselves believe they are Aryans. (*The Windy Sea, Turkmenistan after Independence*. BBC Radio 4, 9.30 a.m, 5.2.1998.)

V.

Vagu: in the Vedic tradition this is a kind of midwife.

Van: town on the SE shore of a salt lake in Eastern Turkey. Important historical associations.

Vanir: Together with the Aesir, one of the very first Paladins in a World History of which there are still many traces.

Vannic insciptions: cuneiform script in a language, deciphered by Sayce. Tells of an ancient kingdom called Biainias which fought the Assyrians and was overthrown by the Phrygians circa 620 BC. The people, called

Khaldis, worshipped the Sun and Air gods, and paid special tribute to the vine.

Vans/Vénètes/Enètes/Oenètes/vaniques/Vanes/Vindes: Mme. Talbot uses all these words at various times to describe the Paladins who prepared the way, inter alia, for the civilisation that would become "Venice". The story of Venice is certainly fascinating, but for the immediate purpose of this study, one point is particularly interesting: the fact that Modern Venice was created in 1310 AD with a **Doge** (Leader) as its titular Head, supported by a **Council of Ten** – very reminiscent of the **Ten Atlantan Kings**, as reported in the old legends. (Shortened, from *Chambers Encyclopedia*.)

Vedas, Indian sacred writings: "This vast amount of religious writings dates back to before the arrival of the Hindus in India, probably to a period when they were living in a relatively cold climate." (*Everyman*, p.227.)

Vénétie bretonne (Fr.): Venetan Brittany.

Veneti (Lat.): Celts of Brittany. Their country was called in Latin: *Venetia*. **also: Veneti**: a tribe in NW Italy. NB: Venetan dialects of NE Italy include the "Venetian" of Venice.

X.

Xuthus: son of Hellen and the nymph **Othreis/Orseis**. Brother of Dorus and Aeolus who was later king of Thessaly and founder of the Aeolic branch of the Greek nation. A descendant of his, also Aeolus, is represented by Homer as the happy ruler of the Aeolian islands, to whom Zeus had given dominion over the winds, "which he might soothe or excite, according to his pleasure". In some traditions, Xuthus is the father of Ion by Creusa but Euripides makes Apollo the father, and Xuthus the step-father. There are also other conflicting versions.

Z.

Zeus (of **Velchanos/Volcanus/Vulcanus**). The fire god, son of Zeus/Jupiter and Hera/Juno. Ancient Roman god of **destructive power**, but also associated with Maia, the month of May, **when plants are growing**. (The *Oxford Dictionary of Classical Mythology* calls this association "puzzling". However, within the context of Mme. Talbot's interest in the Celtic theory regarding **opposites**, it does not seem so puzzling. Translator)

*   *   *